MUV

To my husband John, with love.

MUV

THE STORY OF THE MITFORD GIRLS' MOTHER

RACHEL TRETHEWEY

The
History
Press

First published 2025

The History Press
97 St George's Place, Cheltenham,
Gloucestershire, GL50 3QB
www.thehistorypress.co.uk

Typesetting and origination by The History Press
Printed and bound in Great Britain by TJ Books, Padstow, Cornwall

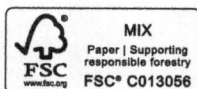

MIX
Paper | Supporting responsible forestry
FSC
FSC® C013056
www.fsc.org

The History Press proudly supports

Trees for Life
www.treesforlife.org.uk

EU Authorised Representative: Easy Access System Europe
Mustamäe tee 50, 10621 Tallinn, Estonia
gpst.request@easproject.com

Contents

Author's Note

The world has changed since Lady Redesdale's time, but many of the sources used in this book were written in her era. In Sydney's circle, gender and race were discussed in ways no longer considered acceptable. Some of the language used in this book when quoting from these sources is authentic to its time and, though difficult to read, it has been left in, as it is necessary to set the story in its historical context.

Introduction

Nancy, Pamela, Diana, Unity, Jessica, Deborah … everyone knows about the six flamboyant Mitford girls, but in fact there were seven exceptional women in the famous family. The seventh was 'Muv', the mother of the notorious sisters. Too often portrayed as different from them and outside the girl gang, Lady Redesdale was really the original and much of her daughters' strong will and self-confidence came from her.

Sydney Redesdale was a divisive figure both among her daughters and their subsequent biographers. Until their deaths, her girls squabbled over what she was really like; their differing views of her persisted even longer than the political divides between them. Each daughter wanted to control the narrative, and they wrote competing novels, memoirs and letters to vindicate their perspective. For Nancy and Jessica, Sydney was often cast as a sinner; for Unity, Diana, Debo and Pam she was more of a saint.

Biographers have been equally divided about how Sydney should be portrayed. Many wondered how such extraordinary children could spring from such ordinary parents, but was Sydney really so 'ordinary'? One thing all her daughters agreed on was that their mother was 'so very unusual'.[1] Muv's granddaughter-in-law, Charlotte Mosley, who has edited the sisters' letters, comments, 'Everything I've seen about her and everything I've heard, which was mainly from Diana and Debo, made me think that she was actually very remarkable.' She considers Sydney a heroine, explaining, 'I think she had a difficult husband to deal with, money was always never sufficient, and she had some very high-spirited children. She went through tragedy after tragedy during the war and came through it still standing.'[2] Mary S. Lovell, author of *The Mitford Girls* agrees that Muv was the heroine of the whole story because of her selfless support of her family.[3] However, Unity's biographer, David Pryce-Jones, saw her very differently. He portrayed Lady Redesdale critically, focusing more on her political beliefs and support for Hitler.

This book explores what Muv was really like, disentangling the real woman from the figure of fun her novelist daughter Nancy turned her into.[4] Sydney was certainly a far cry from the vague, one-dimensional figure of Aunt Sadie portrayed by Nancy in her novels *The Pursuit of Love* and *Love in a Cold Climate*. While the fictional character is a forgettable, flimsy figure compared to her husband the inimitable Uncle Matthew, the real woman was more interesting than their father, or 'Farve'. Sydney Redesdale was as eccentric, opinionated and ultimately misguided as her more extreme daughters. Before they were born she had adventures of her own which rivalled their subsequent escapades. From her youth she was fascinated by current affairs and she passed on her interest in politics to her daughters, although it took them in very different directions.

There have been many biographies of the Mitford sisters, but this is the first full biography of Lady Redesdale. It is essentially a mother's story, exploring what it was like bringing up six exuberant girls in an era of unprecedented social change and international turbulence. No doubt it was exciting and exhilarating to be part of this eccentric clan if you were the one having the adventures – but not so much fun if you were the one who had to pick up the pieces when things went wrong. As Sydney once said, 'Whenever I see a headline beginning with "Peer's Daughter" I know one of you children has been in trouble.'[5]

Lady Redesdale often had to sort out the chaos left in her daughters' wake and she did it without fuss or complaining. Her relationship with her girls highlights the generation gap that developed after the

First World War between the bright young things of the 1920s and their Edwardian parents. She did not always understand or condone their behaviour, but she invariably stood by them.

As a reader might expect from a book about the Mitfords, the inter-war country house atmosphere is present here in all its idiosyncratic glory, but beneath the flippancy and glamour lies a more profound and controversial story which illuminates a crucial period in British history. As Sydney's granddaughter, Constancia Romilly explains, Lady Redesdale was 'an active player in her family at a very complicated historical moment'.[6] It was a time of polarised views, when people were taking sides between two huge political movements: communism and fascism. Lady Redesdale and her offspring were serious women who cared deeply about politics and believed that they could make a difference. They became participants in ideological battles which transformed their lives and took them far away from the sheltered world they had known. There was to be no going back as they found themselves caught up in a destructive maelstrom they could not control and, as her family split down the middle, Sydney found herself on the wrong side of history. Her choice was to have devastating consequences for her marriage, her relationship with two of her daughters and her reputation.

Her support for Hitler is hard for both her family and a biographer to explain. How could an apparently decent woman back such an inhumane dictator? Was it just a blind spot or a deeper indication of her true character? Did her stance change with events or were her fundamental beliefs always the same? These questions are difficult to answer. Even many of her closest family members and friends were perplexed by her views because her standpoint did not seem to correspond with the balanced person they thought they knew. We can find some clues to solving the puzzle in Lady Redesdale's background and personality. The influence of her charismatic and controversial father, Thomas Gibson Bowles, played a large part. She inherited her black and white attitude to life from him and passed it on to her daughters. There was little room for nuance or compromise and, once their minds were made up, nothing would shift them.

Beyond the Mitford mythology, exploring Sydney's political trajectory adds to our understanding of British politics in the 1930s. As leading historian of the era Richard Griffiths writes, 'in their flamboyant way they (the Mitfords) reflected many of the obscure psychological, political and social motives which were to affect certain sections of the British aristocracy.'[7] Although idiosyncratic, even in her own era, Muv's views were far from unique among her class; many of her contemporaries were pro-appeasement, preferred the fascists to the communists, and were impressed by Hitler. Where she differed from most of them was that she did not change her mind during or after the war.

Lady Redesdale's story also has relevance for our own times. In an era when more extreme politics is on the rise, it can be enlightening to examine how people can be won over to support these views. Learning how to cope when families are divided along ideological lines also has a resonance in the modern world. In a time of 'cancel culture', this book raises questions about how we should approach a figure like Lady Redesdale. Should she be outlawed because of her support for Hitler, or can we abhor her views while feeling sympathy for the family tragedies she faced? Can we reject her political beliefs while recognising her qualities of courage and resilience? Her daughter Jessica wrote that she thought of her mother as two different people, one more likeable than the other. Should we do the same?

To answer both the political and personal questions about Lady Redesdale's character involves looking at her from many different angles. Examining the evidence was an emotional rollercoaster – as a biographer, I have rarely had my opinion of my subject fluctuate so much. I admired her as a mother but detested her politics. While researching this book I read hundreds of unpublished letters written by Sydney to her daughter Jessica. They cover three decades from Jessica's elopement to Lady Redesdale's death, and they set out Muv's feelings about the events which transformed her life. Reading them, I felt sympathetic towards a woman who often suffered a raw deal from her husband and her children but never complained. She came across as a loving and self-sacrificing mother. Yet, when I read her political interventions and prejudiced comments, my attitude altered. I was shocked by her letter to the prime minister Neville Chamberlain after the Munich Settlement, which championed Hitler as 'above all a person of heart'.[8] Nor could I understand how an otherwise logical woman could write to a national newspaper supporting the regime and ignoring the horrific reality of what was happening in Germany. My reaction shifted again as I read the unpublished letters between Muv and her niece, Madeau Stewart, which describe Sydney's final years. Reading how she survived after the death of two of her children, I respected her resilience. To help me put these conflicting reactions in perspective, I was fortunate to be able to speak to members of Lady Redesdale's family. Interviewing Jessica's children Constancia Romilly and Ben Treuhaft; Diana's son Jonathan Guinness, Lord Moyne and her daughter-in-law, Charlotte Mosley; and Sydney's great-granddaughter Marina Guinness was invaluable. I gained insight from them into how Sydney came across when you met her and how they made sense of this complex woman.

Drawing on the different perspectives on Lady Redesdale, this book tells her story in full, but the contradictions remain and there is still no consensus. It is now up to each reader to make their own assessment of her. What seems certain is she would not have cared what we thought: she would not have wanted our pity or bothered about our censure. She was a proud woman who greatly valued her independence. All that mattered to Lady Redesdale was that *she* believed she was right, and once she had made up her mind no one would shift her. Like her father, she was at heart a master mariner who steered her own course and faced the consequences.[9]

1

An Adventurous Childhood

As lightning electrified the sky, a hurricane lashed the sails and massive waves swept over the schooner threatening a shipwreck, a brave little girl in a sailor suit stared resolutely at the menacing sea. Eight-year-old Sydney Bowles was not going to cry, nor would she show a flicker of emotion. Instead she carried on with what she was doing: playing dominoes and looking after her little sister. Her father had taken them on an adventure and this hazardous voyage from Alexandria to Acre was just part of it; his daughter accepted it without questioning. Faced with powerful storms it was sink or swim, and Sydney swam; she stayed calm until the storm passed. This experience was to prepare her for the future. As family friend James Lees-Milne was later to observe, she 'looked at life with the philosophic detachment of a mariner and accepted its vicissitudes with a wonderful fearlessness and robust good sense'.[1]

Her stoical attitude was honed during her tempestuous childhood. Sydney's early years were far more dramatic and exciting than her six daughters' upbringing; the Mitford girls were bored by the stability and regular routine their mother provided, but it seems she was determined to give them the secure home life she had lacked. As controversies then tragedies swirled around her, threatening to overwhelm her family, she remained cool, calm and detached. That ability to stand back and observe rather than become fully involved was to prove a double-edged sword: it protected her but also separated her from those she loved. Serene Sydney was to remain enigmatic until the end, a woman who appeared on the surface totally predictable but could spring the greatest surprises.

As Sydney's grandson Jonathan Guinness pointed out, the key to understanding Sydney is her father.[2] The charismatic, self-made magazine proprietor and politician Thomas Gibson Bowles was the greatest influence on her life. His views, rather than her husband's, were to be her guiding light. Thomas, known as 'Tap' to his children, was a talented journalist then later a politician. Always his own man, he was supremely confident and unwilling to toe the party line, instead preferring to ride his own hobby horses. Obstinate to an exceptional degree and always believing he was right, Thomas would pass on many of his views to his daughter and, like him, she refused to accept received opinions.

Thomas was an outsider, a man who never fitted in but who was happy to be a maverick. When addressing an Individualist Club, he told them that he was too much of an individualist to belong to their society; he never spoke a truer word.[3] His unconventional upbringing marked him out as different and made him independent. His father was the politician Thomas Milner-Gibson, who changed parties, leaving the Tories to become a Radical MP because he believed in free trade. He campaigned for the repeal of the Corn Laws and was later made a cabinet minister in Lord Palmerston's government. Milner-Gibson married an heiress, Susannah, who hosted stimulating salons to advance his political career. When her husband got one of their servants pregnant, Susannah proved to have a forgiving nature. The other woman, Susan Bowles, was the daughter of a South London brush-maker. When she was aged about twenty, she began working as a servant in the Milner-Gibson's Eaton Square house. After getting pregnant by her boss, she left the Milner-Gibsons' employment and in 1841 gave birth to a son, Thomas Gibson Bowles, in a lodging house in Whitechapel.[4] In later life, young Thomas could never pinpoint the exact date of his birth. He explained: 'I am no more certain of it than I am of the birthday of Julius Caesar.'[5] Instead, he preferred to portray himself as a unique phenomenon, a truly self-made man. He saw himself as 'Novus Homo', a man who succeeded or failed on his own merit, explaining: 'If that which he has made be good, the greater credit his; if bad, the less discredit – for he started with fewer advantages.'[6]

Fortunately for young Thomas, his father took responsibility for him and, three years after his illegitimate son's birth, Mr Milner-Gibson came to find him. Whatever her emotions, Susan Bowles handed Thomas over to his father believing he would have more opportunities than if he remained with her. From then on, her former lover provided her with a small income and a house where her son could occasionally visit her. Perhaps reflecting his attitude to his own illegitimacy, Thomas never told his children about their real grandmother, and his grandchildren, the Mitford girls, knew nothing about the brush-maker's daughter.[7]

Separated from his mother, the young boy was taken to the Milner-Gibsons' country house in Suffolk. Thomas would never forget standing in the hall waiting to discover whether his stepmother, Susannah, would accept him. Fortuitously, she was a kindhearted woman who welcomed her husband's lovechild into her home. She called the little boy her 'darling Tommy' and would never allow anyone to treat him as a second-class citizen. She told guests: 'This is Tom Bowles. Be civil to him – or leave the house.'[8]

Despite the compassionate treatment, there remained a stigma attached to being illegitimate in the Victorian era and young Thomas could not attend a public school in England, so he was educated in France.

Short, but with a charismatic personality, Thomas was determined to make his mark on Victorian society. In 1868 he launched his own weekly magazine, *Vanity Fair*, which became the scourge of pompous politicians. *Vanity Fair* was best known for its caricatures of famous people by Pellegrini and Ward (known as Ape and Spy), and Thomas wrote witty biographical sketches to accompany the cartoons. Among his contributors were the French artist James Tissot, the author Lewis Carroll, and Oscar Wilde's brother, Willie Wilde. The magazine's sketches and gossip column soon became required reading among the elite. It became a badge of honour – or notoriety – to be featured in its pages; a person was not truly famous until they had appeared.

Believing he could make a difference, Thomas's aim was to create a politics based on principle instead of a government of mediocrity, where the country was ruled by self-serving party hacks.[9] A politician was judged on his personal integrity, adherence to principle and his brilliance of mind rather than his family connections. Fearlessly exposing self-seeking opportunists, he wanted statesmen who would govern in the interests of their country rather than their party.[10] Fearless, he never cared who he offended, even occasionally writing scathing articles about the Royal Family, particularly the louche Prince of Wales.[11]

Thomas was an original thinker, who explored his ideas further in his book *Flotsam and Jetsam*, which recorded his musings on subjects from science to philosophy, politics to religion. He believed in thinking ideas out from first principles and not just accepting other people's theories.[12] Read with his journalism, the book reveals the originality of his mind and emphasises what an effective communicator he was, but it also shows his views were often eccentric and inconsistent. He admired the practical skills of individual members of the working class, for instance the Aldeburgh sailors who crewed his yacht, but he was no fan of democracy, arguing that the masses were too ignorant to vote in the best interests of the country.[13] Disliking the English class system and loathing snobbery, he saw himself as a self-made man and was critical of the powerful families who dominated the Conservative party. Surprisingly, considering these views, he supported the idea of *noblesse oblige*, where there was an alliance between the aristocracy and the masses, and believed that the ruling classes were more likely than self-made industrialists to treat their employees with kindness and respect.[14] In a moment of surprising self-awareness, he admitted that he never acted purely upon reason and rarely followed a principle consistently. He mused, 'I wonder if many other men are as great imposters as I.'[15]

In 1874, Thomas fell in love with Jessica Evans-Gordon, whose father was the governor of the Royal Victoria Military Hospital, Netley, overlooking the Solent. Jessica was descended from an ancient Scottish family, the Gordons of Lochinvar, who inspired many romantic myths.[16] Musical and strong-willed, it was her personality rather than her fair-haired, statuesque looks which attracted her husband. The couple married in 1875, the bride recording (presumably humorously) in her diary 'Married -and-done-for!'[17] Jessica and Thomas moved into Cleeve Lodge in Hyde Park Gate, London, an attractive Regency house with a large garden. They soon started a family. George was born in 1877, then a second son, Geoffrey, two years later. On 10 May 1880, their first daughter Sydney was born at Inchmery in Hampshire, a rented house on the Exbury estate of Thomas's friend Bertie Mitford. The baby girl was named after Thomas's favourite half-sister.

Jessica was a better wife than a mother and she always emphasised to her husband that he was her primary focus. She explained: 'It is you who wish to place children, household and many things first in my heart, and I who have rebelled against them and told you that [...] I married to be with you.'[18] She preferred helping him plot his career to attending to her maternal duties. She held her own views which she argued eloquently in letters to him. Influenced by his wife, in 1885 Gibson Bowles launched *The Lady*, a magazine aimed at a female readership. Combining society gossip, art, music, beauty hints and cookery pages, it soon had a substantial readership.

After giving birth to three children in five years, Jessica was exhausted and became a semi-invalid. Partly due to ill-health but also because she had little interest in her children, Jessica was a kind but distant mother. Sydney's lasting memory of her ailing parent was of her reclining on a sofa in her drawing room.[19] The three children were looked after by their Scottish nanny and a nursemaid, and saw far more of their energetic father than their languid mother. Five years after Sydney's birth Mrs Bowles had another child, Dorothy, who was nicknamed Weenie. Pregnancy and childbirth frightened Jessica and she never wanted to go through another birth. So when, two years later, she discovered she was pregnant again, Jessica was appalled. According to Sydney, who heard the story from her governess, Mrs Bowles tried to take matters into her own hands, with devastating consequences. Early in her pregnancy she tried to miscarry by jumping off a table and rolling downstairs.[20] After this attempt failed, she reconciled herself to her fate, but when she was five months pregnant in June 1887 she went into premature labour.

As it became clear something was seriously wrong, the doctor was called, and he tried to save his patient by aborting the baby.

Unaware of what had been happening, as he had been at work all day, Thomas arrived home to find his wife seriously ill and their baby dead. Furious with the doctor, he chucked him out of the house. As Jessica continued to haemorrhage, infection set in and nothing could be done to save her. Sydney was only seven, and Weenie just two, when Jessica died. It was a terrible time for the whole family; Sydney recalled being sent to see her father, who, overwhelmed with grief, seemed like a stranger.[21] She remembered her mother's funeral with horror, always associating the overpowering smell of stephanotis with that sad occasion.[22] Setting in stone his feelings about their marriage on Jessica's tombstone, Thomas had engraved: 'For eleven happy years were their lives knit together as one; and when she was taken to her rest four children remained to him, among the unspeakable blessings she brought to his home.'[23]

From then on, Sydney's father became the centre of her world. Thomas was a loving, involved father, but he gave his two young daughters a tough childhood, more suited to boys than genteel Victorian girls. After Jessica died, there were no festivities or presents at Christmas or for birthdays. The children missed having a conventional celebration and, wanting to be like everyone else, Sydney used to pretend to her friends that they had received gifts.[24] However, Thomas gave his children something more valuable than material goods: his time. He never left his daughters for longer than a couple of days and insisted on taking them with him to adult social events. Sydney suspected the hostesses did not particularly like two little girls turning up to their sophisticated salons, but for Thomas having his daughters with him was non-negotiable.[25]

As the whole family were devastated by Jessica's death, in September 1888 Thomas decided they needed an adventure: they would take a year out and sail to Egypt and the Holy Land. Dressing his four children in sailor suits, he bought a schooner, *The Nereid*, and manned it with Aldeburgh fishermen. A nursemaid and a governess came along, too, to look after the girls. A sketch of Sydney at the time shows a pretty child with long curly hair, large limpid eyes and a determined set to her mouth – dressed, of course, in a sailor suit.

Thomas wrote about their eventful voyage in his book *The Log of the Nereid*. The book was dedicated to his youngest daughter 'Captain Weenie' in cloyingly sentimental terms. Rather than cute, the spoilt three-year-old comes across as an obnoxious pocket-sized tyrant who enjoyed teasing their long-suffering dog, Smiler, and being rude to the crew. Revealing the characteristics Thomas valued, he wrote that her 'splendid impatience of discipline, entire want of consideration for others, absolute contempt for her elders, complete devotion to her own interests, and utter disregard of all consequences' endeared her to her 'doting father'.[26] Four decades later, this description could have equally fitted several of his granddaughters during their rebellious phases and, unlike her father, Sydney was to find these traits in her children exhausting rather than endearing.

Aboard *The Nereid*, Captain Weenie was treated as the unrivalled star of the show. In her father's book, her babbling baby-talk is treated as though she is an oracle, while 'First Lieutenant Sydney' only merits a cursory mention. As Sydney was so devoted to her father, Thomas's blatant favouritism must have been difficult. Sydney had already suffered the sudden loss of her mother and no longer had a stable home. Perhaps it was at this early age that she learned to detach to cope with the intense emotions which otherwise might have engulfed her. Rather than engage with her feelings, she stood back and calmly observed. It was to prove a protective and perhaps necessary coping mechanism considering the demanding and self-dramatizing characters in her family, both in her childhood and later life.

During the eight-month voyage there were plenty of adventures, which Sydney found exciting rather than frightening. Years later, she wrote a memoir, *The Dolphin*, to entertain her children, which described being becalmed on their way to Gibraltar. It was so hot the children were allowed to sleep on deck under the stars. They loved learning the names of the constellations from the skipper, and thought it was much more fun than being at home in a bed. After a few days with no wind, they were running short of food and water. The only entertainment was the flying fish which occasionally landed on the deck. But then, suddenly, on the third day, a school of dolphins appeared on the horizon. Drawing on nautical superstitions, the skipper killed a dolphin and nailed its tail to the jib. As if by magic the weather changed. First one ripple then another stirred the sea, a breeze picked up and they were able to sail on to Gibraltar.[27] The experience left a lasting impression on Sydney. For the rest of her life the fear of running out of drinking water meant she only ever filled a glass of water one third full, never to the top.[28]

There were many memorable moments which Sydney recalled years later for her enthralled children.[29] A risk-taker, despite a terrible forecast, Thomas decided to set sail from Alexandria to Acre. His actions nearly ended in disaster. Forty ships were wrecked off the coast of Syria in one of the worst storms for a generation, but with his characteristic luck he managed to bring his family safely into port. Sydney was to inherit his obstinacy and pass it on to her daughters, but this inflexibility would have more destructive consequences in the next generation.

The Log of the Nereid provides us with an insight into Thomas's political attitudes and prejudices. An antisemitic diatribe he wrote after observing the Jews at the Wailing Wall in Jerusalem is particularly abhorrent. He shows no sympathy for the plight of persecuted Jewish refugees who had left Russia fearing for their safety after a series of pogroms.*

As well as scorning marginalised Jewish refugees, he was also critical of successful Jewish people, suggesting they pulled the strings on events throughout the world. He then mentioned prominent wealthy Jewish people, including the banking family the Rothschilds, the financier and philanthropist Baron de Hirsch, and the *Daily Telegraph*'s proprietor Mr Levy Lawson, saying that he would only believe they considered there was much to wail about if they gave up their positions in Europe and based their businesses in the Holy Land.

---

*   Pogroms occurred in Russia from 1881 to 1882. There were widespread anti-Jewish riots, which destroyed thousands of Jewish homes and reduced those attacked to poverty. These attacks changed the perception among Russian Jews about how safe they were in the Russian Empire and gave a boost to the early Zionist movement.

This expression of antisemitism was not a one-off for Thomas. When he stood for Parliament in Banbury in 1880, his Liberal opponent Bernhard Samuelson was from a German Jewish background. As the other candidate won, Bowles suggested Russian agents had offered money to the Liberal campaign with the intention that Mr Samuelson would take his orders from a foreign power. There was no evidence for this conspiracy theory and only Thomas, with his overweening confidence, had thought he would win the seat.[30]

Unfortunately, Thomas's hateful prejudices were widely held in the late Victorian era. Negative portrayals of Jewish people were all too common in literature. Charles Dickens's character Fagin in *Oliver Twist*, George du Maurier's caricature of Svengali in *Trilby* and Rider Haggard in *She* drew on similar stereotypes to Thomas's portrayals. After Darwinism, pseudo-scientific theories, which promoted the idea of racial hierarchies and racial degeneracy, built on existing antisemitic myths. Well-established Jewish families who were entering society and politics were also open to attacks. The so-called 'Court Jews' including Baron Maurice de Hirsch, the Sassoons, the Rothschilds and Sir Ernest Cassel, who were in the Prince of Wales' circle, were particularly resented.[31] Rather than being well thought out, there was ambivalence at the heart of *fin de siècle* antisemitism, reflected in the contradictory mixture of attraction and repulsion apparent in portrayals of Jewish people. If they were powerful, they were characterised as threatening, but if they were powerless, they were stigmatised as weak.[32]

Thomas's attitudes reflect this characteristic lack of consistency. In *Flotsam and Jetsam*, he wrote, 'The Jews are the most persuasive race in the world', adding that they were persecuted 'in order to diminish the seductive flow of their speech'.[33] His portrayals of successful Jewish men in *Vanity Fair* were often positive. Between 1869 and 1914, more than seventy Jewish people were featured in *Vanity Fair*, including nine Rothschilds and Edward Levy Lawson, who he mentioned in *The Log of the Nereid*. Ironically, Thomas's first biographical sketch, which helped to seal *Vanity Fair*'s success, was of Britain's first Jewish prime minister, Benjamin Disraeli. The Conservative politician went to school with Thomas's father, and it seems Gibson Bowles identified with Disraeli as a fellow self-made man. He wrote: 'I have the greatest admiration and respect for him.' According to him, Disraeli represented the coming principle of the world, which would be based on personal merit. Even though barriers of 'birth of race of religion of wealth all frowned' on him, he had got over them and he was now 'the first statesman of the day'. No doubt thinking of himself, Thomas concluded it showed that it was possible for 'the man whom Nature alone has made great to win his proper station although other things and men are against him'.[34]

As so often with Thomas, his views do not form a coherent standpoint. At times he seemed to identify with Jewish people as fellow outsiders, who rose by their own merit and should not be discriminated against on grounds of birth, but on other occasions he lashed out at them, reverting to pure prejudice. The views expressed by Thomas and other late Victorians had consequences for the future. As the historian of fascism Martin Pugh explains, 'These debates in the 1890s about moral degeneracy, racial rejuvenation, national unity and the Jews remind us that Britain played their part in laying the foundations of inter-war racist and fascist thinking.'[35]

The *Nereid* voyage was an education for Sydney in many ways. She absorbed by osmosis her father's political views, but she also developed resilience, knowing she could face any challenges calmly. She saw the Holy Land and the pyramids, and sailed on the Nile. She also had some unintended lessons in love aboard *The Nereid*. Sydney and Dorothy's attractive young governess, Rita Shell, known as 'Tello', accompanied them on the voyage. When Tello became Thomas's mistress is open to speculation. She worked for him before Jessica died and chose to leave shortly before Mrs Bowles's death. As soon as she heard of the tragedy, Tello contacted her former employer and offered to come back.[36] Romantic tensions within the close confines of *The Nereid* were intense. She had a flirtation, possibly an affair, with a young naval officer. Sydney remembered the lieutenant visiting Tello on the boat and singing her romantic songs. Apparently, when Thomas found out, he was so jealous he decided to set sail immediately to interrupt the relationship.

After the voyage Tello discovered she was pregnant. When her governess left suddenly, Sydney was very upset, particularly as she did not know why it had happened.[37] She only found out the reason years later, when she saw Tello walking down Sloane Street with four little boys dressed in sailor suits.[38] It was always thought by Tello's family that the naval officer was the father of her eldest son, but in the following years she had three more illegitimate boys by Thomas. He never married her, partly because he had other demanding lady friends, but he bought her a house in Kensington and made her editor of *The Lady*. Sydney liked Tello and was disappointed that her father did not marry her. She remained friends with her former governess for the rest of her life.

As Thomas remained determinedly single, at only fourteen, Sydney was put in charge of her father's large London town house in Lowndes Square. It was a demanding task for an adolescent, which involved managing the staff and finances, but Sydney rose to the challenge. Her only problem was with argumentative footmen and drunken butlers who refused to show respect to a teenaged mistress. This experience left Sydney with a dislike of male servants, and from then on, she employed only women in her house.

As well as their London base, Thomas also rented Wilbury, an exquisite Palladian house in Wiltshire. The symmetrical beauty of the house permanently influenced Sydney's taste; it became for her the gold standard of a perfect country house. She always admired eighteenth-century style, and she passed on this taste to her daughters, Nancy, Diana and Deborah. She found her housemates less harmonious than the house. Wilbury belonged to Sir Henry Malet, but it was so large that the Malet and the Bowles family shared the house. The household was full of eccentric characters. Preferring animals to people, Lady Malet was afraid her horses might be bored in their stables, so she kept them tethered near the entrance of the house so they could be entertained by watching the arrival of guests. The butler, Malpas, would stand on one leg during dinner. When asked why, he answered, 'Because storks do it.' The Malets' daughter Vera, who was a similar age to Sydney, was equally weird. The two girls were expected to be friends, but Vera preferred playing with frogs and newts than with her playmate. Her morbid obsession with ghost stories was also rather disconcerting.[39] Hardly surprisingly, it was at this time that Lady Redesdale first cultivated her lifelong habit of withdrawing into her own thoughts if she was bored. A great reader, she enjoyed making up stories and day-dreaming. Focusing on a painting of a colourful Durbar in India during meals in the dining room, she would block out the people around her and escape to her imagination.[40] One of the highlights of her time at Wilbury was riding every morning with her father to Grateley station, 4 miles away across Salisbury Plain, to collect the papers. Riding sidesaddle, on a sturdy pony called Rowena, Sydney was never a keen horsewoman, but she relished the time with Thomas.[41]

The girls were educated at home by governesses, but Sydney always said she learnt more from her father than any formal education. Despite their brothers, George and Geoffrey, being sent off to preparatory school, the four children continued to form a tight-knit unit. Opposites in personality and looks, the two girls were particularly close. Friends called them Oil and Vinegar, with Sydney soothing and Weenie acerbic.[42] When, aged thirteen, George joined the navy and went to Britannia Royal Naval College, Dartmouth, Sydney worried about him. The discipline was harsh, and she was concerned about how ill her brother looked when he returned home on leave.[43]

Thomas had some eccentric ideas which he passed on to his daughter. He adhered to Mosaic dietary rules, believing they helped Jewish people stay healthy. Pork products were banned from the house, and rabbit, hare and shellfish were never eaten. A great believer in the importance of wheatgerm and bran fibre, Thomas insisted freshly made wholemeal bread was eaten by his family. Fastidious about cleanliness, Thomas relished regular Turkish baths. In London, this involved filling an entire room with steam and then getting his butler to tip buckets of warm water over him. When he was in other parts of the country, he improvised. While in Scotland, a dog kennel was filled with hot bricks to create a steam room. Then, when Thomas emerged, the butler would tip buckets of cold water over him from an upstairs window.[44] The only trouble was this makeshift Turkish bath was near the front door, so unsuspecting guests were treated to the sight of a naked Thomas on their arrival.[45] His children also had an unusual bathtime routine, as he believed they should be rinsed with clean water after bathing to make sure they did not reabsorb dirt from the bath water.

Deeply critical of conventional medicine and believing that 'the good body' would heal itself, Thomas would not allow his children to be given any medicine. Rather than turning to doctors when his family was ill, he called in alternative practitioners. His guru was the Swedish clinician Dr Kellgren, who advocated massage, manipulation of the joints and medical gymnastics as the cure for most ailments. Dr Kellgren would assure his patient that their illness was imaginary, which Sydney admitted was not always the most soothing approach if you were feeling terribly unwell.[46] Nonetheless, trusting to her father's judgement, Lady Redesdale was to apply many of her father's idiosyncratic ideas when she had a family of her own.

Eccentric though it was, the Bowles household was a stimulating environment for Sydney to grow up in. As Thomas took his girls everywhere with him, they met the leading celebrities of the era. Charles Dodgson (better known as Lewis Carroll) sent Sydney a copy of *Alice in Wonderland*, with a whimsical letter, while the Pre-Raphaelite painter Millais used her as a model.[47] While life at home was never dull, Sydney's happiest times were spent sailing with her father and, like him, she developed a lifelong love of the sea. Every year Thomas and his family sailed to Deauville or Trouville in France and spent the summer living aboard their yacht. The experience introduced Sydney to French culture and cuisine and, like Thomas, she became a Francophile.

Back in England, during their daily horse rides or chats over breakfast, her father treated her as his confidante. After selling *Vanity Fair* for £20,000 in 1889, Thomas dedicated himself to getting elected to Parliament. He had stood unsuccessfully as a Conservative candidate several times before, but in 1892, he was finally elected as the Member of Parliament for King's Lynn. With his usual panache, he sailed into the constituency on his new yacht, *The Hoyden*, with his winsome daughters aboard. While in the constituency, the family's home was aboard ship, and the boat also became the campaign headquarters. Sydney enjoyed being involved in the campaign and energetically threw herself into canvassing for her father. On polling day Thomas and the girls drove around the constituency in a large carriage festooned in yellow ribbons, meeting enthusiastic party workers wherever they went. Sydney was disappointed not to be able to go to the count but, on tenterhooks, she stayed up on the boat until the result was in; this time Thomas had won by eleven votes.[48]

Through her father, Sydney found herself at the heart of Victorian political society. She often listened to Thomas vehemently argue his case in heated discussions.[49] At the age of fourteen, she learnt to type so that she could type her father's speeches for the House of Commons.[50] Thomas always emphasised his political independence, telling his constituents that he would put country before party. A charismatic showman, he was a rebel with unpredictable political beliefs. As he was not a party man, although he was exceptionally bright and a forensic orator, he never held the highest office. He often proved to be a thorn in the side of the government, whichever party was in power. A life-long free trader, in 1906 he changed party standing as an independent 'Unionist Free Fooder' in King's Lynn. By doing so, he split the conservative vote and lost his seat.[51] In January 1910, he was briefly re-elected as the Liberal MP for his old constituency, but in the second election of that year he lost the seat and never again sat in Parliament.

During his political career, Thomas was most famous for championing British naval power. Reflecting this, he was portrayed in *Punch* cartoons as 'The Cap'en': a pirate with a peg-leg and a hook for a hand.[52] He argued that the country's power rested in its control of the seas and that it should not undermine its strength by getting involved in struggles between countries in Continental Europe. Near the end of his career, he made history by challenging the government's taxation policy. In 1912, he sued the Bank of England and won. Afterwards, the Bowles Act, which established that nothing less than an Act of Parliament could provide the basis upon which taxation could lawfully be imposed on a subject, went onto the statute books.[53]

As Sydney worshipped her father and never thought he was wrong, she was influenced by his political attitudes. He wrote that he had no patience with 'toleration', stating that it 'can only spring from want of knowledge or want of conviction: it can only grow in laziness and uncertainty of mind. As to the thing we really know, and as to the thing we really believe, no one of us can admit of toleration. To us those things alone are true and to be respected as truths.'[54]

When Thomas died in 1922, *The Times* explained that his temperamental dislike of compromise was the reason why he never held high office.[55] A few years before his death he wrote an essay which is the key to understanding him, 'Whatever I would be or do I must be Myself, and do it as Myself. The Word I have to speak is my Word, and the occasion arising, that Word must be said in my way.'[56]

Many of the seeds which allowed extreme views to flourish in his daughter and granddaughters were sown by him. He could not have foreseen and may not have agreed with the direction their political ideas took them, but his belief that conviction trumped tolerance, and that politics should be defined in black and white rather than shades of grey, paved the way to the polarised paths his offspring would later take.*

---

*   This does not imply Thomas Bowles would have condoned 1930s fascism.

2

Love and Marriage

Fourteen is an impressionable age for a girl; experiences at this time are indelibly imprinted on the memory. Being just about to transform from a child into a woman, beyond her immediate family the opposite sex was an intriguing but largely unknown quantity for Sydney. It was at this moment that she met the man who was to be her future husband. Her father, Thomas, was invited to stay at the large country house of his good friend and Parliamentary colleague, Bertie Mitford. Thomas made it clear that he would only come if he could bring his two daughters, so Sydney and Weenie travelled with their father to Batsford, the Mitford estate in Gloucestershire.

In a memoir written many years later, Sydney recorded every detail of that fateful visit from the aroma of beeswax polish and the wood fire to the welcoming light in the hall. Although she was tired from the journey — first by train and then wagonette from the station through the dark, wintry, Cotswold country lanes — she revived when she entered the library. Her eyes were immediately drawn to the exceptionally handsome young man who was casually standing by the fireplace. Dressed in country clothes of an old brown keeper's jacket, seventeen-year-old David Mitford was totally unaware of the impression he was making, but Sydney would never forget that moment. She wrote in her memoir it was then she first fell in love with him; yet, with her characteristic candour she added that her infatuation was brief, and she soon fell out again.[1] Whether David felt the same we do not know. At fourteen, Sydney was betwixt and between; an awkward teenager dressed in an unbecoming sailor suit, she did not believe she was best equipped to attract David's attention.[2] It would be nearly a decade before this initial attraction was fully played out, but that visit to Batsford was when it all began.

The two families did not form a natural alliance. Unlike Bertie, his more snobbish wife Lady Clementine did not appreciate Thomas's unorthodox behaviour. For her part, nor did Sydney unreservedly admire her future mother-in-law; she thought Bertie was exceptionally handsome, but his wife was too fat. The Mitfords had very different ways of doing things to the Bowles and neither Lady Clementine nor Thomas was willing to back down. When his hostess asked if the children would dine downstairs with the adults, Thomas replied that they would. However, as Lady Clementine did not approve of this arrangement, Weenie had to have supper upstairs as she was considered too young. The dinner was lavish with endless rich courses. As a healthy living proponent, who disapproved of over-eating, Thomas told an obese guest who was about to have a second helping that it would be better for him not to. It was a tense evening for Sydney, made even more stressful when she got a fishbone stuck in her throat. Fortunately, she managed to remove it when she got back to her room.[3]

Over the next few years Sydney grew into a tall, striking girl with attitude. Photos of her as a young woman show a moody beauty, her sulky mouth suggesting a stubborn streak. Languidly staring at the camera, reclining in her chair, she looks as though she cannot be bothered to give even the photographer what he wants. Her relationships with people beyond the charmed circle of her closest family would be on her own terms, and she would please herself, not others. She would always be surprisingly malleable with those chosen few insiders but inflexible with outsiders; few would be allowed into her very private inner sanctum.

The first man to make her feel attractive was an older man, her father's friend, the French artist Paul-César Helleu. The Bowles and Helleu families met every year during their summer holidays in France.

As Sydney grew up the urbane artist enjoyed sketching her; in one of his drawings, he captures her pensive mood: her eyes are cast down as though she is lost in thought.[4] He seemed to understand her complex character, recognising she was not a young woman to be crossed. He nicknamed her '*la Loi*' (the Law).[5]

Losing her mother had made Sydney grow up fast, and she was mature for her age. Her daughter, Jessica, believed that her extraordinary childhood, where she was given an 'unnaturally free rein' from the age of fourteen, made her 'naturally bossy nature' become more pronounced.[6] In most situations, Sydney thought that she knew best. If people did not behave as she thought they ought to, she could be disapproving. As well as being judgemental of others she could also be critical of herself, always analysing her actions in her diaries and noting where she failed to live up to her own exacting standards.[7] Conscientious and dutiful, the natural down-turned set of her mouth made her look more severe than she was. Throughout her life, her lack of a warm smile made her look unapproachable; it suggested a more miserable temperament than she had. In fact, her attitude to life was predominantly positive – she may have been serious, but she was never dull. Sydney had a great sense of humour, but she was an appreciative listener rather than a performer and, while her siblings were always joking, her witty quips were razor-sharp but rare. George teased her relentlessly, saying that she only made two jokes a year, so whenever she came out with one, he would exclaim: 'Oh Hurrah! The Half-Yearly! Applause please, everyone – for Sydney's Half-Yearly!'[8]

Tello had been an excellent governess who provided Sydney with a good grounding. Other governesses were not as impressive or likeable. In 1895, Miss Loraine came to teach the girls for two years. She was a disciplinarian who instilled good manners into her unruly pupils. Sydney described her as 'a dragon', but credited her with turning them from 'savages' into human beings. Hammering out foibles, the governess stopped Sydney's habit of getting up and stretching during mealtimes. This behaviour met with Thomas's approval as it followed Dr Kellgren's principles, but would have been unacceptable in polite society. Academically, Miss Loraine was limited. She could not teach maths but was good at French and she encouraged her pupil's piano playing. Sydney was a talented pianist whose repertoire ranged from Beethoven to popular ballads, and her love of music continued throughout her life: she always enjoyed gathering her family around the piano to sing while she played.[9]

Overcoming the limitations of her education, Sydney became a studious girl with a logical mind. Perhaps inheriting some of her father's journalistic talent, she wrote with clarity and could marshal a well-structured argument.[10] She was so bright Thomas considered sending her to Girton College, Cambridge. This idea was short-lived. After she visited the university, it was instead decided that she should stay at home and be launched into the marriage market of London society.[11] Although ahead of his time in many of his attitudes, Thomas had traditional views about women; he believed a wife's place was in the home with her children. He wrote dismissively that females were 'rendered incompetent' by nature from being involved in the general business of the world, 'to which she can only bring confusion'.[12] Rather than risk Sydney becoming a bluestocking, his daughter needed educating in how to be a wife, but that was one thing Thomas could not do. Lacking the feminine influence of a mother, she remained dressed in a thick serge sailor suit, day and evening, summer and winter, until she was eighteen.[13] By this stage even Sydney admitted the outfit had become a 'sore trial' to her.[14] Finally, a female friend of Thomas's explained to him that his daughter needed a more alluring wardrobe if she was to attract a husband.

Liberated at last, suddenly Sydney metamorphosised from a dowdy teenager into a glamorous young woman. She noted in her diary the many compliments she received and how men in the street would turn around to look at her. Not seduced by the flattering attention, she never lost her self-critical faculty, cautioning herself not to become conceited because probably any reasonably attractive young girl would receive similar attention.[15] The summer of 1898 was a hectic time for Sydney as she had just come out as a debutante. Her first dance was given by the Duke and Duchess of Devonshire in their Piccadilly townhouse. As she had no mother to chaperone her, Thomas escorted her to the ball.

Father and daughter were among the first guests to arrive at 10.30 p.m. and as they entered the grand hallway the strains of a Hungarian band promised a romantic evening. However, when they were presented to their hosts, Sydney was not impressed; she thought the Duchess, with her fixed smile and too much make up, was hideous, while the Duke appeared to be half asleep.[16] It could have been Thomas speaking; Sydney had inherited from her father a sharp tongue accompanied by an inner confidence that she was anyone's equal. Although it was her first dance, she wrote in her diary that she had not felt at all shy, asking why she should be nervous. Father and daughter did not stay long; after seeing a few of her friends they left the ball at midnight.[17]

In between attending parties, Sydney visited her brother George, who had left the navy and was now at Trinity College, Cambridge. Everywhere she went she made an impression. George wrote: 'Even I, as her brother, not given to admiration of my sisters – far from it – nevertheless thought Sydney very handsome.' He added that part of her appeal was that she walked so gracefully and had such a calm presence.[18] Another element of her attraction was that she was unobtainable. When one of George's friends put his hand on her arm Sydney was outraged at his cheek. She stated in her diary that she hated men who behaved like that unless she wished them to. If she disagreed with one of the students, she would tell him straight.[19] There was no feminine guile or fake submissiveness with Sydney. Although she was good-looking, she never bothered about her appearance; her thick wavy hair refused to stay in place and she would leave a trail of hair pins wherever she went.[20]

The centre of Sydney's social life was the ice-skating rink at Prince's Skating Club in Montpelier Square. Rather than the callow youths she met as a debutante, Sydney fell in love with her ice-skating instructor, the tall, elegant Swede Henning Grenander. Seven years older than her, Henning was the undisputed star of the show. He was described in a magazine as 'the most graceful skater' who was 'a poseur in skating'.[21] It is likely that Sydney had already come across him at Dr Kellgren's house, because Henning also gave Swedish massages and was studying medicine at St George's Hospital Medical School.

Like Thomas, Henning was a showman, and on Sunday afternoons he would give extempore demonstrations. All the other skaters on the rink would clear a large space in the middle and Henning would signal to the orchestra to play a waltz or mazurka for his performance.[22] It was no surprise to his fans when he became world champion for his figure skating. Sydney spent hours watching him and, while he was practising, she sketched him. Capturing her complex feelings, one of her drawings is a flattering image of him, but the other is a hideous caricature. Weenie insisted on showing him both versions, and rather than being offended he was delighted with the attention. In her diary, Sydney explored her emotions, analysing every nuance with the characteristic intensity of a teenage girl. She admitted that she was willing to do almost anything he desired, even allow him to call her Sydney or kiss her if he wanted. She even speculated about what it would be like if she married him.[23] His power over her was so great that when she broke her ankle on the ice, she suppressed her pain and stifled her tears while he manipulated it.[24]

Interestingly, with Henning's svelte physique, clad in his black silk tights and coat trimmed with Astrakhan, there is a look about him of Oswald Mosley dressed in his black-shirt uniform. Both mother and daughter had a 'penchant for physical beauty' and were attracted to men who were physically similar.[25] The difference between the two women was that, unlike Diana, Sydney was always in control of her passion, and she rationally balanced the advantages and disadvantages of an alliance with Henning in her diary. Although it made her despise herself for being mercenary, she admitted that if he was English and the same class as her, she would say yes, but as he was not her answer would be no.[26] Clearly, she experienced a powerful physical attraction to the dashing skater, but she distrusted her instincts and crushed her emotions. When it was her daughters' turn to fall in love a generation later, they complained about her appearing disapproving, but it seems she understood only too well how overpowering those emotions could be, and feared them. Whether the relationship with Henning was largely in her imagination is debatable; it seems to have not gone much further than him coming around to her house to tea.[27] Intense though the infatuation was at the time, it did not last. In 1901, her former idol married another adoring admirer whom he had met on the ice.

From August to October, Thomas took his family to stay in Scotland. Across the border, Sydney had plenty of admirers, including a delightfully named Eustace Heaven. Sydney went to Lady Granville's fancy-dress ball wearing an elaborate wig adorned with magpies and cherries. Rather than dancing, the best part of her evening was spent sitting and chatting to Eustace. Their flirtation continued during long walks by the loch or in the mountains. As always, Sydney could not conceal her true feelings, telling her admirer that she preferred him when he was not flirting. The relationship became serious enough for Sydney to meet his parents and attend their Roman Catholic church with them. Prefiguring her daughters' behaviour decades later, as she sat with Eustace's sister, the girls were unable to stifle a fit of giggles during the priest's pompous sermon. He was not amused, furiously denouncing them from the pulpit for insulting God and the holy angels.[28]

Sydney was evidently interested in young men her own age, but her father still came first in her affections. When one admirer wrote her a flirtatious letter, she asked him not to do so again because, even though she enjoyed receiving it, her father would not approve.[29] It seemed no one could challenge Thomas's pre-eminent position for long. She looked at any potential suitor through his eyes as well as her own. In the following years, Sydney's love life did not run smoothly. One boyfriend was killed in the Boer War, and then she fell in love with an unsuitable roué, Edward 'Jimmy' Meade. Her feelings for him were powerful, and in 1903 it seemed likely they would get engaged, but then Sydney found out that he was a womaniser and ended their relationship.[30] Hurt by Jimmy, Sydney needed a man who was totally different. It was at this point that the handsome young man whom she had first met when she was a gauche fourteen-year-old re-entered her life. In the years since their brief encounter, David had gone out to Ceylon as a tea planter, but after a few years he returned. He fought bravely in the Boer War and was badly injured. He had to have a lung removed, which rendered him unfit for military service. Apparently, David had never forgotten the unusual girl he met nearly a decade before and had then seen occasionally at social events. During his long stay in hospital, recovering from his injuries, he realised he was in love with Sydney.[31] Knowing she was the woman he wanted to marry, he dictated a love letter which was to be given to her if he died.[32]

Her self-confidence undermined by Jimmy's betrayal, it seems Sydney needed a man who was reliable and genuinely in love with her. Physically Sydney and David were well matched: both were tall and slim with classical features and striking blue eyes. One of Farve's cousins described them as 'so beautiful they were like gods walking upon earth'.[33] David was certainly very attractive to women. When a girl-friend of Sydney's came to tea, she asked if he would be there, adding breathlessly, 'If I could only just look at him ...'[34]

Despite women swooning over him, David seemed oblivious to his obvious appeal, and lacked confidence. Perhaps it was because he was a second son and his elder brother Clement was the favourite, and was expected to achieve great things. Clement was the heir who would inherit the Redesdale fortune and title. He was his father's golden boy; the one on whom the family hopes were focused. While David was shunted off to board at Radley, Clement followed in his father's footsteps and went to Eton. One reason the brothers had been separated was Lord and Lady Redesdale did not want Clement's stellar career to be affected by his younger brother's behaviour. David was prone to violent temper tantrums. In one furious outburst, he grabbed a red-hot poker from the fire and threatened his father with it until his French tutor intervened.[35] School was a torment to him, as he was a slow learner who never enjoyed reading. One biographer suggests he was an undiagnosed dyslexic.[36] Inevitably, David was well aware of his second-class status, but with his self-effacing nature he never begrudged his elder brother his superior position in the family.

The fact neither Sydney nor David was the favoured child may have been an important bond between them. Their positions in their families were similar. They both had charismatic fathers: Bertie Redesdale was a famous linguist, diplomat and writer, best known for his book *Tales of Old Japan* about the country's culture, politics and legends.[37] More controversially, he wrote the introduction to the English translation of

Houston Stewart Chamberlain's book *The Foundations of the Nineteenth Century*. With his championing of Germany and toxic antisemitism, Chamberlain's racial theories were later to inspire Hitler.[38] Bertie pointed out that he did not agree with all Chamberlain's conclusions about Jewish people, but he added that, 'I go all lengths with him in his appreciation of the stubborn singleness of purpose and dogged consistency which have made the Jew what he is'.[39]

Bertie was elected to Parliament as a Conservative MP at the same time as Thomas. They became good friends, campaigning together against the introduction of death duties.[40] It was while they worked together on this issue that Thomas first brought his children to Batsford. Afterwards, Bertie and Thomas remained good friends, and the two families continued to occasionally socialise together. A known womaniser, who partied with the Prince of Wales, Bertie was as flamboyant in his private as his public life. Apparently, he even had an affair with his wife's sister, Blanche Hozier, and probably fathered one of her children, the future Clementine Churchill. With other members of their family dominating the scene, both David and Sydney were used to keeping a low profile. Neither wished to emulate their parent's unconventional love lives; they were both looking for a partner for life.

Perhaps the greatest attraction between the young couple was their shared sense of humour. With impeccable comic timing, David was so funny he could have been on stage.[41] Sydney was his perfect foil; having played that role with her family, she appreciated a good joke, and could be witty herself. In the Bowles and Mitford clans nothing was ever taken too seriously. When David asked Thomas if he could marry his daughter, his future father-in-law joked, 'Which one?' He then interrogated the young man about how he intended to support Sydney. David told him he had £400 a year, adding 'and these', holding up his strong hands, indicating he was prepared to use them to work hard.[42]

David and Sydney married at St Margaret's, Westminster, on 6 February 1904. The occasion reflected Sydney's taste; the *Daily Mirror* described the ceremony's 'almost austere simplicity'. Avoiding any ostentation, although the groom had seen service in South Africa, there was no military display. Sydney's bridesmaids were her sister, Weenie, and her friend Cicely Haig, with David's cousins Sylvia Stanley and Clementine Hozier, who was to marry Winston Churchill a few years later. According to the *Daily Mirror*, 'it would be hard to find a more sweet-looking and charmingly unaffected bride than Miss Gibson Bowles'. She wore a white satin dress draped with chiffon with a train of antique Limerick lace. To please her mother-in-law, her bouquet included myrtle grown from a sprig taken from Lady Redesdale's bridal flowers.[43]

It seems the bride was not as in love as the groom, because for Sydney her relationship with David was on the rebound. According to society gossip, it was whispered that as the twenty-three-year-old walked up the aisle, she was in tears, weeping for Jimmy Meade. Another story circulated that a few days before her wedding, a married friend told the naïve bride what to expect on her wedding night. Sydney was so shocked she replied, 'A gentleman would *never* do anything like that.'[44]

After a honeymoon aboard the *Hoyden*, the couple began their married life living with Thomas in Lowndes Square, before moving into their own house in Graham Street near Sloane Square. Despite her initial qualms, once Sydney had made a commitment to David, she honoured it. Both husband and wife were determined to do everything they could to make their marriage work, and this involved compromises on both sides. Unlike her daughters, Sydney did not have inflated expectations – she just wanted a normal family life. As Charlotte Mosley explains, 'She came from a background where you married, and you made the best of it. You brought up your children to do the same.'[45]

As a second son, David had no obvious career path and a limited income. With his earnings and Sydney's allowance, they had about £1,000 a year to live on.[46] To help his daughter and her husband, and perhaps to keep control, Thomas stepped in, providing David with a job as office manager at *The Lady*. Few occupations could have been more unsuitable for the ultra-masculine countryman.[47] Working in an office of a ladies' magazine in the capital city was anathema to him, yet he dutifully worked away at his role for a decade. Bringing a touch of his idiosyncratic self into the office, when rats needed catching, he imported a mongoose to hunt them down. One of the bonuses of the experience was that he became great friends with Sydney's brother George, who ran the magazine. Bowles was far more academic and urbane than David, but they shared a sense of humour. George sometimes played on his brother-in-law's gullibility with his jokes. When George assured David that he had written *Alice in Wonderland*, David believed his brother-in-law for years because he lacked any literary knowledge and totally trusted his friend.[48]

Never having mattered much to anyone before, David loved the stability of married life and was content with domesticity. He described the great happiness he experienced during their first years together and complimented his wife for making their home perfect.[49] Sydney was not as sanguine. Although she was loyal to her husband and loved him, in some ways he disappointed her. In the early years of their marriage, when he was working on *The Lady*, David used to bring his wife a peach as a special treat at the end of each week. She never dared to tell him she did not like the fruit, instead pretending to enjoy it.[50] As this anecdote highlights, the young couple wanted to please each other; the trouble was their tastes were different.

One problem was David did not share Sydney's cultural interests, and so she had to shut down her more literary and intellectual side with him. According to family legend, when they first married, Sydney was shocked to discover that her husband had only read one book: Jack London's *White Fang*. Deciding she would educate him by reading him the classics, her first choice was Thomas Hardy's *Tess of the D'Urbervilles*. As David listened to the tragic story, he was so moved by the poignant plot he cried. When his wife tried to comfort him by explaining to him that it was just fiction and not a true story, he was furious, saying that he would never bother with novels again — and he kept to his word.[51]

Sydney and David came from very different backgrounds. He was a countryman to the core; she was used to living at the heart of London society. The men she was used to in the Bowles family had very different interests to her husband. Thomas thought blood sports were wrong and did not take part in them himself because he believed in the interdependence of humans and animals.[52] Sydney's brother George described the country as 'all muck and blood', and his interests were academic, political and musical.[53] Sydney was sociable and enjoyed meeting different people, but David was content to spend time at home with just his wife for company. The perfect evening for him was sitting in the drawing room in front of the fire, wearing their dressing gowns and eating a simple supper of bread and milk off trays on their laps.[54] Reflecting the balance between the sexes in the Edwardian era, Sydney accepted his wishes and lived a quieter life than she had known with her gregarious father.[55] Her marriage involved Sydney submerging some parts of her own personality and developing new elements. She was willing to do it, because she had always been the undemanding member of the family who fitted her needs around others, but it would be at some cost to her true self.

3

Motherhood

Endlessly conscientious, Sydney did what was expected of her and, almost immediately after her wedding, she got pregnant. During the pregnancy she was so certain she was having a boy that she named him Paul and knitted him blue outfits.[1] David was also delighted at the news and anticipated having a son and heir. He wanted to be with his wife every step of the way, so when she went into labour in November 1904, he remained with her throughout and even administered the anaesthetic.[2] During a fourteen-hour difficult labour, Sydney was characteristically courageous, but when her first-born finally appeared, the nine and a half pound baby was a girl instead of the expected boy. Although she did not complain, it took Sydney some time to get over the whole experience.[3]

At first, the couple thought of calling their daughter Ruby, but eventually they decided on Nancy, the name of a sailor's wife in seafaring ballads, because of Sydney's love of the sea.[4] With her curly dark hair and green eyes, the little girl never looked like a typical blonde, blue-eyed Mitford. Her father thought she was the prettiest child he had ever seen, but her mother was less smitten.[5] Pictures of Sydney as a young mother show a lack of *joie de vivre* in her expression, as though she might have been suffering from post-natal depression. In a photograph of her with Nancy as a toddler, Sydney is turning away from her child. Looking miserable, she stares into the distance, as though she wishes that she was somewhere else. In contrast, David holds his daughter's hand and looks down affectionately at their little girl. Unlike his wife's cool attitude, he was delighted with Nancy and always doted on her.

Growing up as a tomboy, Sydney was unsure about how to deal with girls. She dreamt of having six sons, but over the next sixteen years she was to have five more daughters and only one boy. In 1907, Pamela was born; then two years later Sydney gave birth to her only son, Thomas. There was just a short gap of a year before Diana was born. The Mitfords' bevy of daughters continued to increase over the next decade, with Muv giving birth to Unity in 1914 followed by Jessica (Decca) three years later and finally Deborah (Debo) in 1920. The demanding cycle of pregnancies and births began when Sydney was twenty-four years old and only finished when she was nearly forty. We get an idea of what Muv felt about childbirth from Nancy's novel *The Pursuit of Love*. The character based on her, Aunt Sadie, told her daughters that it was the worst pain in the world, but the strange thing was that she forgot what it was like afterwards. She only remembered when she went into labour again, but by then it was too late.[6]

According to her daughters, Sydney was never maternal, dismissing most of her babies as 'too ugly for words'.[7] Her reserved personality meant she was not tactile or overtly affectionate. Nancy could never remember being hugged or kissed by her mother.[8] With his childlike quality, Farve was more physically affectionate and much better at relating to his daughters. When he came home there were riotous games of hide and seek and a great deal of laughter. However, seen from Sydney's perspective, her perceived failings as a mother are understandable. As her mother had died when she was young, she did not have a maternal role model. She received advice from various members of her husband's family on how to bring her children up, but it was not the same as having her own mother to trust. Inevitably, she only learnt by trial and error, and some of the advice she was given was not helpful. Perhaps the most counter-productive advice came from David's sister Frances, known as Aunt Puma. When Nancy was born, she advised Sydney that her daughter should never hear an angry word. Muv blamed this approach for turning Nancy into a spoilt brat, who threw horrendous tantrums and could not cope with the competition when her sister Pam was born.[9]

As an Edwardian upper-class mother, Sydney was able to delegate the day-to-day care of her children. Her growing brood were handed over to nannies, and time with her children was strictly rationed to first thing in the morning and an hour at teatime. Unfortunately, several of the nannies Sydney chose were far from perfect. The first one was Lily Kersey, whose only qualification for the job was being the daughter of Thomas Bowles's skipper. Although she was untrained and knew nothing about babies, she worked reasonably well until Pam was born. With Lily's attention turned elsewhere, Nancy became jealous that their nanny preferred the new baby. Not wanting her eldest daughter to feel displaced, Sydney dismissed Lily. Her replacement, Norah Evans, stayed for a few years with the Mitfords, but when she left the new nanny was a disaster. Known in family folklore as 'the unkind nanny', she used to bang Nancy's head against the bedpost as a punishment for misbehaving. When Sydney discovered what had happened, she was so upset she retired to bed, leaving Farve to sack the woman on the spot.[10] In later life, Nancy claimed to friends that either 'the unkind nanny' or a nursery nurse had suffered from syphilis which she may have passed on to her, leading to her infertility problems.[11] The story seems to have been one of Nancy's fabrications, but it highlights her resentment towards her mother for the repercussions of her upbringing.

The Mitfords were not the only children in their extended family to have negligent nannies. The older Churchill children had a sadistic nanny who issued harsh physical punishments to Randolph when he was cheeky. Even worse, it was rumoured that George's son, their Bowles cousin Michael, developed rickets because his nanny never fed him properly.[12] These experiences reveal the dangers inherent in the separation of drawing room and nursery; the less involved the mother was, the greater the risk of things going wrong. It was the structure of child-rearing in this era as much as the individuals involved which was at fault. Women were taught to put their husbands first as they depended on them for their status and financial security; this left limited time and emotional energy for their children.

For the Mitfords the situation only changed when the quiet but firm Laura Dicks joined the household. Coming from a staunch non-conformist and liberal background, her values were very different from her conservative employers', but she became a firm ally of Sydney. The two women worked as a team trying to keep the Mitford girls on the straight and narrow. The children depended on their nanny, whom they nicknamed 'Blor', more than their mother. Nearly fifty years later, Nancy wrote an essay in praise of Miss Dicks which was deeply critical of her mother. While Nancy accepted Sydney's distant approach to motherhood was typical of her class and generation, she claimed that her mother was 'abnormally detached' even by the standards of the era. Muv remained unruffled through every crisis. The girls had plenty of anecdotes to illustrate their mother's casual approach. When Unity rushed in to tell her that Jessica was standing on the roof threatening to commit suicide, Sydney's response was, 'Oh, poor duck. I hope she won't do anything so terrible.' And then she carried on writing.[13] When Jessica broke her arm for the second time, Muv was equally unfazed, saying with a sigh, 'Poor Little D; she doesn't seem to have much bounce.'[14] Debo recalled that if she told her mother something frightening or exciting, she would just say, 'Orrnnhh, Stubby, fancy,' or, 'Did you really? I do hope not.'[15] Sydney's sangfroid was due to her temperament and upbringing as well as society's mores. What had perhaps begun as a necessary protective mechanism in her youth did not endear her to her children, who wanted a reaction and went to increasingly extreme lengths to get one.

Nancy was not alone in finding her mother wanting; four of Sydney's daughters later complained that she was a cold, undemonstrative parent.[16] However, judging by biographies of other children brought up in this era, complaints about maternal parenting skills were common. Farve's cousin, Clementine Churchill, was criticised in similar terms by two of her daughters.[17] Edward VIII levelled the same charge against his mother, Queen Mary. In their offspring's eyes these women were unloving; in fact, it seems that they loved their children deeply, but because of their undemonstrative personalities they had problems expressing it. Another part of the problem was that they had large families and demanding husbands, which meant they were over-stretched. Diana's daughter-in-law, Charlotte Mosley, says, 'I don't think Muv was an unloving mother, I think she was dealing with seven children. She did have help but nevertheless, it was very hard work. Diana once said to me, "There were too many of us." Lady Redesdale did not have the leisure to give the attention which Nancy might have craved to each of her children.'[18]

Whatever the reasons for the lack of bonding, it was to have long-term consequences both in these children's relationship with their mothers and with their future partners. Whether Sydney loved her elder daughter or not, Nancy did not feel loved.[19] In the opening paragraph of her novel *The Pursuit of Love*, there is a family scene where Aunt Sadie, who is based on Muv, and her children are sitting around the tea table, which focuses on her as an inept mother. She has her baby on her lap but seems uncertain how to hold him, and a nanny hovers in the background ready to take the child away when necessary.[20] The fact this is our first intro-duction to the family, and the focus is on the mother, suggests that what subsequently happens to the children stems from the inadequate parent-ing they received. In later years, when Nancy asked her mother what she did all day, Muv replied she lived for them all. Her eldest daughter com-mented that perhaps she did, but she certainly did not live with them.[21] This was unfair as, like her father, Sydney rarely took time away from her children. Nonetheless, it seems that for Nancy the problem was her mother was physically present but emotionally absent.

Interestingly, Sydney's nieces and nephews disagreed with Nancy's view of their aunt; they thought Muv was the good mother in their family, much better than her sister Weenie and her brother George's first wife, Joan.[22] Julia Budworth, George's daughter, described her Aunt Sydney as strict but doting, while she said Weenie was a bad mother and Joan was cold and contemptuous towards her children, preferring her horses and dogs.[23] Debo also disputed her eldest sister's assessment. She felt their mother's life revolved around the needs of her family and she described her as particularly selfless.[24]

Sydney had inherited firm ideas on child-rearing from her father. She continued his adherence to Mosaic dietary laws, but the main consequence of her ban on pork was that her daughters' craving for this forbidden fruit became an obsession.[25] When Jessica visited a friend she was so excited to be allowed to eat a sausage she cut it open, put butter and clotted cream inside it and ate it as if it was the greatest delicacy.[26] Except for her prohibitions, in other ways Sydney demonstrated a more lenient attitude towards diet than many of her generation. She declared that her children should never be forced to eat anything they disliked. According to family folklore, this led to Unity living on milk, bananas and chocolate for a year.[27]

Potentially more damaging was her opposition to conventional medicine. She was willing to go against received wisdom and even defy the rules. When testing cows for tuberculosis became mandatory, three of her Guernseys tested positive. Even after this diagnosis, she refused to get rid of them and continued to let her children drink their unpasteurised milk.[28] Debo developed a lump in her neck from a permanently inflamed gland, but Muv was unrepentant.[29] She wrote to the *Daily Telegraph* advocating giving unpasteurised milk to children from cows who were reactors to the TB test, explaining, 'There is nothing in all this to worry about, but if we begin to dwell on such matters there will be no end to our fears of disease. A healthy body has ways of dealing with these dangers (if they are dangers), and to be continually in a state of fear of illness is all against health.'[30] She would not have her children vaccinated, and even when they had broken bones she left 'the good body' to heal itself. Like Aunt Sadie in Nancy's novel *Love in a Cold Climate*, she seems to have believed there was no illness except appendicitis.[31]

Sometimes her theories appeared to work, but at others her unscientific attitude had long-term repercussions for her children. When there was a measles epidemic shortly after Jessica had her first baby, Julia, neither mother nor child had immunity because they had never been vaccinated against the disease. Tragically, Julia died from complications following the illness.

Stubborn though Sydney was, in an emergency she put aside her principles. When Pam was three years old, she caught polio. Muv was so worried she called in doctors, but they could do little for her seriously ill daughter. As conventional medicine failed, Sydney turned to her father's trusted osteopath, Dr Kellgren. His recommendation of massage and exercise worked, and Pam was left with just a slight weakness in one leg.[32] When Diana developed appendicitis, once again Sydney had to call in a conventional doctor to operate. The procedure was carried out at home, and it was a success. A few years later, when Jessica had an acute pain in her stomach, she immediately thought it was her appendix. Muv was not unduly worried.

'Poor little D, I expect you ate too much,' she said. 'If you really have an awful pain, I expect we should call the doctor.'

There was no sense of urgency, and she went off to feed her chickens. Not willing to wait, Jessica phoned the doctor herself. When he arrived, he confirmed it was appendicitis and carried out the operation immediately.[33]

Muv's unscientific approach to illness did not endear her to other parents. Her refusal to have her children vaccinated meant they were not invited to some parties. No matter how contagious the illness, the Mitford children carried on with their plans. They would appear at weddings, Christmas festivities and birthday parties with chicken pox, whooping cough and streaming colds.[34] Sydney's cavalier attitude did not take into consideration other people's feelings. Like her father, Muv always believed she knew best, even if the majority disagreed with her and evidence disproved her theories.

4

The Family and Other Animals

Despite the family foibles, on the surface the Mitfords had an enviable life. Until the First World War they continued to live in London, but often escaped to the country at weekends. Sydney rented and then later bought Old Mill Cottage in High Wycombe, Buckinghamshire, as a holiday home. In the summer the family decamped to the picturesque house. Made up of two cottages joined at right angles around an open yard, the third side of the building was a working mill still used by a miller. The cottage had six bedrooms and three sitting rooms as well as a rambling garden, orchard and a tennis court.[1] Each year, the Mitford menagerie, which included three dogs, several hamsters, grass snakes, mice and a miniature pony as well as the family and their staff, all travelled by train to High Wycombe.[2] They must have appeared like an upmarket travelling circus as they crowded into a carriage.

The family also descended on David's parents at Batsford in the Cotswolds, or Sydney's father in his seaside house, Bournhill Cottage in Hampshire, overlooking the Solent. During these visits the Mitfords would get together with their brothers and sisters. Family was always more important than friends to David and Sydney, and they formed a tight-knit clan. As David's eight siblings and Sydney's three had more than twenty children between them, it was a large circle. Sydney, her sister Weenie and sister-in-law Joan all had children at about the same time, so the cousins saw a great deal of each other. Second cousins were also often thrown into the mix, and Winston and Clementine Churchill's children, Diana and Randolph, became great friends with Tom and Diana.

Sydney was at her most relaxed with her own family. George was a keen photographer, and his snapshots capture happy holidays with their children dressed in striped bathing suits, and the adults playing tennis, eating outside and chatting together over tea. One of the few photographs where Muv looks totally relaxed and happy is taken by her brother. Sitting in a deckchair on a beach wearing a cardigan and straw hat, she is really laughing, and her usually stern face softens and is completely transformed.[3] The family was a self-contained unit which left scant need for additional friends. In Nancy's novel *Love in a Cold Climate*, which captures the atmosphere of this family, the aunts knew the latest gossip, but they were never particularly interested in it because they did not care much about what people outside the family circle were doing.[4] Aunt Sadie, who is based on Sydney, was bored by strangers and only enjoyed being with people with whom she shared day-to-day interests; this was essentially her neighbours and relatives.[5]

The extended family formed an eccentric clan who provided endless source material for embryonic authors. Sydney's brother Geoffrey never married and lived on his own in a flat in London. Inserted in the front door he had a 'go-to-hell-door' to deter unwanted visitors. If someone he disliked appeared, he would look through this trapdoor and then slam it shut. Sydney was usually welcome, but once even she was turned away. After the maid had taken her into the drawing room, Geoffrey refused to see her. Just speaking to her from his bedroom on the telephone, he said hello and then goodbye. She was annoyed but also amused by his bizarre behaviour.[6]

Like his brother and sisters, Geoffrey had inherited many of his father's quirky ideas. Some of his opinions now seem ahead of their time, but it was the way he argued his case as much as what he said that labelled him a crank. He frequently wrote to the newspapers about 'murdered food', believing that the decline in use of natural fertilisers on the soil was at the root of the country's problems. Opposing processed food, particularly pasteurised milk, refined white flour and sugar, he encouraged everyone to eat bread made with wheatgerm. He published his diatribes in a book entitled *Writings of a Rebel*.[7] Although Sydney never thought of herself as a rebel, she agreed with her brother and supported his crusades by occasionally writing to the papers about the importance of eating fresh food, particularly homemade bread. In one article she staked her claim to fame as 'the only peeress who has made all the bread eaten by her family for years'. She concluded by suggesting that women should devote their attention to acquiring a scientific knowledge of diet.[8]

Another important member of Sydney's inner circle was her oldest friend, Violet Hammersley. The two women met as teenagers when their families lived near each other in London. Violet used to join Sydney on her yachting holidays to France. They were very different characters, and yet their friendship was to survive until their deaths, just months apart. A widow after her much older banker husband died, Violet was habitually dressed in black and became known as 'The Wid' or 'Mrs Ham' to the children. A drama queen, she was a pessimist who always looked on the dark side of life, but she was also a good listener and fascinating raconteur. Mrs Ham was well connected in literary circles, counting among her friends Somerset Maugham, Arnold Bennett and the Sitwell siblings. The author Rosamond Lehmann described her as like a witch with her low voice and saturnine appearance, but Sydney's daughters grew very fond of Violet, considering her to be much more sympathetic and intriguing than their own mother.[9] In fact, with her daughter Monica, Mrs Ham was no more maternal than Muv. A photograph of Violet with her baby on her lap shows a woman who is completely disinterested; she is not even bothering to hold the precariously balanced child. It seems other people's mothers always appeared more appealing than their own to this generation of children.

According to her daughters, Sydney was vague and always seemed preoccupied with something else. Nancy wrote that when this happened it was as if her spirit had absented itself.[10] Most people who knew her noted her dreaminess, as though she was in a world of her own. She knew her reputation for vagueness and even joked about it. When their groom, Hooper, wanted to see her, he asked one of the children, 'Is her ladyship vacant?' Sydney overheard and replied, 'No more than usual.'[11]

If Muv appeared preoccupied, maybe that was partly because she was so busy with her growing family, but also due to not always being particularly happy herself. Many years later, Nancy wrote to Jessica that her mother once told her that, in the early days of her marriage, she nearly left David for another man. She only ended the relationship because Nancy was a toddler. It is worth remembering that Nancy was known to make up good stories and Diana and Debo never heard about this from their mother.[12] If it is true, it would explain Muv's miserable expression in the photo of her with Nancy and her husband at this time.

A very loyal person, it seems unlikely Sydney seriously considered an affair. Even after the birth of several children, Muv and Farve remained physically very compatible. David's aunt described them as 'the greatest lovers'.[13] His eyes would follow her as she left the room, and after dinner in the evenings he would stand by her chair, just waiting for her to be ready for bed so he could run her a bath. She accepted his devotion without appearing to notice it.[14] Even later, when she was middle-aged and did not bother much about her appearance, he would tell Sydney that her hair was like 'molten gold' and that she was 'more beautiful than the day', which made her daughters laugh.[15]

Despite his undoubted admiration for her, Farve was not always an easy man to live with, as his temper was hard for his wife to handle. Strong-willed herself and not brought up to be a submissive wife, she was unwilling to just acquiesce and be a passive victim. Years later, Debo wrote about her father's 'terrifying temper' and realised that her mother 'never would be a nondescript agree-er'.[16] However, he was the ultimate authority in the household, and she never questioned his word.[17] Rather than scream and shout, she just withdrew into chilly vagueness. Husband and wife were opposites: while she was cool and logical, he was hot-headed and emotional. As several of her daughters inherited their father's volatility, Muv tried to remain the equable force at the heart of the family. As the girls grew older, if they stormed out of meals, banged doors, burst into tears or giggled uncontrollably, she ignored it.[18] If they went too far, she would just tell them not to be silly.

Mealtimes were a particular minefield when all the family foibles were on full display. Farve had some pet aversions which were not compatible with dining with young children. He hated unpunctuality and could not bear any messiness at the table. If these red lines were crossed, he would explode in a furious outburst calling the culprit a 'filthy beast', which either traumatised or amused the children and their cousins depending on their temperament.[19] Perhaps to relieve the tension, and recalling Dr Kellgren's tips, Lady Redesdale would stretch during meals. Spreading out her arms and making circles in the air, she explained it was good for her digestion.[20] Although he certainly made his wife's life more stressful, Farve's bark was always worse than his bite, and his sense of humour was as much a feature of family life as his temper. The house was filled with shrieks of laughter as often as floods of tears, because they all had great senses of humour. The funniest members of the family were David and Nancy, and with her teasing and his reaction, they played off each other as if they were a professional double act.

Friends who stayed with the Mitfords considered it to be a happy household.[21] The nicknames used within the family suggest this informality; the girls felt safe to tease their parents and be cheeky. They called their father TPOM (The Poor Old Male), the Old Ape, Forgy, Forgery and, of course, Farve. Their mother was Muv, TPOF (The Poor Old Female), Sydney or Aunt Syd. The cheekiness of the names hardly suggests they were afraid of their parents. Lord and Lady Redesdale just accepted it, but Sydney did once punish Jessica for calling her father 'a feudal remnant', withholding her pocket money after telling her not to call him 'a remnant'.[22] The girls had a variety of nicknames, which altered over time. For instance, when she was a small child, Nancy was Koko to her parents and Blob Nose to Farve. Jessica was called Decca, but Little D to her mother. Unity's nickname was Bobo, but Jessica called her Boud. Deborah became Debo, but Muv called her Stubby.[23]

With six daughters, competition was rife, and the girls were always vying for attention. According to Nancy, Farve had favourites, but the chosen one would change regularly. In contrast, Muv tried to treat all her children equally and be scrupulously fair, but Nancy believed she was greatly influenced by physical beauty and secretly preferred who-ever was the prettiest sister at the time.[24] Unlike her husband, Sydney did not lose her temper with the children, but she could be strict and severe if they behaved badly. Her daughters were less forgiving of her sarcastic put-downs than their father's rages.[25] As Charlotte Mosley points out, 'He was a much more difficult character but never came in for the same sort of criticism Muv did. He was let off much more lightly. I think that happened in families, it is the mother who gets a lot of the controversy.'[26]

Nancy believed that Lady Redesdale was far more relaxed with her younger daughters than her older ones. In *Love in a Cold Climate*, she claimed Muv's alter ego, Aunt Sadie, was rarely severe with her young-est children and was more 'human' and 'companionable' with them. She had always treated the six girls as if they were the same age, so the younger ones benefited from receiving the same concessions as their older siblings.[27] Perhaps this alteration in attitude was just because Sydney was now a more experienced mother and had learnt by trial and error what worked. When Aunt Sadie's brother-in-law Davey says she spoils them, she admits it is true but says it was the result of having so many children; she had forced herself to be strict for a few years with the older ones but eventually it became too much effort.[28]

Rather than deal with the underlying family tensions, the Redesdales minimised any problems and turned difficult situations into a good joke or an amusing anecdote. In the short term it worked, but it stored up problems for later life. Looking back, Diana wrote that she believed it had been a failing in their upbringing that they were always expected to put on a brave face, and it was considered wrong to admit to vul-nerability or despair. When both Sydney and her daughters later faced tragedies, they hid their grief and were remarkably resilient. Few people saw behind the mask: it remained so rigidly in place that at times it became hard to confide their true feelings even to those closest to them.[29]

Another source of tension was finances, which were tight by the standards of their class. Having run her father's household for so long, Sydney knew exactly what she was doing. Her days were spent managing her home and staff, shopping in Harrods or the Army and Navy Stores, visiting friends and keeping meticulous accounts to make sure the family stayed within budget.[30] Unfortunately, David's attempts to become an entrepreneur only proved that he had an unerring eye for a white elephant. Over the years he got involved in a series of schemes which lost money. From 1912, Muv and Farve visited Canada to prospect for gold. While his neighbour Harry Oakes struck the jackpot, discovering the largest gold mine in Canada just a mile away from the Mitford mine, David was not so lucky. The 40 acres he had bought near the small town called Swastika in Ontario only yielded minimal traces of gold.

Nancy believed her father would have been much more fulfilled living in Canada than the Cotswolds.[31] Sydney and David's trips to Ontario were among the happiest times the couple spent together. They enjoyed roughing it; they built a wooden cabin which was known by the locals as 'Redesdale Castle'.[32] Without any servants, Muv did the cooking and housework while Farve enjoyed the hard physical labour.[33] As Sydney had never learnt to cook there were some disasters; when she roasted her first chicken she did not realise you needed to remove the gizzards, which were full of corn, and it then floated unpalatably in the gravy.[34]

It was a sharp learning curve, but in many ways the demanding outdoors lifestyle suited them more than their pampered aristocratic existence in England.[35] They were both practical people who were willing to work hard, and it gave them a shared purpose. Left at home under the supervision of nannies and grandparents, Nancy enjoyed her parents being away. She secretly fantasised about their ship sinking, which would leave her in charge of the family and able to boss her siblings about like Katy, the heroine in *What Katy Did*.[36] Her childish daydream nearly came true, because Muv and Farve were booked to sail on the *Titanic* until a crisis at home prevented them from going.[37]

Although Sydney and David never made their fortune in Canada, one prospecting trip did lead to a change in the family circumstances which was to have huge consequences. During their visit to Canada in 1913, their fourth daughter was conceived in Swastika. The following year, just a few days after the First World War broke out, Unity Valkyrie Mitford was born. Her first name was after her mother's friend, the comedy actress Unity More,[38] but the place of her conception, the timing of her birth and her second name, which was chosen by her Wagner-loving grandfather, Bertie, after the war maidens, foreshadowed her transgressive life.

5

Lady of the Manor

The First World War changed everything for David and Sydney and their young family. When war was declared David insisted on joining up with his old regiment, seemingly undeterred by the fact that he was classified as unfit for service by virtue of having only one lung. On one occasion, when he came home on leave, he received an unpleasant shock. Sydney had gone to stay with the children at her father's seaside home, but while they were there a fire broke out. When David arrived in London and first heard the news from the cook that Thomas's cottage had burnt to the ground, he did not know if his family had survived. Fortunately, no one was hurt; only Diana's teddy bear perished in the flames.[1]

Farve served bravely in France, but in January 1915 his health broke down and he was invalided home. It was while he was recovering that he received the news which would change his family's future. David had never expected to inherit his father's title or estates, but tragically, in May 1915, his eldest brother Clement was killed in action. The whole family was devastated. Pam would never forget seeing her parents openly crying when they were informed.[2] Clement and his wife Helen had one daughter, Rosemary, but were expecting another baby when he was killed. If Helen gave birth to a boy, he would have become Lord Redesdale's heir. When she gave birth in October to another girl it meant that the estate and title would pass to David. It was not something her brother and sister-in-law had sought, but Helen became irrationally angry with them.[3] The change in their status was of no immediate benefit to the couple; in fact Sydney was already finding it hard to manage their finances. As soon as he was well enough David returned to France, where his role was to get supplies through to his battalion every night. When he was on leave in Paris, Sydney visited him, but her news from the home front was not positive. His army salary was less than he had been paid at *The Lady* and her father was cutting her allowance because of increases in taxation. To cut expenditure, Sydney decided to let out their London house and move with the children to a house on the Batsford estate.[4]

Bertie, Lord Redesdale, never recovered from the death of his eldest son and ten months later, in August 1916, he died. Sydney and David became Lord and Lady Redesdale and took over the whole estate. Their inheritance proved to be a mixed blessing; the family finances had been seriously depleted by Bertie's building projects. In 1880 he had knocked down the Georgian house at Batsford and spent a fortune building a late Victorian mansion. Although they were aristocrats, who now owned an extensive estate in the Cotswolds and more land in Northumberland, Sydney and David did not have a ready supply of income to match their new lifestyle and maintain the estate. They moved into Batsford, but much of the vast house had to be shut off because it could not be fully staffed or heated. While their parents worried about how to finance the daunting pile, the children had a ball running up and down the five staircases and exploring the many rooms. Wracking her brains about how to save money, Sydney came up with changing to Bromo lavatory paper and no longer using napkins at meals because the cost of laundering the dozens used every day was so expensive. Her economies caused much amusement; she appeared in a *Daily Sketch* story headlined 'Peeress Saves Ha'pence'.[5] Unfortunately, even her attempts at austerity could not save Batsford, and the Redesdales soon realised they could not afford to keep the house. Shortly after the war was over, they sold the house and many family heirlooms, including pictures by Sir Joshua Reynolds, Sir Godfrey Kneller and Poussin.[6]

Their next move was to Asthall Manor, near the village of Swinbrook. It was a magical place and in later years Sydney looked back on it with nostalgia. She wrote, 'What happy days they were […] when we seemed to live in sunshine with all the children and their friends.'[7] She wrote that time seemed to have been 'all summers'.[8] Asthall Manor was a quintessential Cotswold gabled manor house, built in the seventeenth century. The house was next to the church and close to the River Windrush. Rumoured to be haunted, the house was adored by the whole family, except for David. Like his father, the new Lord Redesdale had a penchant for building projects, and he soon began a programme of improvements. Panelling, battlements and a new ceiling were added to the building. He also built a covered walkway, which became known as the cloister, between the main house and the converted barn which housed a wonderful library. This room was the older children's favourite place; with comfortable sofas and a grand piano, it became their space where they could escape from adults.[9] Lady Redesdale had a gift for interior design and improved every house they lived in with her faultless taste. Her favourite period was the eighteenth century, and at Asthall she used French furniture and pictures from that era to furnish her drawing room.[10]

Lord Redesdale did not like having guests to stay. As Jessica explained, he disliked 'outsiders' which included 'not only Huns, Frogs, Americans, blacks and all other foreigners', but also other people's children and most young men.[11] In contrast, Lady Redesdale enjoyed having visitors, but she accepted her husband's rules and narrowed down her social circle.[12] Even though it was less varied than Sydney might have liked, it was hardly an isolated existence as their extended family and a few carefully chosen friends were always visiting. David and Sydney were seen as the stable couple – the ones other relatives gravitated towards in times of trouble. Close-knit as ever, Sydney's siblings chose to live near her. Her younger sister Weenie and her husband Percy Bailey, with their four sons, moved to Maugersbury in the Cotswolds. When George and his wife Joan decided to divorce, he spent a great deal of time at Asthall. He preferred Sydney to Weenie, considering Sydney to be more sympathetic.[13] When he met his second wife Madeleine, the Redesdales were among the first people she was introduced to, and after their marriage they chose to live near their in-laws. David and Sydney had never directly encountered divorce or a second wife in their circle before, but they handled it with tact. Muv was welcoming to her brother's new wife while remaining on friendly terms with his former one.[14]

George's daughter, Phyllis, who was a good friend of Nancy's, also preferred Asthall to her own home. On one visit, when she was sixteen, Phyllis was so unhappy she self-harmed, digging her fingernails so hard into the vein in her wrist that the blood poured out. When her aunt Sydney asked her why she had done it she explained that she did not want to go back to her mother. Showing the lackadaisical attitude her daughters complained about, Sydney ignored her niece's cry for help and Phyllis had to return to Joan.[15] This approach of being aware that something was wrong but turning a blind eye to it was a recurring theme in Sydney's life. She was equally unsympathetic when David's cousin, Nellie, who was Clementine Churchill's sister, came to her about her gambling debts. A young unmarried woman in her twenties, Nellie begged Sydney to lend her eight pounds to pay them off. Rather than helping her, Muv went straight to her mother and told her what Nellie had done. In later life Jessica thought this incident illustrated her mother's disapproving quality.[16]

As mistress of a large staff, Lady Redesdale exuded authority. At first one of the parlourmaids, Mabel, considered her employer a proud, unapproachable woman who was much less friendly than Lord Redesdale. Yet, as they got to know each other better, she broke through that reserve. When Mabel had worked for them for many years, Muv would give her a big hug. Once, when the family were having a fancy-dress party, Sydney said to Mabel that she wanted to dress up as her, so Sydney borrowed Mabel's uniform and sat at the dinner table dressed as her maid.[17] The uniform was particularly fetching because Muv had carefully chosen it for her staff. The maids wore a blue and white toile de Jouy dress with a traditional bird pattern on it, accessorised with a white linen apron and a white organdie cap threaded with black velvet.[18]

David and Sydney got thoroughly involved in the local community. Many years later, Debo described Asthall as a perfect English village with its vicarage, manor, church, school, pub, farmhouses and cottages all in proportion. There was a sense of continuity as the villagers quietly continued in the same occupations which had taken place in the agricultural community for centuries.[19] Every year the Redesdales held a large Christmas party for their tenants, staff and children. Ninety guests were given a delicious tea before gathering around the Christmas tree in the large drawing room.[20] Lady Redesdale created a magical atmosphere; the room was dark except for a few candles, then hand bells rang and Father Christmas (alias the vicar) came through the window with a large sack on his back. Sydney carefully selected a toy or outfit for each of the children, making sure never to repeat the same gift they had been given the previous year.[21] Later in the evening a conjuror entertained the party, then, before leaving, the guests gave three cheers to thank their hosts.[22] This was emblematic of the society the Redesdales admired: it was unchanging, conservative and hierarchical, but it was at odds with the modern world.

Unlike their fathers, David and Sydney were outwardly conventional and, in many ways, they were typical of their generation and their class.[23] The Redesdales believed in a paternalistic society where the upper classes carried out their civic responsibilities and helped the deserving poor. Sydney regularly visited Swinbrook villagers who had fallen on hard times, bringing them small gifts of charity. However, the poverty of these families worried Jessica even as a child. As she walked home with her mother after a visit, she questioned her about the disparity between the villagers' lives and their own. Jessica asked her mother why the wealth of the country could not be divided more equally to end poverty. Lady Redesdale replied that this was what socialists wanted to do, but a redistribution of wealth would not be fair to people who had carefully looked after their money. For a time, this argument appeased Jessica, but as soon as she was old enough, she investigated her initial idea further and no longer found her mother's justification satisfying.[24]

Muv became a stalwart of the newly formed Women's Institute. She set up the Asthall and Swinbrook branch and gave lectures on her favourite topics: Nelson, Queen Victoria and bread-making.[25] As Lady of the Manor, she supported worthy local charities and often opened events. All the children were expected to play their part in the fundraising fetes held in the Redesdales' grounds. One year, just before the

63

garden party opened, Sydney thought the White Elephant stall looked sparsely stocked. Gathering random items from around the house, she inadvertently included priceless family heirlooms her father-in-law had brought back from the Far East. When her husband and children real-ised what she had done they rushed around buying back as many pieces as possible from their guests. Forewarned, in future years the children used to hide their favourite toys when it was time for the annual fete.[26]

Anecdotes like this, which became part of family folklore, suggest Sydney was a scatter-brained woman. In her writing, Nancy portrayed her mother as a rather ineffectual aristocrat who floated around lan-guidly doing nothing much. This picture could not have been further from the truth.[27] Unlike her husband, Muv had an excellent business brain and was an efficient organiser. She was a meticulous bookkeeper and in a different era could have been a successful businesswoman. She inherited nearly a quarter of her father's £60,000 estate, including a 19 per cent share in *The Lady*.[28] If she could have used this legacy to start a business, the family fortunes might have been very different. Sydney was good at accounting, and she told her youngest daughter Debo that if she could have chosen a career, she would have liked to be 'the woman at the *caisse*' at a French restaurant who collected the money from diners.[29] To finance her daughters' education, she kept 500 hens and sold their eggs. After washing each egg herself they were carefully packed in boxes; then the Mitford's groom, Hooper, would drive them to the station in a horse-drawn float to be sent to London.[30] Every year she made a profit of at least £100 from her enterprise.[31]

Influenced by her father, Sydney was also a political woman who had many of the skills which could have made her an effective politi-cal wife or even politician in her own right. Throughout the 1920s she was deeply involved in the local Conservative party. She always got her children to help her run a stall stocked with produce from her garden and eggs from her hens at the annual fete. Perhaps recalling happy memories of campaigning with her father, during elections she had her car decorated with blue ribbons, pinned blue rosettes on her daughters and took them canvassing with her. Their task was to visit voters in the villages and persuade them to vote for the Tories; if they agreed the Redesdales' chauffeur would drive them to the polling station on election day. Sydney was no fan of the local Conservative MP, thinking him a 'dull little creature', but she was loyal to the party.[32] When she became first chairman and then president of the Ladies' Association in the constituency, she showed her skill at organisation, increasing the membership to 3,000 members and strengthening the branches. She was thanked by party supporters for the excellent work she had done and the impressive ability she had brought to her role.[33]

Despite living in the Cotswolds rather than the capital, Lady Redesdale was not cut off from the latest political ideas. She attended party conferences in London and large political rallies. Leading Conservative politicians came to the constituency to speak about topical issues. During the 1920s there was a feeling among some right-wing traditionalists that the country was perpetually on the edge of crisis. They were constantly looking out for signs of national degeneracy and international conspiracies which they imagined to be orchestrated by Bolsheviks and Jews. The election of the first Labour government in 1924 accentuated these fears, then the General Strike two years later was viewed as another major threat to the established order.[34] As tensions mounted before the General Strike, the Conservative Home Secretary, Sir William Joynson-Hicks, gave an address about the coal crisis in the Banbury constituency.[35] On another occasion, the Minister for Pensions, George Tryon, came. Attacking the Labour Party's ideas as 'not British', he claimed that they got their ideas 'from abroad'. He believed the British did not want 'foreign ideas' and the socialists would destroy Parliamentary Government and set up 'a tyrannical order of things'.[36] Another visiting Conservative MP called on party members to put their country and Empire first. He did not believe they could keep the Empire if there was a Labour government in power.[37] Sydney was prominent at these events, often sitting on the platform next to the speaker.

As Thomas Bowles's daughter, the ideas Sydney heard would not have been alien to her; they were to feed into her worldview, which became more extreme in the next decade. Communism, which had overthrown the monarchy and aristocracy in Russia less than a decade before, seemed a real threat to Lady Redesdale. Nancy later recaptured her mother's paranoia about communism in the character of the widowed country landowner, Lady Bobbin, in her novel *Christmas Pudding*. Lady Bobbin attributed every problem in society to the Bolsheviks and believed in the most bizarre conspiracy theories. When her livestock developed foot-and-mouth or her favourite pastime, hunting, was cancelled, she blamed 'the Bolshies'. She believed they were planning to assassinate even the most insignificant politicians. This eccentric character was even willing to believe that the government was in the pay of 'the Reds'.[38] In the novel, Lady Bobbin's cranky views are put down to her being out of touch with the world for years; it seems Nancy attributed her mother's idiosyncratic ideas to living in a similar bubble.[39]

Sydney brought up her daughters to share her fears. Jessica recalled, at the time of the General Strike in 1926, when she was nearly nine, Sydney was afraid she would be shot by the 'Bolshies'. If there was to be a class war in the 1920s, there was no doubt which side the Redesdales would be on. During the General Strike, several of the sisters volunteered in the strike-breakers' canteens, while their parents anxiously read the news bulletins, concerned about what would happen next.[40]

Unlike many women of her generation, Lady Redesdale relished public speaking. She spoke regularly at Conservative events and even took part in a debating competition organised by the local Conservative party. In an era when women in similar social positions to her, including Lady Astor and the Duchess of Atholl, were entering Parliament for the first time as Conservative politicians, Sydney would have made a competent MP. As a confident public speaker and an efficient organiser with strong opinions, she had many of the necessary skills. Nonetheless, she never followed in her father's footsteps. Her large family left her with little time, and no doubt her husband's aversion to women in Parliament also deterred her. His sexist attitude was obvious when he opposed peeresses being able to sit in the House of Lords. According to Nancy, his stance was because there was only one lavatory in the upper house and he was concerned ladies might use it.[41] Instead of putting herself forward, when the Oxford constituency was looking for a Conservative candidate to stand for Parliament, Sydney promoted her brother George. Jessica remembered villagers gathering on the lawn to hear their uncle give a speech.[42] Despite his sister's support, George was not chosen by party members because he was divorced.[43] Muv's other brother, eccentric Geoffrey, was also active in the Conservative party and addressed Tory campaign meetings locally. Like his siblings, he detested socialists, telling villagers: 'The trouble with the Labour Party is that they want everyone to be poor, but we want everyone to be rich.'[44]

Lord Redesdale was far less interested in politics than the Bowles brothers and sisters,[45] but he had a political platform because he had a hereditary seat in the House of Lords. When he attended, he took up idiosyncratic causes which made him a joke rather than a serious political player. The zenith of his political power was becoming chairman of the House of Lords' Drains Committee. His greatest claim to fame was when he opposed a proposal to reform the upper chamber and limit its powers. He made a speech, saying, 'May I remind your lordships that denial of the hereditary principle is a direct blow at the Crown? Such a denial is, indeed, a blow at the very foundation of the Christian faith.' His view was so bizarre it was mocked in the newspapers. *The Observer* described his speech as having 'the genuine ring of "Iolanthe"', a Gilbert and Sullivan comic opera which satirised many aspects of British government.[46]

Lord Redesdale's political creed was to hold on tightly to traditional, conservative values, including an unwavering support of the monarchy, church and state. The family was made to attend church every Sunday and Lord Redesdale took a great interest in the choice of vicars and orders of service. Lady Redesdale also attended church, but her attitude to religion, like everything else, was more complicated. Her father never went to church, not because he was without religion but because his beliefs were too individual to fit into even the most non-conformist chapel. Sydney became a regular churchgoer mainly because she saw it as her patriotic duty.[47] Like her husband, she believed that for the stability of the country, the security of the monarchy, the House of Lords and the Church of England should be maintained. Nancy explored her mother's views through the character of Lady Chalford in her novel

Wigs on the Green. The fictional figure had no personal feelings towards God, just regarding him as the head of the Church of England, jointly with the king.[48] Influenced by her father, Sydney did not approve of evangelising and was open-minded about different faiths.[49] In Nancy's novel, Lady Chalford shared this attitude, considering religious fervour to be as shocking as sexual abandon and linked with it.[50] According to her grandson, Jonathan Guinness, Sydney had an aversion to the sense of sin associated with traditional Christianity; this attitude came from Thomas and was passed on to her children.[51]

Even though every hour of the day was taken up with organising her home, caring for her large family and running her small business, not to mention her political and charity work, an observer cannot help feeling Sydney was capable of more. It filled her time, but did it really fulfil her? Life with her father always had a purpose: he wanted to change the world, and she was his helper. With her husband there was no long-term aim or wider crusade, except to maintain the status quo. During the turbulent 1930s, Sydney's daughters were to show their compulsion to find a cause to fight for; that instinct, which lay dormant in their mother for much of her married life, revived in the next generation. Although in later years, Sydney described the Asthall era in her life as a halcyon time, in photographs she never looked happy. In the group family photos taken annually as her children grew up, she stands slightly aloof, a solitary unsmiling figure set apart.

In retrospect, her daughters thought there was something missing in their mother's life. Many years later Diana wrote to Debo that she thought their parents were 'bored stiff' but did not identify the problem.[52] Did her daughters, in their youth, subliminally pick up on their mother's frustration and become determined never to live such a restricted life themselves? Rather than not seeing themselves in her, did they realise how similar to Sydney they really were – and thus what could lie ahead for them, too, if they did not break free from a traditional upper-class English life? Sydney had the potential to be a rebel too, but while they were growing up, she tried to rein in any rebelliousness and conform. Eventually something had to give, and when it did the repercussions were devastating.

6

Home Education

Nancy and Jessica's greatest complaint against their mother was that she failed to send them to school and provide them with the education they desired. When writing her autobiography, Nancy told family friend James Lees-Milne that this was her parents' most fundamental mistake; their daughters were highly intelligent and needed to be intellectually stretched.[1] If their potential was not channelled in the right direction, it risked diverting to the wrong path.

While the girls were taught by a series of often inept governesses, their brother Tom was sent to Eton. Jessica and Nancy resented this sexist approach, which limited the opportunities open to them in later life. In contrast, Debo, Pam and Diana appreciated their free-range home schooling. It was also much more thorough than Nancy or Jessica would ever admit. Muv's scheme for her daughters' education was neither chaotic nor irrational. She was as thoughtful and thorough in her attitude to their schooling as she was in every other aspect of her life. Her approach worked; as Charlotte Mosley points out, 'You have to look at the results'. Four of Sydney's six daughters became published writers.[2]

Neither Lord nor Lady Redesdale wanted their daughters to go to school for a range of reasons. According to Nancy and Jessica, their parents' motivation was a mixture of sexism, snobbery and economy. In Nancy's novel *The Pursuit of Love*, Uncle Matthew loathed clever women; it seems Farve felt the same.[3] David and Sydney believed school would turn their girls into bluestockings, which would make them less marriageable. They were concerned that their daughters would become less attractive because the school uniforms were hideous, and playing hockey might leave them with chunky calves. They also feared that mixing with a wide assortment of pupils from different backgrounds might have a 'vulgarising effect' on their daughters.[4] There were also financial considerations, and the cost of sending six girls to boarding school acted as a deterrent. Paying for a governess to educate them at home was more cost-effective.

Reading Lady Redesdale's letters, there seems to have also been another more endearing reason for her decision. Like her father, Sydney wanted her children with her as much as possible. During the Spanish Civil War, she thought it 'so dreadful' that children were 'torn' from their parents and brought to Britain.[5] In the war years, when she heard of some wealthy contemporaries sending their offspring to America to safety, she was equally appalled. She thought it barbaric to separate children from their parents. When her grandchildren left home for either boarding school or university for the first time, she always commiserated with her daughters, drawing from her own experience to emphasise how much they would miss them.* Farve was also motivated by wanting to keep his girls at home. He had loathed his time at boarding school and did not want his daughters subjected to the same ordeal.[6] He once told his sister-in-law he never had a single happy day at his school, Radley. His niece Julia Budworth believed that by preventing his daughters going to boarding school, he was protecting, not depriving, them.[7]

Rather than some badly thought-out plan, it seems Lady Redesdale carefully weighed the advantages and disadvantages of the different

---

* Lady Redesdale wrote to Jessica saying how Debo would miss Emma 'terribly' when she went to Switzerland, and Decca would miss Dinky too, while she was away. She wrote, 'It is too horrid when they have to go.' Sydney Redesdale to Jessica Mitford, 17 September 1958. Jessica Mitford correspondence, Ohio State University, Special and Rare Manuscripts, 0089, Box 205, Folder 1.

options. She wanted to do the best thing for her girls, but unfortunately the conclusions she came to and what they wanted did not always coincide. It was hard for Sydney to win, because what was right for some of her daughters would have been wrong for the others. Each of the girls had different needs. While Nancy and Jessica believed they would have thrived at school, Debo, Diana and Pam were happiest at home. Diana described dreading the thought of being separated from her animals and comfortable life.[8] Unity's needs were unique, and she never fitted in at home or school. When Sydney's daughters complained about her decision, she told them: 'The fact is children always want to do something different from what they are doing. Childhood is a very unhappy time of life; I know I was always miserable as a child. You'll be all right when you're eighteen.'[9] In her view, they just had to get on with it, like she had done.

Nor was the education they received as clear-cut as it is portrayed by Jessica and Nancy. It is true that most of Sydney's daughters' education was at home, but there were brief interludes when they went to school. When Nancy was a small child, the family lived in London, so she was sent to the Frances Holland day school close to her home. Later, when she was sixteen, she went to Hatherop Castle to be 'finished'. With about twenty pupils from neighbouring county families making up the school, it hardly offered the stimulus Nancy desired, but she enjoyed her time there.[10] When governesses found Unity too hard to control, she was also sent off to boarding school. As Unity was unable to conform, she did not last long. She was asked to leave St Margaret's Bushey because her rebellious behaviour was too disruptive.[†] Jessica and Debo also briefly tried going to school. Jessica loved it but Debo loathed the experience; she fainted in her geometry class and was sick after the school meals.[11] Rather than making her youngest daughter continue, Lady Redesdale promptly removed her. Debo's aunts thought Sydney was wrong to pander to her child's whims and that it would make her

---

†   Her rebellions were not major, but the final straw was when she refused to be confirmed.

spoilt, but Muv stuck to her decision. Debo was eternally grateful to her mother for listening to her needs.[12]

Sydney's experiment in home-educating her daughters evolved over time. Her younger daughters had better experiences than her older ones. Once the Mitfords moved to the country during the First World War, it became practical for Sydney to educate her brood herself until they were old enough to be taught by a governess. Whether this was a good decision depended on whether Lady Redesdale had the skills to teach her children as well as a professional teacher; as usual, opinions differ. Nancy portrayed her mother as a complete philistine, who never read books when she was young and in adulthood preferred reading tomes on Victorian clergymen to anything else.[13] In her novel The Pursuit of Love, the figure based on Sydney, Aunt Sadie, had to conceal her ignorance as absent-mindedness during a conversation with a more erudite guest.[14] Once again, Nancy's version is far from the truth. Known as a bookish girl, Sydney became a cultured and well-read woman. Sydney enjoyed teaching, considering it to be probably the most interesting and useful thing she did in her life.[15] Her youngest daughter, Debo, described her as a natural teacher who never made anything seem hard and was much more inspiring than the governesses.[16] According to family friend James Lees-Milne, Sydney's daughters were lucky to have her as their role model. Although she was not an intellectual, she was 'acutely perceptive, well read, fastidious, yet surprised by nothing and amused by practically everything'. He claimed that nothing could be further from the truth than the image of her as 'a philistine mother with hide-bound social standards'. Instead, she 'encouraged her children's interest in music, the arts and reading, and probably inculcated the mental independence which has distinguished them'.[17]

Sydney started teaching her children when they were five years old. Her aim was to give them a good grounding in the basics; their first goal was to be able to read The Times leader by the age of six.[18] Trying to capture her children's imagination, she taught history from the patriotic book Our Island Story. Jessica later recalled how her mother was able to bring the stories of Empire and monarchs alive with her vivid descriptions and her interpretations. Like her father and husband, Sydney believed in British exceptionalism and was an ardent imperialist. She tried to pass on her pride in what the Empire-builders had achieved to her children. According to Jessica, Lady Redesdale's worldview was simplistic, 'the good so good, and the bad so bad, history as taught by Muv was on the whole very clear to me'.[19] She believed children only needed to remember the information which seemed important to them, so she used the teaching method of narration. She would read an excerpt from a book then her daughters would tell her what they remembered. It proved more productive with some of her daughters than others. In one session, she asked Jessica what she recalled. When she replied, 'Nothing', Sydney pushed her, saying that she must remember at least one word. Her daughter responded, 'Very well then, "THE"'.[20]

Once her girls reached the age of eight or nine, they were taught by a governess. Muv employed a series of tutors who varied widely in quality: while Miss Mirams and Miss Hussey were outstanding, others were academically average or inadequate. According to Jessica, the only skill they learnt from one governess was how to shoplift. Few of the teachers lasted long once they were subjected to their pupils' rebellious behaviour and frequent pranks. However, the expertise of their teachers mattered less than Jessica and Nancy suggested because Lady Redesdale had given them a good foundation. Miss Hussey described Muv as 'wonderful': she had taught her children their sums and time-tables, and they could read well before they entered her schoolroom. She described their English as better than her own.[21]

With her youngest daughters, Lady Redesdale made sure that whomever the teacher was, the girls followed a properly structured programme.[22] Inspired by Charlotte Mason's book *Home Education*, she turned to the Parents' National Educational Union (PNEU) scheme, which had been set up for military families and people living abroad. This type of home education became another of Lady Redesdale's causes which she promoted. Writing to *The Times* emphasising its benefits, she explained: 'The advantages of this to a parent who wishes to start her children's education herself, [...] are obviously very great, as there is something definite and very carefully thought out to work on.'[23] A programme of work was provided, and a timetable; then progress was measured by independently marked exams. It was based on a structured curriculum which included English, mathematics, history, geography and some science, as well as music, art appreciation and dance. The ethos was particularly suited to the Mitfords' free spirits, because it was based on pupils conducting their own independent study. They were encouraged to learn through their senses and nature, rather than just being given information by their teacher.[24]

The PNEU system was supplemented by many extra-curricular activities. As well as a governess, an additional French tutor was employed in the summer holidays to make sure the girls became fluent in the language. With an extensive family library at their disposal, they had access to a wide range of literature which they read voraciously. In retrospect, as an autodidact, Diana appreciated the education her mother had given her. She wrote that once a child had learnt to read, she could teach herself many of the subjects taught in school by reading books in a well-stocked library.[25] Muv tried to make her daughters' lives as stimulating as possible. There were regular trips to nearby Stratford-upon-Avon to see Shakespearian plays. Lady Redesdale also encouraged them to get involved in activities with the local girls. When Nancy wanted to set up a Girl Guide group, including her sisters and girls from the village, Sydney enthusiastically supported her, and even the reluctant Diana was forced to take part.[26]

Their education enabled them to become cultured young women, but Jessica and Nancy believed that it narrowed the career opportunities open to them. Later, Jessica complained that she had wanted to become a scientist and go to university. To make this possible she had secretly visited the headmaster of the local grammar school and asked about studying there. She was excited at the prospect, but when she put the proposal to Muv her face 'turned to disapproving stone' and her only comment was, 'Little D, being a scientist! What nonsense, no, of course you can't go to the grammar school.'[27] Jessica recalled that this refusal 'burned into my soul'.[28] Jessica began to actively dislike her mother. She later wrote that she seemed 'cold, strict, unapproachable, a person to whom one could never open one's heart or confide one's dreams'.[29] Nancy felt the same; she also blamed Sydney for preventing her from fulfilling her potential. Despite later writing accomplished historical biographies, she believed that she did not have the intellectual rigour of some of her rivals. In her novel *The Pursuit of Love*, she states that because of their free-range education, the Radlett children had not developed the habit of concentrating and they lacked any mental discipline.[30]

Nancy and Jessica were not the only ones limited by their mother's attitude. When Diana was sixteen, she wanted to learn German, but her parents refused to allow her.[31] Debo had been such a talented skater that she was approached to join the junior British team. Despite her ability, Sydney believed the training involved would take over her youngest daughter's life, so she stopped her taking up the opportunity.[32] Debo only heard of the offer years later and was angry she had been denied the chance.[33] It seems Lady Redesdale lacked the imagination to think her daughters might be most fulfilled by living a life that was drastically different from her own.

Part of the clash between mother and daughters about what constituted a suitable education was generational. Born in the Victorian era, Sydney brought up her girls to be aristocratic wives and mothers. However, this limited view of a woman's potential was becoming increasingly out of date. Feminist thinkers like Virginia Woolf would challenge it in their writing. The Bloomsbury author was the same generation as Sydney, but Woolf shared Jessica and Nancy's resentment that her brothers had been given a boarding school education while she was taught at home, just because she was a girl. In Woolf's extended essay *A Room of One's Own*, written in 1928, the section on 'Shakespeare's sister', Judith, the girl who was as intelligent as her brother but not given the same opportunities, could have been written for Nancy. A cornerstone of Virginia's feminist ideas was that women should be given the same education as men and be able to enter the same professions, not just become wives and mothers. Nancy and Jessica felt the same and much of their resentment towards Muv was because she had failed to change with the times. Whether they were influenced by Virginia Woolf's ideas we do not know, but certainly Nancy read her work and admired her as a writer. The modernist author is mentioned in *Love in a Cold Climate*, as a novelist everyone is talking about, and Woolf's novel *Mrs Dalloway* is praised.[34] In a letter written in 1930, Nancy wrote that she saw financial independence as vital for human happiness.[35] Although she would never call herself a feminist, on a personal level Nancy was fighting the same battles.

In Nancy's novel *The Pursuit of Love*, we get an idea of the attitude to schooling she would have liked her mother to have pursued. Aunt Emily values female education so highly that she moves house so that Fanny can attend a good day school.[36] She has a modern attitude, stating that although a girl may marry a man who can support her financially, she may need to earn her own living. A good education would make that possible, but it would also turn her into a more fulfilled, mature, interesting person.[37] Aunt Emily's model of parenting is contrasted with Aunt Sadie's and Uncle Matthew's failure to send their daughters to school. Only half joking, Nancy writes that if they had been poor children Uncle Matthew would have been sent to prison for refusing to educate them.[38]

Rather than wanting her daughters to be intellectuals, Muv intended them to become practical women. With varying degrees of success, she tried to instil in them the importance of managing their finances carefully. When they were old enough, she got all her daughters together and offered the prize of half a crown to the one who could draw up the best budget for a young couple living on £500 a year.[39] She suggested they consider what proportion they would spend on wages, rates, rent, heating, cleaning materials, food and travel. When Nancy triumphantly read out her proposal, 'Flowers: £499. Everything else: £1', Muv realised she was fighting a losing battle.[40] She also encouraged entrepreneurial skills by training her children to keep pigs, hens and calves. To put it on a businesslike footing, they paid 'rent' to their father for the land and stables and then sold what they produced. As an incentive, they could keep any profit they made. Trying to maximise her earnings, Pam challenged her father when she discovered that she was paying proportionally more rent for her small piece of land than his other tenants.[41] Pam and Debo excelled in this life lesson, and both were to use the skills they learnt later.

For the Mitford girls, the social consequences of home education were as important as the academic. On the positive side, it meant they could develop as individuals unfettered by any pressures to conform. Nonetheless, there was a downside, because instead of mixing with other children from different backgrounds the girls were isolated with each other for long periods. Stuck in the schoolroom with just Unity and Debo for company, Jessica found this stultifying, but Muv believed that being with other children would have been 'overstimulating'.[42] This rarified existence reinforced their eccentricity: Jessica described them as like 'a lost tribe separated from its fellow men'. They developed their own private language, Boudledidge, and a distinctive way of talking, which could appear affected when they entered the outside world.[43] Constantly thrown together, the sisters were always competing for attention among themselves, rather than with classmates. It also meant that, unlike schoolgirls who could turn any resentment towards their teachers, for the Mitford girls Muv became the authority figure who was the focus of their discontent.

Nancy, Diana and Jessica emphasised the tedium of their teenage years and the boredom of their country life, but that was not how it appeared to observers. Looking back, their cousin Julia Budworth pondered what exactly they had to moan about.[44] Debo could not understand her sisters' desire to escape from home.[45] With countless relatives frequently coming to stay there was always something going on. When the clan got together, there were tennis parties, cricket, picnics and dancing, while at Christmas, fancy-dress parties became a tradition. The girls put on plays, and sometimes Muv took part; on one memorable occasion Jessica played St George while Sydney was typecast as the dragon.[46] There were also occasional trips abroad, including family holidays to Dieppe and St Moritz, where the whole family enjoyed skating. Once the girls were old enough, they were allowed to visit Europe with their friends or to attend a finishing school in Paris.

Jessica admitted that Muv was always organising activities for them, and it was not outward circumstances so much as a deeper issue which caused her *ennui*.[47] The problem was not the lack of activity so much as the type. For the daughters like Pam and Debo, who loved a traditional country life, their upbringing was idyllic. Debo described her childhood as 'paradise'.[48] In contrast, Nancy, Diana, Jessica and Unity felt differently; they had inherited the Bowles genes, which made them restless and drove them to seek a more cosmopolitan and intellectually stimulating environment. Jessica described feeling cut off from real life and from contact with people outside their privileged circle. In the cocoon her parents had spun around their daughters, it was safe, but it was unreal, ignoring the 'poverty, hunger, cold, cruelty' that other people were suffering.[49]

Whatever the pitfalls of their education, the Mitford girls grew up to be exceptionally confident young women.[50] As Jessica later wrote, her upbringing had given her the feeling that she could 'walk unscathed through any flame'. However, she added that 'the instinctive respect for the fundamental dignity of every other human being – even his enemy – so often displayed by the Negro or Jew in his fight for equality, were on the whole conspicuously lacking in us, or only present in the most undeveloped form.'[51]

Inevitably, Sydney made mistakes as a parent, but she did her best and conscientiously weighed her actions. Muv and Farve were well-intentioned and tried to learn from their own far from perfect upbringings, but it did not always work. By trying to keep their children in a rarified upper-class orbit and protect them from the childhood experiences which had scarred them, they stored up problems for the future. As soon as they were old enough, their daughters could not wait to escape from home and launch themselves on the wider world.

7

Escapades

The Mitford girls' belief that their parents restricted them made them crave freedom from their gilded cage. Nancy was the first to spread her wings and seek out broader horizons but, although she liked to portray herself as a rebel, she did not fly very far. She was to remain, albeit resentfully, under her parents' roof and subject to their discipline until she married in her late twenties.[1] This perceived restriction resulted in a battle for control between the two generations. As the younger daughters watched their older sisters come into conflict with their parents, marriage seemed the only feasible escape route.[2] Jessica believed that Nancy was trapped because she lacked financial independence and the education to be able to achieve it.

The first step on Nancy's road to liberation was her coming out party, which was recreated in her novel *The Pursuit of Love*. The reality was very similar to the fictional version. Muv tried to give her daughter the best possible launch in society, but she failed as the party at Asthall was limited to their narrow circle, and Nancy's dance card was full of ageing uncles and immature cousins. Dissatisfied with the far from stimulating set her parents had to offer, Nancy was determined to make friends of her own. She was soon mixing with a group of young aesthetes. Many were from the *Brideshead Revisited* era at Oxford University; her set included Harold Acton, Evelyn Waugh, Brian Howard and Cecil Beaton. When she brought them home to meet her parents a clash was inevitable. The effete young men with their anti-imperialist, pacifist or socialist views could not be more different from her conservative, hyper-masculine father. The younger generation's frivolity jarred with the older generation's serious-minded approach to life. Nancy's friends mocked everything Farve held dear. They called the Boer War, in which Lord Redesdale was badly injured, 'the Bore War', and challenged English exceptionalism by changing Blake's 'green and pleasant land' to 'green unpleasant land'.[3]

For Sydney, the young women of her daughters' generation were equally alien. From their shingled hair to their painted toenails, these bright young things could not have been more different from Lady Redesdale's tightly corseted, blowsily coiffed contemporaries. The flippancy of the flappers was at odds with their straightlaced, Edwardian mothers. This incomprehension between the generations was commonplace in interwar novels, but no one captured it better than Nancy.[4] In her novel *Wigs on the Green*, Lady Chalford, the character based on Lady Redesdale, is described as being like a relic from a previous era. It was not because of her age – she was in her prime – but because of her outlook and way of speaking and dressing, which had not changed since before the First World War.[5]

Nancy also brilliantly captured the generational clash in her first novel, *Highland Fling*.[6] The heroine, Jane Dacre, is based on Nancy. The character shares the author's attitude to her parents and the stratified society in which they lived. In her book, Nancy sets out her generation's argument with their elders through the character of Albert Memorial Gates. As a cosmopolitan, artistic character, he questions the concept of patriotism. He claims the older governing class started the First World War, and if they carried on with their outdated xenophobic attitudes there would be another war, which none of the young men would want to fight. Rather than criticise the Germans, the British should befriend them as another civilised nation. The long-term aim should be a United States of Europe under one government and a permanent peace.[7]

Farve, more than Muv, found it hard to move with the times and was bewildered by the postwar era. At first, he reacted with furious frustration to the young upstarts his daughter brought home. He would get out his horsewhip to punish louche young men who dared to put their feet on the sofa. During dinner, while the girls teased him about every topic from politics to sex, their guests discovered that it was best to keep their opinions to themselves.[8] Calling these languid youths 'sewers' he would lambast their arguments until he made it clear it was time for them to leave by shouting down the table to his wife, 'Have these people no homes of their own?'[9] There were sometimes embarrassing clashes over the dinner table, most notably when Tom's friend James Lees-Milne suggested that it was time Britain stopped producing anti-German propaganda. Having fought in the First World War, Lord Redesdale was incandescent, describing 'the Huns' as like 'devils in hell'. He shouted at his antagonist to be quiet and not talk about what he did not understand.[10] Lees-Milne was chucked out of the house and could only creep back later when the coast was clear. By this time the storm had blown over, and Lord Redesdale characteristically greeted him like a long-lost son.[11]

When rows broke out, Lady Redesdale tried to smooth over the surface and calm the situation down. During an explosion from Lord Redesdale, a pained expression would cross her face. Then she would put a hand on her husband's arm and say in a plaintive drawl, 'David'. Her intervention would usually stop him and rather than continue to rant he would leave the room.[12] Even though she was rather bemused by the antics of Nancy's facetious friends, commenting to her younger daughters, 'What a set!',[13] she found them amusing and insisted they should be allowed to visit.[14] While Lord Redesdale was viewed with a degree of trepidation, Lady Redesdale inspired admiration. One young man, Michael Mason, who lived on a nearby estate Eynsham Park, Witney, developed a crush on her. Despite being twenty years younger than Sydney, many years later, he confessed to her:

You (why should I seek to conceal it?) I always loved and admired beyond measure, chiefly, perhaps, for your good looks and secondly perhaps because you never smiled unless you were pleased to see someone and so, when you smiled that was something. And you smiled at me often enough to make me feel honoured, and I have not forgotten.[15]

He was not Sydney's only admirer: James Lees-Milne described her as like Persephone, Queen of the Underworld, because of her 'statuesque, melancholy beauty'.[16] Many years later he wrote:

> To their callow and unsophisticated guests their home seemed a perfect Elysium of culture, wit and fun. The source of those cloudless days was [...] that enigmatical, generous great-minded, matriarchal figure, with her clear china blue eyes and divinely formed, slightly drooping mouth, which expressed worlds of humour and tragedy.[17]

As an observer, James Lees-Milne did not feel the Mitford girls had much to complain about. Muv 'presided' over them with 'unruffled sweetness, amusement and no little bewilderment'. While Farve, even though he could be fierce with outsiders, was indulgent towards his daughters, and allowed them to say and do whatever they liked.[18] To a degree, Nancy knew James was right; in *Highland Fling* when she described her heroine Jane Dacre's critical attitude to her parents, she wrote that she regarded them with bitterness for no apparent reason. While Jane's friends thought they were charming and cultured people who were clearly devoted to their daughter, she portrayed them as narrow-minded, 'aged half-wits with criminal tendencies'. She always wanted to shock them and cause a scene. For Jane, like Nancy, it was all a pose, and beneath the glib comments she was extremely fond of them.[19] It was as though Nancy could only see her parents clearly when she distanced herself and looked at them through the filter of fiction. Revealing though her writing was, the self-awareness revealed in her novel did not prevent her negative feelings continuing to surface.

In retrospect, no matter the tensions that were clearly present, Sydney looked back on the family's six years at Asthall manor as the happiest time in her family's life. She believed that none of their troubles would have happened if they had stayed there.[20] Inevitably, her husband's desire to sell the manor house and build a new house for the family nearby caused resentment. Nancy always claimed that her father took on this costly project because he did not have enough to do. If he had a proper occupation, they would have never left Asthall.[21] Perhaps marking her disapproval, Lady Redesdale left her husband to oversee his pet project on his own. She bargained with him that she must have a London base from which she could launch her girls in society.[22] They bought a six-storey house, 26 Rutland Gate, Knightsbridge, which conveniently had its own ballroom as well as enough bedrooms for the whole family; there were also a mews, garage and flat behind for their staff. The house was decorated to Sydney's taste. Painted pale grey, the airy drawing room had pale-blue taffeta curtains and eighteenth-century gilded French furniture; to make it comfortable as well as elegant there were pink chintz sofas.[23] Skilfully mixing old and new, Sydney was delighted to find the dining room was decorated with stippled paint, which imitated stone and was the height of fashion in the 1920s.[24] Lady Redesdale was in her element in her London home; there is a photograph of her looking regal, sitting on her stylish canopied bed.[25]

While Lord Redesdale was developing his grand design and the renovation of Rutland Gate was completed, Sydney took the girls to Paris for a three-month holiday. Influenced by her Francophile father, Muv loved the city and enjoyed the change of scene.[26] Unfortunately, Lady Redesdale had made a fundamental error by leaving her husband in charge. She was the one with a good business head who could have kept the project within budget; she was also the partner with a gift for interior design. The result was Swinbrook, a house completely designed and decorated by David. Farve had planned what he believed would be the ideal home for his family, with a bedroom for each person, tennis and squash courts, but neither Sydney nor most of her daughters ever liked it. The house looked like a large barracks and was very cold in winter. The consequences of building Swinbrook were to be costly and long lasting; neither the family finances nor the Redesdale marriage ever fully recovered.

While Sydney was annoyed by the expense of the project, which they could not afford, David was hurt by his wife and daughters' rejection of the home he had created for them. In the aftermath, the couple began to live more semi-detached lives. After they first moved in, Lord and Lady Redesdale were hardly on speaking terms. Farve was well aware of what his wife thought. When Nancy commented that their pictures looked awful, Muv replied tartly that of course they did in that sort of room. To escape the oppressive atmosphere, Farve spent most of the summer shooting in Scotland.[27]

After the Swinbrook debacle, Lord Redesdale must have felt he could never please his wife, but he kept on trying. Every year he bought her a Christmas present at the Army and Navy Stores but, knowing that she would not like his taste, he told the shop assistant that his wife would return it after the festivities were over. He was right, and his gift was always immediately exchanged.[28] Unlike in the early years of their marriage, when Sydney had pretended to relish the peaches David gave her, she could not be bothered to conceal her feelings anymore. A degree of cynicism tinged her attitude to marriage. In *Love in a Cold Climate*, Aunt Sadie wonders why young girls expected perfect happiness once they are married. She describes this naïve hope as 'Dame Nature's' way of trapping them.[29]

The cost of building Swinbrook was more than the Redesdales could afford. According to Lord Redesdale's grandson, Jonathan Guinness, the family finances were always opaque. It was considered bad form to talk about money, so the subject was never openly discussed in the family. Lord Redesdale would ricochet from either thinking he was poorer or richer than he was. Like Uncle Matthew in Nancy's novel *Love in a Cold Climate*, every few years there would be a financial crisis during which Lord Redesdale thought his family would end up in the workhouse.[30] Years later, in a letter to her friend Evelyn Waugh, Nancy described what it was like when the family faced these periodic financial crises. Her parents would be closeted in a room for hours with an adviser; then there would be trivial economies which never made any real difference. She remembered the anxious atmosphere lingering for several months.[31] The true state of Farve's resources was never clear to his children, and perhaps not even to himself. He was rich enough to buy Rutland Gate and build Swinbrook simultaneously, but the cost of the building project ended the period of financial stability the family had experienced since the sale of Batsford. From this time onwards, Lord Redesdale was increasingly worried about money.[32]

Farve was not the only aristocrat to have financial problems. Between 1914 and 1925 the number of people in Britain whose annual income exceeded £10,000 fell by two thirds from around 4,000 to 1,300. Price rises, super tax, death duties and income tax undermined the financial and eventually the social position of these aristocratic families. Despite many of them pleading poverty, they were far from impoverished, but they were not as wealthy as they had been before the First World War.[33]

What revenue Farve had was further threatened by him embarking on more hare-brained business schemes. Completely honest himself, he was naïve about people and often taken in by charlatans.[34] Listening to wacky Uncle Geoffrey instead of his canny wife, he made many disastrous investments.[35] One of his most counterproductive entrepreneurial escapades was with a dubious South American aristocrat called the Marquis De Andia-Irarrazaval, who claimed to have a right to the Spanish throne and that he was a hereditary Knight of the Garter. At first Lord Redesdale believed him and was attracted by his concept of manufacturing wirelesses concealed in *papier mâché* jewelled caskets in the shape of a Spanish galleon or a Buddha. The intention was to make an ugly object more attractive, but unfortunately the caskets were more grotesque than the wirelesses.[36] Hardly surprisingly, the scheme did not work out; not only did he lose money, Farve also ended up in court, threatened with a potentially costly slander case. When Lord Redesdale lost faith in the product and his business partner, he began to question whether the Marquis was really a nobleman, or whether he was an imposter. It was alleged that David and another director of the company had said that the Marquis and the woman who claimed to be his wife lived together but were not married. They described her as 'no better than she ought to have been'. Defending her honour, the outraged lady claimed damages for slander.[37] When he took to the stand, Farve made an impressive witness. Diana Churchill, who attended court with the rest of the family, described him as looking like 'God the Father'.[38] The judge believed Lord Redesdale and found in his favour, but it had been an embarrassing and expensive experience.

Equally galling were the opportunities Farve missed. He became friends with William Morris, Lord Nuffield, when he ran a bicycle shop in Oxford. William had asked him if he would like to invest in his scheme for a car factory, but unfortunately, Farve turned the offer down. If he had been more financially astute, he could have shared in the car magnate's success.[39] For someone as cautious with money as Sydney, watching her husband squander their savings on hopeless projects and missing out on profitable ones must have been frustrating. In her household account books she recorded every penny she spent. She was never extravagant, but nor was she mean. When her brother George faced financial problems after the 1929 Stock Market Crash, he offered his siblings shares in *The Lady*. Even though at the time the magazine was making a loss, Sydney loyally bought some shares while both Weenie and Geoffrey refused. Eventually, when the magazine's fortunes improved, Muv's generous investment paid off.[40]

Throughout their married life, Sydney paid the emotional cost of David's financial adventures. Her home mattered to her; it was no coincidence that her memoir was entitled *Five Houses*, charting her life through the places in which she had lived. Found among her papers was a memo in which she listed a husband, children and a house in order of importance, although she added that at times the order altered. Describing their house as 'a casket' to contain the family, she explained that interior design was the way a woman with no ability to paint or write could express herself and create something beautiful. Perhaps the fact she used the word casket suggests that, consciously or unconsciously, her husband's foolish entrepreneurial adventure still rankled. She prided herself in making a beautiful environment for her family and putting down roots, but because of their financial circumstances and Lord Redesdale's restlessness, she often had to move. In her memoir, she admitted she was sorry that it had been her lot to live in many houses, because she would have liked to have stayed in the same one and passed it on to her descendants.[41] However, whatever frustration she felt, she internalised it, and her children never heard her complain.[42]

Rather than moan, Lady Redesdale devoted herself more to her daughters. This shift in Muv's priorities from her husband to her children is captured in Nancy's *The Pursuit of Love*. When Aunt Sadie is organising Linda's coming out ball, she opposes Uncle Matthew for the first time because his prejudices threatened to prevent her asking suitable suitors who would make her daughter's party a success.[43] Over the next few years, Sydney's life revolved around bringing her girls out in society, and then coping with their ever more daring escapades. It was to be time-consuming and emotionally exhausting and left her with little time or energy for her own life.

As one after another of her daughters went through the same routine of their debutante season, she was by their side. Her first duty was to organise a coming out party for each of her girls. Although she had less money than many of the other mothers, her creativity made these memorable events. Next came a succession of balls, house parties and lunches where the same people mingled day after day. For Sydney and the other chaperones, evenings were spent sitting chatting until the early hours while their children danced the night away. During the season, Muv faced a gruelling and repetitive schedule, particularly as by the time her last daughter came out, she was in her late fifties, but she did it because she thought it was her maternal duty. Only in later life did Diana and Debo acknowledge how good she was to do it for them.[44]

While her daughters enjoyed lying in in the mornings, Lady Redesdale was always up at 8.30 a.m., sitting ramrod straight at her desk dealing with her morning letters and then phoning Harrods to give the food order for the day.[45] The only luxury she allowed herself to keep her going was chocolate; she kept a box of Terry's *langues de chat* and chocolate pastilles in her desk drawer.[46] Once her work at home was done, she would go shopping, walking down to the fishmonger's on the Brompton Road or to Mrs Munro's on Montpelier Street to select chintzes for the house. She was always looking for a bargain and the drapers, Owles and Beaumont, near Harrods, often provided one.[47]

The Mitford girls were soon making their mark in London society, but their behaviour was hard for their parents to handle. The world had changed so much from their youth three decades earlier that they hardly recognised it. They tried to control the situation by imposing the strict rules they had abided by, but that approach often backfired.

They would perhaps have been more successful if they had picked their battles rather than fighting on all fronts. In her novel *The Pursuit of Love*, Nancy described Aunt Sadie and Uncle Matthew's standards of chaperonage as positively medieval. A young woman could not meet a young man alone unless they were engaged.[48] This meant that in London the Redesdales' daughters had to be accompanied by a chaperone, even if they were only walking the short distance from Rutland Gate to shop in Harrods. There were also certain streets where it was not suitable for a young lady to be seen. Sloane Street was allowed, but Jermyn Street was not.[49] When in the street, the youngest girls were told by their mother never to speak to anyone not in uniform. Rather than this making them fear strangers, the girls half hoped they would be abducted by a notorious white slave trader because it would be thrilling.[50]

In her memoir, Jessica analysed the flaws in her upbringing. She wrote, 'Too much security as children coupled with too much discipline imposed on us from above by force or threat of force, had developed in us a high degree of wickedness, a sort of extension of childhood naughtiness.'[51] There were many petty skirmishes over issues that did not really matter. Rather than treating her daughters as independent adults, Sydney tried to control them as though they were still wayward children. After Nancy broke the rules and secretly went to Oxford for an assignation with a male friend, which involved having a harmless walk, she was harangued by her father and told no one would want to marry her. Similarly, when Nancy disobeyed her parents and had her hair fashionably shingled, Muv told her that with her new short haircut no one would look at her because, whereas she was plain before, she was now positively ugly.[52] Even though Nancy was now in her twenties, Sydney tried to stop her mixing with people she thought would be a bad influence. After Lady Redesdale read Evelyn Waugh's novel *Vile Bodies*, he was added to the banned list.[53] Her eldest daughter ignored her, but she resented not being able to socialise freely with her mother's blessing.[54]

Nancy was not the only sister to find herself in conflict with her parents over some minor misdemeanour. When Sydney read in Diana's diary that she had gone to the cinema alone with a man while she had been studying at the Cours Fenelon, a day school in Paris, Lady

Redesdale overreacted. Although the outings had been harmless, she prevented her daughter returning to France and instead made her go on holiday to Devon with her younger sisters and their nanny. The invasion of privacy involved in reading the diary, accompanied by the infantilising restriction of freedom, was deeply resented by the girls and added to Muv's reputation as a censorious parent who was out of touch with the modern age.

As the eldest, Nancy was the trailblazer for her sisters, fighting the battles which would make life easier for her successors. In 1928, at the age of 24, she had a pyrrhic victory against her parents. Following furious rows with her father, she finally persuaded her parents to let her go to the Slade School to study art and live in a furnished bed-sitting room in Kensington. Her quest for freedom did not last long because she found life away from her home comforts much harder than she expected. After three weeks living in a flat in London she returned, explaining to Jessica: 'Oh darling, but you should have seen it. After about a week, it was knee-deep in underclothes. I literally had to wade through them. No one to put them away.'[55]

As the project to become a Bohemian artist had failed, she turned to writing to supplement the allowance she received from her parents. First, she contributed articles to *Vogue, Harper's Bazaar* and *The Lady*. She then turned her gift to writing fiction. Her first novel, *Highland Fling*, published in 1931, parodied her family. General Murgatroyd and Admiral Wenceslaus bore striking resemblances to Farve and her uncle George Bowles. A joke figure, Wenceslaus was a pompous armchair admiral who liked his drink and was obsessed with the navy and blockades, while General Murgatroyd was a philistine squire who lived for his fishing and shooting. Muv showed some interest in the novel, suggesting its title should be *Our Vile Age* as a pun of their nineteenth-century ancestor Mary Russell Mitford's book *Our Village*. However, her idea was soon rejected because it was too like Evelyn Waugh's title *Vile Bodies*.[56] Concerned about publicity and upsetting their relatives, Muv told Nancy she must not publish the book under her own name. As usual, her daughter ignored her.[57] It turned out Sydney was far more upset about the caricatures than her brother or husband; Farve was amused by his portrayal, while Uncle George seemed to relish his unflattering alter ego. He told his sister the novel was 'awfully indecent', but he hoped that it would sell well.[58]

Like most mothers, Sydney wanted her daughters to be happily settled, but the girls had other ideas – they wanted adventures. Nancy was always bad at picking men. Her first great love was the totally unsuitable Hamish St Clair Erskine, son of Lord Rosslyn. Five years younger than Nancy, he was homosexual, and at Eton he had a fling with her brother Tom. Both his parents and hers disapproved of the match, but it dragged on for four years. He often made Nancy deeply unhappy, which led to her trying to end her own life by switching on the gas fire in her room but not lighting it.[59] Not much was made of her suicide plan as, typical of her generation, her mother did not seem to understand mental health issues. She had no time for psychologists, writing a few years later that they were 'ridden by Freud's fantastic ideas and forget ordinary things like good food and air and water'.[60] Sydney wrote to Diana that she hoped Nancy would not consider marrying Hamish until he had a job. Justifying her attitude, she explained she would not be bothered about the money if only she thought he could make her daughter happy. She thought it would inevitably end badly.[61]

When they finally split up, Muv could only pick up the pieces. After one break-up between them, Sydney encouraged Nancy to get engaged to a more suitable young man who seemed to love her. The only problem was that Nancy was not attracted to this alternative, and when she rejected him there was a heated argument with her mother. Sydney told her daughter she was in danger of becoming an old maid. Years later, Jessica remembered the incident, too, and was very critical of Muv.[62] In retrospect Nancy was more forgiving, admitting that Sydney never tried to push her into a loveless marriage. She added that to her credit, her mother was not mercenary and did not seem to know or care if a suitor was wealthy or not.[63] In her novel *Highland Fling*, the heroine based on Nancy, Jane Dacre, expects her parents to be difficult when she introduces her arty fiancé, Albert, to them, but in fact they are charming because they just wanted to see her happily married. She wrote that any respectable young man with a reasonable fortune would have been accepted by them. This desire for her to marry was not because they wanted to get rid of their daughter, but rather that her recent erratic behaviour had caused them a great deal of worry and they thought marriage would steady her.[64] It seems deep down, even at the time, Nancy realised that Lady Redesdale was acting from the same motivation.

Perhaps remembering her own youthful frustrations, Sydney always attributed moodiness or boredom to needing a husband.[65] Her standpoint is explored through Aunt Sadie in Nancy's novel *Love in a Cold Climate*, who suggests the need to marry is causing Polly Hampton's malaise. When Aunt Sadie's brother-in-law, Davey, suggests she sees sex as a cure-all, she immediately denies it. Sex was not the motivating force for her; instead, marriage meant that a girl could leave home and embark on her 'career' of managing her own household and having a family.[66]

Sydney did not find it easy to discuss her children's love lives with them. Her daughters thought she was too unworldly to understand. Like the Radlett children in *Love in a Cold Climate*, they found it hard to believe their mother even knew the facts of life.[67] However, her own passionate feelings when she was young suggest she understood more than her daughters would ever acknowledge. Perhaps she just chose to turn a blind eye to matters she did not want to deal with directly. As a schoolboy at Eton, Tom had had some homosexual encounters, which his sisters knew about, but his parents did not. It caused great hilarity when Tom brought a male friend home to stay but, because the house was packed, Muv asked if the young man would mind sharing a room with her son. Inevitably, she wondered why her daughters could not contain their laughter.[68]

In her novel *The Pursuit of Love*, Nancy wrote that it was difficult for the Radlett girls to talk to Aunt Sadie about sex. The nearest they got to it was discussing babies. Aunt Sadie felt that she should discuss the subject more with her children but was too embarrassed. Instead, she gave them a textbook to read, which left the girls with only a hazy understanding of what the act involved. They got much more helpful information from a book entitled *Ducks and Duck Breeding*.[69]

Once again, Sydney's reserve got in the way of close relationships. Her daughters recognised this was a problem for her. In *Love in a Cold Climate*, Nancy wrote that Aunt Sadie was too shy to talk directly to Polly about intimate subjects and instead just dropped hints into the conversation about what marriage entailed.[70] Looking back, Debo described her mother as distancing herself from their romantic relationships; she was amused by them but remained detached. She was well aware if her girls were unhappy, and tried to understand what was upsetting them, but did not get too involved.[71] There were enough other people available to dramatise every situation. As Sydney found emotional intimacy difficult, the girls turned elsewhere. They discovered an avid listener in Muv's friend Mrs Hammersley, who wanted to know every detail of their romances.

It was not just Nancy who proved a worry. The Redesdales' second daughter Pamela experienced a broken engagement. Pam was very different from her sisters; she did not vie for the limelight and was happiest living in the country surrounded by animals. In her steadiness and love of her home, she was the daughter who was most like Muv.[72] She got engaged to Oliver Watney, the heir to a brewing fortune, but he then decided to end their relationship. It was an embarrassing incident because the wedding presents had to be returned and the story was widely covered in the newspapers.[73] Despite the inconvenience it caused her, Muv was relieved because she knew the couple were not in love.[74]

In contrast, Diana had no lack of admirers. As soon as she came out as a debutante in 1928, she was feted as one of the most beautiful girls of her era. By the end of her first debutante season, Bryan Guinness, the twenty-two-year-old heir to another brewing family, proposed to her. The Redesdales considered the couple too young and said they must wait a year, but Bryan's parents supported the match. As Diana sulked and threatened to pine away, eventually Muv and Farve backed down. No one could accuse Sydney of being materialistic; unlike many mothers, she was concerned that Bryan was just too rich, and she feared that such vast wealth would corrupt her daughter. In spite of her concerns, faced with a *fait accompli*, as usual she gave in.

The date for the grand society wedding was set for January 1929. Unusually for such traditionalists, Lord and Lady Redesdale objected to a church wedding because Diana had largely lost her faith. However, Bryan and his parents insisted, so the service was held at fashionable St Margaret's, Westminster.[75] The reception was to be held at the Guinnesses' London house because Rutland Gate was let out, but Lady Redesdale and her daughters were totally immersed in preparations. There were guest lists to prepare, menus to select, a trousseau for the bride and bridesmaids' dresses for her sisters needed. In Rutland Gate the excitement was reaching boiling point, when just before the wedding Jessica and Debo fell ill with whooping cough. With her eccentric attitude to germs, Lady Redesdale was quite happy for her infectious daughters to still attend the service and then go back to bed. Sensibly, the Guinness family outlawed her reckless idea.[76]

As an eighteen-year-old married woman with a stimulating social life, Diana was initially very happy. She was delighted to no longer be under her parents' control and instead now able to live by her own rules. Concerned about how her daughter would handle her newly discovered freedom, Lady Redesdale tried to steer her in the right direction. She explained to her daughter that one of her duties as mistress of the house was to choose menus, but when Diana was faced with the task, the only dish she could think of was dressed crab – it appeared often because it was one of Muv's forbidden foods. One of Sydney's parting gifts to Diana was a blue leather account book with her initials embossed on it in gold, intended for recording detailed household accounts.[77] However, with a large fortune and four homes at her disposal, Diana had little incentive to emulate her mother's frugality, and the book was seldom opened.

The balance between mother and daughter had changed. Now, Lady Redesdale and her younger children came to stay with Diana at Biddesden, her country house in Wiltshire. It was supposed to be haunted so Diana did not want to be there alone. During one visit, Sydney made a good impression on her daughter's friend and neighbour, the artist Dora Carrington, who was part of the Bloomsbury set. Carrington noted in a letter to Lytton Strachey that she thought Lady Redesdale was 'remarkable, very sensible and no upper-class graces'.[78]

It did not take long for Muv's qualms about the Guinness marriage to be proved right. On the surface, Diana seemed to have everything she could possibly want. She was at the centre of a glittering circle of bright young things, adored by her husband and admired by his friends. Within a few years of her marriage, she had two sons, and, unlike Sydney, she immediately adored her babies and loved motherhood.[79] Despite her pleasure in her new role, it was not enough to completely fulfil her. Diana and her sisters desired more from life; they needed a hero and a crusade. During the next decade, a heady cocktail of politics and passion were to lure Sydney's daughters on to adventures which would create even greater challenges for their mother to handle. Describing what happened to Aunt Sadie in *The Pursuit of Love*, Nancy recreated her mother's experience. Her children had broken free from her control, and if they made mistakes, there was nothing she could do about it; she had become a mere spectator.[80]

8

Political Divides

D uring the 1930s the polarisation in international politics was reflected in the Redesdales' home. While Stalin's communist dictatorship ruled in Russia, from January 1933, Hitler controlled Germany with his authoritarian fascist regime. In a Britain badly affected by an economic depression, to some people, particularly the young, the old political solutions no longer seemed adequate; people began to look elsewhere for answers. No family was to be more divided by the ideological clashes of the era than the Mitfords. While Jessica turned to communism, Unity, like her elder sister Diana, was attracted to fascism. What at first seemed like yet another family joke proved to be far from funny.[1] Through their daughters, Muv and Farve were sucked into the vortex which swallowed up their world. There was to be no going back and not their marriage, family nor reputations would be left unscathed by the devastating forces unleashed.

Observers have often found it hard to understand why this bevy of aristocratic beauties became so entwined with the politics of the era. Superficially, the Mitfords seemed like frivolous party girls: the most radiant stars in the firmament of the bright young things. But beneath that sparkling veneer they had a far more serious side, one which could never be fully satisfied by skating across the shallow surface. As Sydney's grandson Jonathan Guinness argues, to understand where this came from involves looking back into their family history.[2] They were

Thomas Bowles's granddaughters, and as such they were not content to be just social butterflies: they needed a purpose in their lives. To the world they looked like the ultimate insiders, but the maverick inheritance from their maternal grandfather meant they liked to see themselves as outsiders. They relished being irreverent and questioning standards just because they were accepted.[3] They wanted to be rebels with a cause.[4] As Thomas's old butler Caddick commented, when he heard of their political forays in the 1930s, 'Well they are Mr Bowles' grandchildren. What else do you expect?'[5]

Biographers have often portrayed this political gene as skipping a generation, but that was not the case. Despite being outwardly so different from her father and daughters, beneath the surface Lady Redesdale was more similar than anyone was aware, and so, when she came out in her true colours, it was more of a shock. In her seemingly conventional, quieter, less outrageous way, Sydney set the precedent for being politically involved; she was the link between Thomas and her daughters. Muv had been brought up by a man who was willing to break away from mainstream politics to promote his own ideas. He believed that the individual could make a difference, and so did she, which is why she intervened in the politics of her era, writing to the newspapers and politicians to make her views known. Thomas never admired most of his fellow Parliamentarians. It was no coincidence that Lady Redesdale and her daughters were also attracted to unorthodox politicians.

Brought up in this environment, as Diana's son Jonathan Guinness explains, his mother was 'a political animal with a potential for extremism'.[6] She led a luxurious and glamorous life married to Bryan Guinness, but she needed more stimulation. She had a social conscience and was 'vaguely liberal', admiring David Lloyd George.[7] As she looked at the state of the country, she thought it needed drastic change. When she met Oswald Mosley in 1932, she believed she had found the man to bring about that transformation. Mosley had been elected to Parliament as a Conservative in 1918 and, aged just 22, he became the youngest MP of the time. He later changed parties, sitting first as an independent then loosely allied to the Liberals. In 1924, he joined the Labour Party and was treated as a rising star, later becoming Chancellor of the Duchy of Lancaster in Ramsay MacDonald's government. During the Great Depression, he produced a memorandum to help the unemployed, but his party ignored his advice. Frustrated, he resigned from the government and launched his New Party in 1931; a year later he founded the British Union of Fascists (BUF).[8] The BUF was radical without being revolutionary: it did not challenge the monarchy, the Church or capitalism. Influenced by European fascist parties, it supported an authoritarian concept of government and nationalism.[9]

Just as his political career entered a new and exciting phase, Mosley met Diana. Although they were both married with children, they fell passionately in love. There was no suggestion he would get divorced; instead, he remained married to Cynthia 'Cimmie' Curzon, daughter of a former Viceroy of India. Undeterred by his commitment to his wife, from then on Diana dedicated herself to the man and his movement. She left Bryan and moved into a house in Eaton Square. As usual with the Mitfords, the drama became a family affair. At first Lady Redesdale hoped her daughter could be persuaded to go back to her husband. In an insightful letter, she told Diana that she thought that Bryan's worst fault was being too fond of her. She begged her not to throw away a fundamentally good marriage for a bad relationship. Perhaps thinking of her own challenging marriage, she encouraged her daughter to try again, because there was genuine affection between husband and wife.[10] While Sydney took a measured approach, David charged in. He went with Bryan's father, Lord Moyne, to see Mosley to ask him to give Diana up, which Mosley bluntly refused to do. Partly as a joke but also to create mischief, Unity told Muv that Diana was laying up a store of diamonds and furs for when she got divorced. Believing her daughter, Lady Redesdale told her husband, who then passed the story on to Lord Moyne, which stirred up animosity towards Diana among her in-laws.[11] The scandal escalated further when Cimmie unexpectedly died from peritonitis and Diana got divorced from Bryan.

Lord and Lady Redesdale were horrified by the whole situation and banned their two youngest daughters from visiting their notorious sister. Debo recalled that, like any unpleasant matter, her parents did not discuss Diana's love life in front of her. She was just aware of how upset they were, while only vaguely understanding the reason.[12] It seems that the Redesdales' outrage was more social than political. In the 1930s there was still a stigma attached to divorce, and Sydney was terrified Diana's behaviour would jeopardise her other daughters' marriage prospects. Nancy parodied her mother's abhorrence of divorce in the character of Lady Chalford in her novel *Wigs on the Green*. When Lady Chalford's son got divorced she was so mortified she never set foot outside the park gates of her stately home again.[13]

Even after Diana married her great love in Goebbels' house in Germany in 1936, Lord Redesdale refused to meet 'that man Mosley'. As the marriage was kept secret, to the world it appeared that the couple were still 'living in sin', so, for appearance's sake, Muv continued to ban Debo from visiting them. Determined to keep in touch, Diana regularly came to see her parents without her husband. In her novel *The Pursuit of Love*, Nancy suggests that her heroine, Linda, was allowed back into the family fold after her unsuitable marriage because her parents missed her too much to keep up the quarrel.[14] It seems that the motivation was the same for the Redesdales. Looking back, in her memoir, Diana wrote that she now understood her parents' actions and her sympathy was with them; they thought she was ruining her life and had only wanted the best for her. However, at the time, she found it harder to see the situation from their perspective.[15]

Like her older sisters before her, Unity was bored and frustrated. She had always been a worry for her mother; as a small child she was introverted and shy, but as a teenager she became disruptive. If she did not like what Farve said, she would just fix him with her large blue eyes and glare at him; he would glower back and become increasingly angry. She rarely rebelled against Muv, but she could be badly behaved with other people.[16] Sydney had always appeased Unity and ignored her abnormal behaviour, but it proved to be the wrong tactic to deal with such a turbulent spirit. When friends visited, to prevent her from throwing a tantrum, they were told by Muv never to tease her.[17] Left unchecked, Unity became increasingly out of control, leading to one friend describing her as having 'an element of sadism' in her character.[18]

When Unity came out as a debutante in 1932, her rebellious attitude was another form of attention-seeking. Rather than dress demurely, the almost 6ft-tall deb decked herself in fake jewels from a theatrical costumier. She took Enid, her grass snake, or Ratular, her pet rat, to parties and would sit stroking them. When she was presented at Buckingham Palace, she stole the writing paper to use at home. Sydney was horrified, but that was part of Unity's intention: to shock.[19] Early in 1933, she began attending the London County Council's Art School in Vincent Square. Rather than studying she had lunch and went to the movies with friends, so her stint as an art student did not last long and she left at Easter.[20] She used to invite her friends to Swinbrook for the weekend, but Lady Redesdale nicknamed them the 'Saturday afternooners', because by that time Unity had become bored with their company so Muv had to entertain them for the rest of their visit.[21]

With not enough to do, Unity longed for a new interest to give her life meaning. When she met Mosley on one of her visits to Diana, she immediately converted to his cause.[22] In June 1933, aged nineteen, she joined the BUF without telling her parents.[23] Knowing that Lord and Lady Redesdale would not approve, she would change into her black shirt at a friend's house before charging off to the East End to play ping-pong with some fascist boys.[24] When she went on a BUF recruiting march through London, she made up an elaborate story about what she was doing to deceive her mother.[25]

While Unity's life began to revolve around the fascists, Jessica took the opposite stance and became fascinated by communism, as Jessica's daughter Constancia Romilly explains:

There was the truism about Unity and Dec [Jessica] taking their diamonds and carving a swastika and a hammer and sickle on their windows. All that was a symbol for little girls, it was their way of understanding what was going on politically around them, what they heard in the discussion.[26]

At first, their different ideologies did not come between the two sisters, and they were still united against the grown-ups. When Lady Redesdale left them in charge of her produce stall at the local Conservative fete, they conspired to share the profits rather than let it go to 'the beastly old Conservatives'. Jessica took half of it for a communist newspaper while Unity donated her share to the BUF.[27] What began as a bit of a tease and part of their sibling rivalry soon escalated into an obsession for Unity and a crusade for Jessica.

In 1933, Diana took her younger sister to Germany, where they attended the Nazi Party Congress, or *Parteitag*, in Nuremberg. At first, Lord and Lady Redesdale opposed Unity going; Farve wrote to Diana saying they did not want the girls associating with a band of thugs, and the idea of it made both parents thoroughly miserable.[28] As usual there was no stopping the headstrong young women, so David and Sydney had to accept the situation. After the trip, Muv was so angry she told Unity that she would never let her go abroad again.[29] Her attitude changed once she realised her problematic daughter was transformed by the experience. When Unity told her parents she wanted to return to Germany to attend a finishing school and learn the language, Lady Redesdale could not think of a valid reason why she should not go.[30] Perhaps Muv was just glad Unity was enthusiastic about something and relieved her oddball daughter had finally found somewhere where she belonged. She later wrote to Jessica that Unity had discovered her 'spiritual home'.[31]

After moving to Munich in May 1934, Unity became as infatuated with Hitler as Diana was with Mosley. She stalked the Führer when he lunched at a local restaurant, the Osteria Bavaria, watching him from a distance. When she came back to England for the holidays, she was full of enthusiasm for the regime. Gradually, the Redesdales' attitude to the Nazis also began to alter. Coming from their background and with their existing views, in many ways this is not a surprise. Lord Redesdale had always expressed anti-foreigner attitudes and a British jingoism, which Jessica believed was remarkable even for his class and generation. She noted that Unity and Diana used to describe him as 'one of Nature's fascists'.[32] However, since fighting in the First World War, he had hated 'the Huns', so the change to admiration of the Germans was a major transformation. Lady Redesdale had also always held strong right-wing political views, but she was not an authoritarian as she believed in the freedom of the individual. During the Great Depression of the early 1930s, she was an ardent opponent of communism and disliked any form of socialism. She disapproved of unemployment benefits because she believed they removed the incentive to work. She also opposed the eight-hour day, claiming it dictated to free-born Englishmen how many hours they could work.[33]

It seems likely that Unity influenced her parents' attitudes towards Nazi Germany. Both Jessica and her cousin Joan Farrer noticed that Unity had become a great favourite with Lord Redesdale. Her sister described it as a shift from 'total loathing to adoration', and Unity became his favourite daughter. Both Muv and Farve were infected by Unity's newly discovered excitement.[34] They became curious to find out for themselves more about Nazi Germany. When they visited, they were won over by what they saw, but Sydney's conversion was more gradual than her capricious husband's. Her views on international politics had already begun to shift: she became more sympathetic to Germany after reading Maynard Keynes's criticism of the Treaty of Versailles; and she believed that the post-First World War settlement, with its demands for harsh reparations, had been unfair to the country.[35] However, when she first visited Unity in Munich in summer 1934, she was still sceptical about the regime. Brought up to be a Francophile, she wrote about having 'rather a contemptuous' attitude to the country, thinking it would be aesthetically unappealing and charmless.[36] She also wondered why the Germans put all their trust in one insignificant looking man, with his odd moustache and scruffy hair, dressed in a macintosh. Curious, she hoped to see Hitler and make her own assessment.

During her stay with Unity, Sydney liked what she saw. The beautiful architecture of the baroque theatre at Bayreuth and the ornate churches charmed her. Politically, she remained more sceptical, and she did not approve of the authoritarian aspects of the Nazi regime. She had an argument with Unity because, as an English citizen, she refused to give the Nazi salute outside a building where a plaque commemorated the men who died in the 1923 Beer Hall Putsch. To retaliate, Unity ran away from her mother and caught the tram home, leaving Sydney completely lost. Unable to speak German, it took Lady Redesdale hours to find her way back to their base.[37] After this experience, Muv walked on the other side of the road when near the memorial to avoid further confrontations with her obsessive daughter. At this point Sydney was open-minded; it was only later that she became an ardent supporter of Hitler.[38] When a friend of Unity's, Peter Hesketh, criticised the Nazis over dinner at Rutland Gate, Muv seemed pleased to hear his opinion. She told him that she only heard the other side, and his point of view was interesting because it was so different.[39]

Lord Redesdale was also keen to see for himself what was happening in Germany. After Unity's Christmas holiday, in January 1935, he took her back to Munich. During the visit, his daughter took him to the Osteria Bavaria, where they saw, but did not speak to, the Führer. With his usual gullibility and penchant for charlatans, Farve approved of what he saw and admitted he had been wrong about Hitler.[40] Never intellectually questioning it, he was soon totally taken in by Nazi propaganda. Delighted at her father's conversion, when Unity finally met Hitler in February 1935, she wrote a euphoric letter to Farve first instead of Muv. She thought her mother would describe her as hysterical while her father would be a more sympathetic audience. Describing herself as 'the luckiest girl in the world', she told Lord Redesdale that it was the best day of her life.[41] When Unity finally wrote to her mother a few days later, she explained that she suspected that to Muv's balanced mind the meeting would not seem very important, but surely even she had to admit it was interesting?[42]

Whether it was her Aryan looks or her aristocratic connections, Hitler was flattered by Unity's admiration, and he soon included her in his inner circle. When Lady Redesdale next visited her daughter in April 1935, Hitler said he would like to meet her. She was introduced to the Führer over tea at the Carlton Tea Room. As Lady Redesdale did not speak German, her daughter had to translate between them. Unity found it embarrassing because at first no one could think of anything to say and everything she translated sounded stupid. To her relief, when the regional commander arrived the conversation flowed more easily. After an hour, Sydney tactfully left while Unity stayed with her idol.

Unlike her husband, Lady Redesdale did not completely fall under the Führer's spell. She commented that, although no doubt he was good for Germany, there were aspects of his regime of which she disapproved.[43] Her main concession was that he had a very nice face. Unity complained to Diana that her mother lacked feeling because she did not sense Hitler's 'goodness and wonderfulness, radiating out'.[44]

Despite her lukewarm comments, when Lady Redesdale later wrote about this visit, she described Hitler in more flattering terms. She compared him to Nelson, who was both her father's and her great hero. She criticised Britain's 'contemptuous' attitude to the nationalist fervour which was sweeping through Germany. She admitted it could be seen as a form of hysteria and it would be better if the Germans exercised more self-control, but she suggested that a similar hysteria had inspired the British when Nelson embarked on the *Victory*. Sydney added that in Britain the Führer was viewed as a cruel tyrant, but during her trip to Germany she was only aware of adoration for him. She explained that her visit had prompted her to find out the truth, and over the next few years she made up her mind about the regime.[45]

During the 1930s, 'fascist tourism' became fashionable; Lady Redesdale was one of many British political tourists visiting Germany at this time.[46] Among them was the society hostess Mrs Greville, who came back from Nuremberg singing Hitler's praises 'long and loud' at dinner parties.[47] The British naturalist Henry Williamson was also won over at a Nuremberg rally. He described Hitler as 'an essentially good man who wanted only to build a new and better Germany'. At this stage, the Foreign Office seemed unconcerned by these pro-Hitler British visitors, with one official just recording in an intelligence report, 'there were a number of particularly silly people at Nuremberg'.[48] Other interventions were more serious and of great propaganda value to the Germans. In a speech to the British Legion, in June 1935, the Prince of Wales promoted friendship with Germany and encouraged former servicemen to visit the country. The following month a delegation from the British Legion travelled to Germany. They had an audience with Hitler and visited Dachau, the first concentration camp where political detainees were imprisoned. During the visit, the prison guards dressed

as prisoners to conceal what was really happening.[49] As this propaganda stunt showed, during these fact-finding missions Lady Redesdale
and her fellow travellers only heard what the regime wanted them to
hear and saw what they allowed them to see. This selective 'research'
airbrushed the cruelty which lay at the heart of Hitler's dictatorship.
Political violence was already routine under the Nazi regime. During
the recent Night of the Long Knives, the SA brutally killed opponents
on Hitler's orders.[50] In 1935, Hitler introduced the Nuremberg Laws,
which took many human rights away from Jewish people. It changed
the legal status of German Jews from citizens to 'Jews in Germany',
which established a framework for persecution.[51]

Unity openly supported Hitler's antisemitic policies. She became a
friend of Julius Streicher, one of the most virulent racists of the regime,
who promoted the Nuremberg laws and revelled in sadistic acts against
Jewish people. At his invitation, Unity attended a Nazi festival at
Hesselberg, near Nuremberg, where she spoke to the masses, alongside
Göring and Streicher, about her hope for lasting friendship between
Britain and Germany.[52] Afterwards, she wrote ecstatically to her mother
about the event. When her antics were covered in the British press, her
parents were not pleased. They cancelled a trip they had planned to see
her in Germany, and Farve wrote an angry letter to his daughter ordering her to come home. Defending herself, in a reply to her mother,
Unity claimed it would have been impolite to refuse Streicher's invitation. She remained unrepentant and continued to voice her hateful
opinions. In July 1935, a rabidly antisemitic letter written by her was
published in Streicher's newspaper *Der Stürmer*. After attacking British
Jews, claiming that 'the English have no notion of the Jewish danger',
Unity signed off, 'I want everyone to know that I am a Jew hater'.[53]

Unity was back in England in time to experience the fallout in a
critical British press. Afterwards, Farve was in a terrible temper with
her, mainly because of the letter.[54] Nancy wrote to Unity expressing
her disapproval and mocking both her and the regime.[55] Jessica was so
shocked by what was happening to Jewish people in Germany that she
showed Lord and Lady Redesdale *The Brown Book of the Hitler Terror*.
Compiled by an organisation called the World Committee for the

Victims of German Fascism, it was published by a respected publisher, Victor Gollancz. It was one of the first accounts of the effects of Nazi antisemitic laws, recording how German scientists had been driven out of the country for either their left-wing beliefs or 'reasons of ancestry'.[56] It also contained graphic photographs of the brutal persecution of Jews by Hitler's Stormtroopers. The book was mainly distributed through communist organisations and left-wing bookshops, so the Redesdales brushed it aside as just exaggerated communist propaganda. According to their daughter, they claimed that 'anyway the Jews had brought all this trouble on themselves, apparently by the mere fact of their existence'.[57] Their reaction sickened Jessica, and years later she explained in an interview, 'People say they didn't know what was happening to the Jews until after the war, but they did know because it was all there.'[58]

Unfortunately, the Redesdales' response was far from unique. Reports about the humiliation and persecution of Jewish people in Germany appeared in mainstream newspapers, but many readers turned a blind eye, taking the attitude that it was not their business.[59] This view was expressed by Edward, Prince of Wales, to the Kaiser's grandson, Prince Louis Ferdinand, when he claimed that Britain should 'not interfere in German affairs either re-Jews or re-anything else'. Other people refused to believe what they read because they accepted pro-German propaganda, which claimed that the press was run by 'the Jews' and the newspapers were lying to discredit the Nazi regime.[60]

Historians debate the extent of antisemitism in Britain in the interwar years. Martin Pugh describes it as rife throughout British society and across the political spectrum. This prejudice promoted stereotypical views of Jewish people, which blamed them for virtually all disasters, from the Boer War to the Russian Revolution.[61] Andrew Roberts agrees that antisemitism was quite widespread across all parts of society, adding that it was 'not worse among the aristocracy than say among the lower middle classes. As always it thrived amongst the ignorant and under-educated.'[62] Richard Griffiths distinguishes between different degrees of prejudice, claiming that antisemitism of a political and active kind was 'a minority interest' in Britain, although what he describes as 'parlour' or verbal antisemitism, involving social ostracism and a 'distaste for things Jewish', was more widespread.[63]

Many people were shocked by the Nazi antisemitic measures, but at this stage only a few politicians actively defended the rights of German Jews. Leading the way in highlighting their plight and warning the country of the threat posed by the Nazis was Winston Churchill. He was one of the rare philosemites in his class. Brought up by his father to like Jews, he admired them for their ethics and supported the Balfour Declaration.[64] His attitude allowed him to understand sooner than most other politicians the true nature of the Nazi regime.[65] When asked by one of Hitler's henchmen to meet the German leader, Churchill told him to tell the Führer that 'anti-Semitism may be a good starter, but it is a bad sticker'. He wanted to ask Hitler, 'What is the sense of being against a man simply because of his birth?'[66] However, the days when the Churchills and the Mitfords socialised frequently were over, and Lady Redesdale now considered Cousin Winston to be 'a dangerous man'.[67]

Attitudes to Germany's policies split the Mitford family down the usual fault lines. Oswald Mosley shared the prejudices about Jews that were common in Britain at the time, but they hardly featured in his early writing and speeches.[68] From 1934 his party, the British Union of Fascists, became increasingly antisemitic and his tone changed. When Julius Streicher congratulated Mosley on a speech he made in Leicester, the BUF leader wrote back to him, 'the power of Jewish corruption must be destroyed in all countries before peace and justice can be successfully achieved in Europe'.[69] Where Mosley led, Diana usually followed. Questioned during the war, Diana admitted that she had seen *The Brown Book of the Hitler Terror*, but she had not paid much attention to it.[70] In contrast, her brother Tom's attitude was more nuanced. While he was impressed by the economic transformation of Germany under the Nazis, he opposed their antisemitism.[71] For Jessica, the *Der Stürmer* letter was a turning point in her relationship with her family. She admitted in her memoirs that all the Mitford children, except Tom, were 'terrific' haters. Nonetheless, Unity's antisemitic diatribe was on a different level. Jessica explained: 'I felt she had forgotten the whole point of hating, and had for once and for all put herself on the side of the hateful.'[72] Nancy coped in her usual way by turning the situation into a joke. She teased Unity and Diana, saying that she had discovered a Jewish great-grandmother called Miriam Schiff, whose brothers were all rabbis.[73] She told them that she was going to start a rumour and tell Hitler that they were one sixteenth Jewish.[74]

Nancy had not veered to the same extremes as her sisters. Instead, she remained a socialist, although not an active one, leading Jessica to describe her as 'a drawing-room pink'.[75] In 1933, Nancy married Peter Rodd, son of a former ambassador, Lord Rennell. He shared her more moderate political beliefs. The Rodds had attended some BUF meetings, but the extreme right-wing never appealed to them for long. Observant as ever, Nancy satirised her sisters' fascism in her novel *Wigs on the Green*, published in 1935. The eccentric heroine Eugenia Malmains is based on Unity, while her grandmother, Lady Chalford, shares many characteristics with Lady Redesdale. Described as 'batty', Lady Chalford is also nicknamed 'The Poor Old Female' (TPOF).[76] Like Muv's treatment of Unity, the grandmother indulges Eugenia, while her granddaughter finds her all too easy to deceive. When Eugenia plans to organise a rally in her grounds for the thuggish Union Jack Movement, based on the BUF, Lady Chalford agrees because her granddaughter has never shown any interest in a cause before.[77] A friend of Eugenia's thinks that TPOF seems quite enthusiastic about Union Jackshirtism, but Eugenia assures her that her grandmother thinks it is the Women's Institute and is just glad she is doing something for the village at last.[78] It seems that Nancy preferred to think her mother was unworldly and slightly mad rather than admit she could genuinely support fascism. *Wigs on the Green* widened the split in the family. Nancy subsequently removed some passages Diana considered damaging to Mosley, but her mockery of his movement caused a rift with both Diana and Unity.

Parting of the Ways

While Diana and Unity flew the fascist flag in the family, Jessica was going in the opposite direction. Nancy teased her about being 'a ballroom Communist', a cut below a 'drawing-room pink', but Jessica was deadly serious about her political convictions.[1] Looking at the problems in the outside world, away from her comfortable home, Jessica developed a social conscience which could not be reconciled with her parents' beliefs. As she read widely, she realised that she was a pacifist, who was attracted to communism. The idea of redistributing the wealth of the richest people in society by transferring ownership of the land and factories to the workers appealed to her.[2] After her revelatory political awakening, Jessica accused her mother of being an enemy of the working class. Lady Redesdale seemed to be genuinely hurt by this accusation, replying, 'I'm not an enemy of the working class! I think some of them are perfectly sweet!' Her daughter imagined that she was thinking of the 'perfectly sweet' grooms, nannies and gamekeepers she had known.[3] Sydney's response was reminiscent of her father Thomas's logic, which involved him revering hard-working men like his Aldeburgh crew but fearing the political and economic power of the working classes *en masse*.

Reading about the Nazis' action in Germany and Europe, Jessica became increasingly appalled that her sisters and parents could support the regime. Rather than listen to her views, to her disgust, Lord and

Lady Redesdale were both becoming more actively involved in politics. On 7 March 1936, Hitler marched his troops into the Rhineland in a direct contravention of the Treaty of Versailles. He then offered Britain and France a non-aggression pact, claiming that Germany would make no territorial demands in Europe. A week later, in a letter to *The Times*, Lord Redesdale praised the Führer, describing him as 'a right-thinking man of irreproachable sincerity and honesty'.[4] Later that month, in a speech in the House of Lords, he supported Hitler's right to have German colonies restored. Gone were the days when he lambasted 'filthy Huns'; now he claimed that it was time 'to let bygones be bygones' and to extend the hand of friendship to Germany. He explained: 'We have no quarrel with any nation. We have no hatred for Germany. Why should we? Where hatred exists, it is bred of fear. Why should we take any part in the apparent desire at present for the encirclement of Germany?' He argued that any attempts to 'trample on her and bottle her up indefinitely' would be doomed to failure and would only lead to an explosion. As for Germany's human rights record, he claimed that the country's internal policy was of no concern to Britain. Hitler desired peace and Britain should help him attain it. He concluded, 'Why cannot we do something generous and do it off our own bat?'[5]

A similar line was taken by two other peers. Lord Londonderry, the former Secretary of State for Air, and Lord Mount Temple, a former Conservative MP.[6] They both wrote to *The Times* supporting Germany's actions in the Rhineland. The Redesdales were soon socialising with these like-minded aristocrats in the newly formed Anglo-German Fellowship, which aimed to promote understanding and trade between the two countries and prevent another war. At a dinner at the Dorchester, held in honour of the Duke and Duchess of Brunswick, the Redesdales mixed with other notable diners.[7] Unashamedly elitist, within two years the fellowship boasted 600 members, including aristocrats, Members of Parliament, leading businessmen, city financiers and members of the armed forces. Not all members were pro-Nazi enthusiasts; instead, they were an eclectic group with mixed motives. There were some antisemites and conspiracy theorists, but there were also well-meaning pacifists and Germanophiles.

The Anglo-German Fellowship was a controversial organisation. A recent historian, Charles Spicer, argues that many of its members acted as 'amateur British intelligence agents', who built relationships with the Nazi regime in a bid to entice Germany back into the fold of civilised European nations in the hope of averting war.[8] He believes that the majority of them were decent individuals who, due to 'varying degrees of naivety and gullibility', were taken in by the Nazi regime.[9] However, other historians have not viewed the fellowship so sympathetically. Lawrence James describes the group as a 'knot of peers adrift in an uncongenial world, united by paranoia, pessimism and panic'. These alienated aristocrats blamed 'the misfortunes of their times and class on an immensely powerful but clandestine Judaeo-Bolshevik global conspiracy, which could be thwarted only by Fascism and Nazism'.[10]

The Redesdales were soon leading lights in the society. In November an article by Lord Redesdale appeared in the first edition of the magazine the *Anglo-German Review*. He asked, 'Has any one of [Hitler's] critics stopped to consider [...] what Europe would be like today if Germany had gone Red? By holding Bolshevism on the flanks of Western civilization a tragedy was averted.'[11] In December Lord and Lady Redesdale, accompanied by Unity, attended another dinner of the Anglo-German Fellowship, held at Grosvenor House. Reflecting their prominence in the organisation, they were seated at top table alongside the new German Ambassador von Ribbentrop. In his first formal speech in Britain, the ambassador attacked the Bolsheviks and raised the spectre of international communism destroying everything his listeners held dear. He emphasised Germany's need for the return of its colonies, and he reassured his audience that Germany was willing to co-operate with other nations to establish a lasting peace.[12] This dinner was just the start of Ribbentrop's charm offensive on the British aristocracy. He soon won over many of the leading hostesses, such as Mrs Greville, Lady Cunard, Lady Astor and Lady Londonderry. The Member of Parliament and diarist Harold Nicolson complained, 'the harm these silly hostesses do is immense'; he believed they were giving the Germans the wrong impression that British foreign policy was made in their drawing rooms.[13] Lady Redesdale was to develop a similar misguided view, thinking international politics could be conducted along the same rules as polite society.

The Redesdales' attitudes were moving in the opposite direction from Jessica's, but her alienation from her parents was on a personal as well as a political level. Like Nancy, she believed the roots of her problems lay in her relationship with her mother. She later wrote: 'I actively loathed her as a teenager (especially an older child, after the age of fifteen) and did not respect her. On the contrary I thought she was extremely schoopid [sic] and narrow-minded – that is sort of limited minded with hard and fast bounds on her mind.'[14] After Diana married, Jessica felt increasingly depressed living at home. From 1929 she began putting money into a 'running-away account' at Drummonds bank. Lady Redesdale was aware of her daughter's unhappiness but did not take it too seriously, attributing it to normal teenage moods. When Jessica told her about the running-away money, Muv just said, 'Well darling, you'll have to save up a nice lot: you have no idea how expensive living in London is these days.'[15] When her daughter later told her she was a communist, Lady Redesdale was equally nonchalant, commenting that she thought a communist would be more considerate to the members of the working class she came across, thus, surely Jessica would become tidier and make less work for the servants.[16]

When Jessica came out as a debutante, she could not be bothered with the whole charade and annoyed her mother by never making any attempt to remember the names of the young men she met. It was partly because she was not interested in any of them, but also because she could not see very well. Jessica was very short-sighted, but Lady Redesdale would not take her to an optician to be prescribed glasses because she thought they were hideous and costly. As usual, she just told her daughter that 'the good body would heal itself' and she would probably be able to see better as she got older. By the end of the season, neither Jessica's eyesight nor her mood had improved. She wrote about the 'boredom that was enveloping me like a thick fog, out of the trivial, dull daily round of activities in which I found myself'.[17]

Lady Redesdale was aware of Jessica's malaise, but she never tried to talk to her about the underlying cause.[18] This was probably because

Sydney considered it would be an invasion of her daughter's privacy, but also because she found it hard to establish emotional intimacy with her children. No doubt Jessica would have rejected her attempts, but Muv did not try. Instead, she turned to practical rather than psychological solutions. Trying to alleviate the boredom for Jessica with more trips abroad, in April 1936, Lady Redesdale took Unity, Jessica and Debo on a Hellenic cruise of the Mediterranean. Making sure it was educational, Sydney chose a voyage which included lectures and visits to historic sites in Spain, Greece and Turkey. As usual, her girls were badly behaved as they competed to find ways to embarrass Muv. On board the ship, they made up rhymes about their fellow passengers and told crude jokes. Sydney did her best not to rise to their teases, but at times it frayed her nerves. Trying to pre-empt them, after an outing to a hareem in Istanbul, she called them into her cabin to insist that they did not mention at dinner the eunuch they had seen.[19]

Even on a cruise there was no escape from politics. The voyage was just a few months before General Franco attacked the Spanish Popular Front Government and the Spanish Civil War began. Tensions were already running high in the country. When Sydney and her girls visited the Alhambra in Granada, a group of Spaniards became furious as they spotted Unity was wearing a gold swastika badge. They shook their fists and tried to attack her, but the family managed to make it back safely to their car. Afterwards, Sydney told her daughter to remove the inflammatory emblem.[20] In the car on the way back to the ship, Jessica and Unity had a fight and Muv had to separate them.[21]

A fellow passenger on board the ship was the Duchess of Atholl, a Conservative MP who had recently been involved in a heated argument in the newspapers with a peer and newspaper proprietor about the respective merits and demerits of Germany and Russia. The Duchess had attacked Hitler, quoting from *Mein Kampf* to expose the true nature of the Nazi regime.[22] The controversy continued at sea. During a fiery debate on the advantages or disadvantages of the governments in Italy and Germany, Unity and Sydney argued on one side against the Duke and Duchess on the other. The anti-fascists won with a large majority. Afterwards, the Duchess wrote a placatory note to Unity congratulating her on her oratory and sincerity. She added that anything she said was not out of personal animosity but because, as a Member of Parliament at a time of great national anxiety, she believed it was her duty to make people aware of the facts, as she saw them.[23]

It seems Lady Redesdale was not appeased by the Duchess's gesture. They were a similar age and from similar backgrounds, but they saw international politics in diametrically opposed ways. 'The Red Duchess', as the Duchess of Atholl became known, actively supported the Spanish Republicans in the Civil War, arguing that Britain should not allow another democracy to be overthrown by a dictatorship. Back in England after the cruise, Sydney remained critical of her adversary. The following year, she attacked the Duchess's humanitarian crusade to bring Basque refugee children to England. When the Basque leaders appealed to foreign governments to accept child refugees to keep them safe from the civil war, at first the British government refused. In response, the Duchess of Atholl launched a campaign to change the government's policy. She succeeded and in May 1937, after the devastating bombing of the market town of Guernica, 4,000 Basque children arrived in Britain.[24] Lady Redesdale did not approve; she wrote to Jessica about 'the poor Basque children, torn from their parents and brought over here, really so dreadful'.[25] A few months later she publicly criticised the Duchess and her committee in the *Daily Telegraph*, suggesting that 600 of the parents now wanted their children returned but the committee had not acted on their wishes. She proposed that the government should intervene and insist on their immediate repatriation. She asked: 'I wonder if the parents knew that, the danger over, their children would not be returned to them, but would be kept here indefinitely. The poor children since they came here have done their best to show their feelings but what can children do?'[26]

On their return from the Mediterranean cruise, Sydney decided she would take Jessica and Debo on a world cruise to keep them entertained. Looking back, in her memoirs Debo describes this plan as an example of how their mother showed concern for each of them when they most needed it. Sydney did not particularly want to go on the voyage herself, but she did it to cheer up Jessica.[27] Although she constantly picked rows with her mother, Jessica also vaguely realised that she was doing her best to try to help her.[28] However, holidays could never be enough to satisfy Jessica's need for a sense of purpose. She was looking for a means of escape from her aristocratic life. She had watched Nancy during the period when she was trapped at Swinbrook constantly clashing with Muv, and she was determined not to share the same fate.[29]

Jessica found the ideal route to freedom when she met and fell in love with her second cousin, Esmond Romilly. He was the son of Nellie Romilly, Clementine Churchill's sister. The Mitford girls had never met Esmond because Muv disapproved of Nellie, whom she considered to be feckless.[30] Her curiosity already aroused, Jessica had been fascinated by her intriguing relative since she heard about his rebellious actions. Esmond had run away from boarding school and ended up in a remand centre because his mother could not control him. He then set up an anti-establishment newspaper and wrote a book which attacked the public school system. As a pacifist and communist, his values were in tune with Jessica's attitudes. When the Spanish Civil War began in the summer of 1936, he was one of the first to join the International Brigade organised by the communists to fight against General Franco and the nationalists. Having fought on the frontline, Esmond was seen as a hero by Jessica.[31]

The couple met at a house party at a mutual cousin's house. The attraction between them was instant and they immediately hatched a plan which would involve Jessica's greatest rebellion yet. In February 1937, Jessica eloped with Esmond to take part in the Spanish Civil War. Esmond and Jessica had plotted every detail of their escape, which involved a complicated deception of Lady Redesdale. Sydney was busy preparing for her world tour with her daughters, which was due to begin in March, when Jessica told her that she had been invited on a trip to France with her friends, the Paget twins. Although it was just a short time before Lady Redesdale and her daughters were due to set off, Muv agreed to let Jessica go. Debo suggests this was partly because she just wanted her daughter to enjoy herself, but also because it would be a relief not to have Jessica's discontented presence in the house for a fortnight.[32] In fact, there was no holiday with the Pagets and, instead,

Jessica planned to meet Esmond and travel to Spain. The elaborate plan worked well; once the young couple were across the Channel, Jessica even fabricated postcards to her mother, telling her what she was doing with the twins. As the time drew closer for the world trip, Sydney felt Jessica should be coming back to England. When she received letters from her daughter from all over France, she gradually became suspicious. She phoned the address in Dieppe where Jessica said she had been staying, and they had never heard of her. She also contacted the Pagets' aunt, who had no knowledge of any trip.

Understandably, Muv went into panic mode because she had no idea where her nineteen-year-old daughter was. Farve contacted Scotland Yard and the Foreign Office but there were no immediate leads. Finally, on 23 February, Jessica and Esmond's friend, Peter Nevile, visited the Redesdales and gave them a letter from their daughter explaining her elopement. Jessica wrote to her mother in the hope she would understand her actions and forgive her. Explaining that she had felt awful deceiving her, she admitted that she had not told Sydney because she thought she would disapprove and try to stop her. Attempting to reassure Lady Redesdale, she told her that she would be in no danger and there was no point trying to get her back because Jessica did not want to be associated with Unity's fascist connections.[33]

Farve and Muv had been worried their daughter had been kidnapped by white slave traders or joined a communist cell, but when Lord Redesdale heard the truth, he complained, 'Worse than I thought. Married to Esmond Romilly!'[34] No doubt, his reaction was as much politically as personally motivated, because Esmond and Farve held opposing views on the Spanish Civil War. Lord Redesdale believed General Franco was leading a crusade for all that the British held dear. Right-wingers like Farve saw the Republican side as a form of Bolshevik conspiracy.[35]

For once Muv did not just put on a brave face; the anguish she experienced is captured in her desperate letters. That day, she wrote to Jessica:

My darling,
   We have been in such agonising suspense about you not knowing where you were. Now I have your letter. Esmond will, I am sure look

after you but please come home. I cannot do more than <u>beg</u> of you to return. [...] Please write immediately and often or I cannot bear it.[36]

Sydney was stripped bare in a way she had never been before, and any reserve fell away as she openly expressed her emotions. So much for not being a loving mother; her genuine devotion comes across in every word. Turning her anger inwards, rather than castigating her daughter, Muv blamed herself. Her daughters knew this was how she reacted. In *The Pursuit of Love*, Nancy writes that Aunt Sadie, the character based on Muv, did not say much if her children did something wrong, but she brooded over it and took it to heart. She wondered if it was her fault because of how she had brought them up.[37] Reflecting this reaction, Lady Redesdale wrote to Jessica:

> Darling beloved Little D,
>
> I woke up just now and just for a moment I had forgotten and thought all was as it was before you went away. Then it came back to me. I think I am living in the most frightful nightmare and half expect to wake up and find it never happened and Little D is here. [...]
>
> It is something to know where you are, I nearly went mad when it seemed you had quite disappeared (...) I can't help blaming myself terribly for it all. [...] Of course, I knew you were unhappy but the cause of it was beyond me, except that like many girls you had nothing definite to do. I ought to have been able to help you more. I think it all over and over in my mind and think of nothing else night and day.[38]

Acting as though there had been a bereavement, the whole family gathered at Rutland Gate. Every few minutes flowers with messages offering condolences arrived as if it was a funeral. Unity came back from Germany, and Tom, Diana, Nancy and her husband Peter were on hand to offer advice. Lord and Lady Redesdale's siblings also gathered to commiserate. Muv's brother, Uncle George, described Jessica as 'a heartless little thing to put her family through all that', while Farve's brother, Uncle Jack, thought his errant niece should be flogged.[39]

Aunt Weenie was particularly vitriolic, saying it would be better if Jessica was dead. However, she thought the same about Diana and Unity, too, and blamed them for setting a bad example.[40] One person seemed to enjoy the drama; Muv's oldest friend, Mrs Hammersley, came around to the house about five times a day and insisted on seeing everyone individually to get the inside story.[41]

Despite what her daughter was putting her through, Sydney never said anything against Jessica or blamed her. Lady Redesdale's old ally, Nanny Blor, tried her best to persuade her rebellious charge to come home, telling her they would have no peace while she remained in Spain.[42] She described to Jessica the effect her elopement had on her mother, writing: 'If you think for one moment of all the changed plans and the anxiety we are still feeling you would come if only for your mother's sake, she is looking so sad and ill at times.'[43] Lord Redesdale was devastated too; Sydney wrote to Nancy that she had never seen him so upset. He had lost his buoyancy, and he was never fully to regain it.[44] When Muv cried all night, Farve would stagger downstairs and make her a pot of tea.[45] The situation was made worse by the newspapers' interest in the story; once again there were lurid headlines about 'Peer's Daughter' getting into mischief.

The Redesdales did everything they could to try to prevent the marriage. It seems Farve was more rigid than Muv about their course of action: he was furious while she was just worried. On Peter Rodd's advice, Lord Redesdale made a move which was counterproductive, stoking the resentment felt by the young couple. As Jessica was under the age of twenty-one, she could not get married without her parents' consent, so Farve had her made a ward in chancery, which meant the judge became her guardian. If Esmond married her without permission, he would be in contempt of court and could be imprisoned. On receiving a telegram from her parents' solicitors informing her of the court action, Jessica was furious. She later wrote 'this then, meant total war'.[46]

When Jessica and Esmond were found to be living in Bilbao in Spain, where he was writing articles for a British newspaper, the consulate asked her to return home. When she refused, at Muv's suggestion, Nancy and Peter were dispatched to try to persuade the family's red sheep to come back to the fold. On meeting Jessica in the South of France, Nancy told her how awful it had been at home, explaining, 'Poor Muv has been in floods ever since you left.'[47] The Rodds' arrival only made the situation worse, and Esmond and Jessica refused to return. Not satisfied with second-hand accounts, Muv could not wait to go out herself. Nanny told Jessica that her mother could not rest until she had seen her.[48]

The Redesdales' reaction to Jessica's elopement had backfired. Their daughter was not the first member of their family to make the grand romantic gesture of eloping. Perhaps she got the idea from two of her cousins. A decade before, Phyllis Bowles, Uncle George's daughter, had left home when she was twenty-three because she was having an affair with a married man who was thirty-six years older than her. She left a letter for her parents saying she did not want to see them again and they heard nothing from her for years.[49] In 1936, Sarah Churchill, Winston and Clementine's daughter, ran away to America to be with her older, married lover, the comedian Vic Oliver. She later married him, and even though they did not approve of him, her parents had no choice but to accept her husband.[50]

It seems Sydney and David may have initially overreacted and made the situation worse. After all, Esmond was unmarried and a similar age to Jessica – not to mention, he was part of the extended family. When she heard of the effect of her elopement on her parents, Jessica was surprised. She found it extraordinary that they could make themselves so unhappy about it. She felt it was a shame that she could not be true to herself without causing so much pain for them.[51] However, for Sydney, as a mother, the worry of not knowing where her daughter was must have inflamed the situation. As soon as she had calmed down, she acted as peacemaker in the family, trying to achieve a reconciliation. Jessica later wrote, 'I got the impression from my mother that, although she was too loyal to Farve to criticize any of his decisions, she really regretted the severity of the measures he had taken.'[52]

At the end of March, while Farve remained in London, Lady Redesdale travelled across Europe to see her daughter, who was now living in Bayonne. Sydney tracked the young couple down to a cheap room above a café. When she met Esmond, she immediately launched into an angry attack on his behaviour, telling him that he was a coward not to face Farve and ask to marry Jessica. She told him that his 'conduct was what you would expect from a communist'. To Lady Redesdale's surprise, he agreed with her that they had behaved badly but told her it was the only way.[53] Mother and daughter had just one day together, but during that time Jessica made it plain to her mother that she had slept with Esmond and was probably pregnant, so marriage became the only respectable option. Muv promised to do everything possible to make it happen. Even Esmond was impressed with Sydney's calmness and sense of humour during a difficult situation.[54]

When Lady Redesdale returned to England, she acted as go-between for her daughter with Lord Redesdale. She went to court with Farve and Tom to see the judge who had become Jessica's guardian. Sydney explained to him that she thought they should be married and Farve made no objection. Thanks to Muv's intervention, the judge revoked the order which he had made for Jessica's immediate return. Once financial arrangements were sorted out, he also agreed to lift the ban on them marrying. Rather than being antagonistic, Sydney appeased her daughter, writing to her, 'I hope darling this is much what you were hoping to hear from me. It was not a very easy task, but I am happy to have so far succeeded on your behalf and especially to be of one mind now with Farve.'[55]

Once Sydney knew Jessica was pregnant, she was keen the wedding should go ahead as soon as possible. She claimed it was because of her plans to go abroad with Debo, but it seems more likely she did not want the stigma of people guessing their baby was conceived out of wedlock. Knowing how to upset her, Esmond played games with his future mother-in-law, suggesting that they might not bother getting married after all. In response, Lady Redesdale bargained with him, writing: 'Old as I am I cannot agree with the unconventional idea of you living with Decca not married to her, and I could never in a thousand years get used to this idea, it seems to me extremely wrong. I have done all I could to help you and I much hope therefore you will do as I ask.'[56]

Unfortunately, Farve aggravated the situation by writing to his daughter telling her that she would never receive any financial help from him while she was with Esmond. Nancy and Peter Rodd made it worse by suggesting that Esmond was keen to make money from the situation. The implication that Esmond was motivated by mercenary considerations annoyed the young couple so much they did not reply to several of Sydney's letters. Once again Muv had to calm the situation down, explaining that she had never thought this was true and she admired her future son-in-law's independent spirit very much.[57] When they did get back in touch, Esmond suggested that, as the Redesdales had such a low opinion of him, they should not come to the wedding.[58] This rebuff made Lady Redesdale so sad Nanny Blor intervened, imploring Jessica to let her mother come. She wrote, 'I ask you again to write soon to Muv. I'm sure she wants to be with you again, especially for your wedding and I know how she is feeling all this but only wants what is best for you.'[59] When Jessica got back in touch, allowing her mother to come, Sydney had to walk on egg shells; she weighed every word she wrote, anxious she might offend her daughter again and be cut out of her life.

Before Jessica's wedding day, Lady Redesdale attended the coronation of George VI. As the wife of a peer of the realm, she dressed in a robe of ermine-trimmed red velvet with a 3ft train. Trying to economise, she had her dress made by a dressmaker rather than buying it from a shop. The day before the event she had her hair and make-up done in a beauty parlour in Dover Street and, to Debo's amusement, slept in her makeup. On the morning of the coronation, once she had put on her robe and the family jewellery, even her daughter admitted she looked wonderful.[60] As Lord Redesdale refused to attend the service in Westminster Abbey with her because 'he always hates such doings', Sydney went to the ceremony with her son, Tom. They had to be in their seats by seven in the morning and then after the service went to the House of Lords for lunch.[61]

Shortly afterwards, Lady Redesdale trekked across Europe to Bayonne for Jessica's wedding, bringing presents, including a gramophone and records. She also brought a silk dress from Harrods for

Jessica to wear at her wedding. Once in Bayonne, Muv rushed around with Jessica buying her a hat, brown coat, shoes and gloves for the day.[62] In May 1937 the young couple were married at the British Consulate in Bayonne. Esmond's mother, Nellie Romilly, came to the wedding too, but Farve would not join them. A small crowd gathered outside the consulate, and journalists and cameramen were there to get a good story. When one hack asked Lady Redesdale if he could ask her when the Redesdales had given their consent, she replied sharply, yes, he could, but she would not answer.[63]

At the ceremony, the groom described their two mothers as looking 'more like chief mourners at a funeral than wedding guests'.[64] After the ceremony, Nellie and Sydney took their wilful children and their friends out to lunch at a hotel. Unfortunately, as the mothers took a circuitous route to avoid the press, they lost the wedding party. Arriving at the venue to find no one else there, Mrs Romilly took the initiative and went out into the town to find the bride and groom and their guests. Afterwards, Sydney wrote to Jessica, 'I thought it was a very nice wedding and you and Esmond both looked sweet. [...] I know you are both happy and so I am happy now.'[65] She was amused by the reports that appeared in a French newspaper telling the story of the lost wedding guests and describing Nellie as '*forte et exuberante*'.[66]

Trying to normalise the situation and treat Esmond like her other sons-in-law, Muv wanted to pay for Jessica to have a studio photograph done of her with her new husband, so that she could display it.[67] However, a combination of the family's reaction to the elopement and Esmond's hatred of everything the Redesdales stood for meant that the breach was irreconcilable. It seems that for both Sydney and Jessica it was their husbands who were most intransigent. In her memoir, Jessica wrote that she was 'secretly shocked and disturbed' that Esmond assumed she would never see her family again. She had expected there to be a terrible row but then the situation would be accepted, like it had been when her sisters brought home husbands who Lord Redesdale disliked. Her hopes were in vain – it was not to be. Jessica explained that Esmond's 'extraordinary single-mindedness and direct purpose would have rendered all this impossible. He regarded my family as the enemy.'[68] Although mother and daughter always remained in touch, exchanging regular letters, Jessica was never to see her father again.

Lady Redesdale just wanted to keep her increasingly fractured family united. Impressed by a painting the artist William Acton did of Diana, she commissioned him to draw a sketch of each of her daughters. Framed in red brocade, Nancy described the pictures as looking like Bluebeard's chamber, but the drawings captured the Mitford girls at their peak. Muv was so pleased with the likenesses that she displayed them in her drawing room.[69] Poignantly, it was now the only way she could gather all her girls together. Nevertheless, even when her daughters were separated from her, wherever they were in the world, Sydney's influence remained. When Unity was sunbathing nude in a secluded spot in a public park in Munich, she wondered if somehow Muv knew what she was doing. The thought of her mother's shocked reaction made her laugh so much it hurt.[70] When Jessica took a job in a bar which involved looking after women who had passed out in the ladies' restroom, she also wondered 'What would Muv say?'[71] Whether they liked it or not, mother and daughters were so inextricably interwoven there was no permanent escape.

10

On the Move

After Jessica's wedding, outwardly, life for the Redesdales returned to normal. Sydney carried on as though nothing had happened. Putting the crisis, which had rocked her emotional stability, behind her, she took Debo on a scaled-down version of their planned world tour, travelling to Italy, Austria and then Germany. Rather than the philistine of Nancy's caricature, Sydney comes across in her letters as a cultured woman. She relished seeing the art in Florence, and while in Venice wrote with romantic verve that 'the spirit of Byron still hovers here, in what he called "The grandest isle of my imagination"'.[1]

Once in Germany, they met up with Unity and had 'great fun' touring around the countryside near Munich in Unity's little car. As there was a heatwave, they swam in the lakes on the outskirts of the city. It was too hot to do much sightseeing, so Lady Redesdale turned it into a fact-finding visit. They went to a china factory and then visited a work camp for boys. Impressed by what she saw, Lady Redesdale wrote admiringly, 'It must be immensely good for them physically to do all that hard manual work, they were all working naked to the waist and were quite brown. [...] I do think too it is <u>such</u> a good thing for everyone to have once in their lives done hard work with their hands, to know what it is like.'[2]

The highlight of the visit was tea with the Führer in his flat. Debo recalled that as they went up the stairs, Unity was trembling with anticipation.[3] When they arrived, they were tired and dirty from travelling, so Hitler showed them into his bathroom, where they freshened up.[4] The Führer had been planning to go to his house at Berchtesgaden, but he delayed going to meet them. During the two hours they spent with him, Hitler seemed very fond of Unity, never taking his eyes off her. He talked to them about the Spanish Civil War and the bombing of Guernica. Inevitably, Muv raised her favourite topic, asking him if Germany had any laws to guarantee the use of wholemeal flour.[5] At the end of their time together, he told them they must all come to the next Parteitag; then he shook hands twice with each of them and said goodbye. Afterwards, Lady Redesdale wrote to Jessica about their encounter, making Hitler sound like just another of her daughters' boyfriends. She explained, 'He is very "easy" to be with and no feeling of shyness would be possible, and such good manners.' Tactlessly, she told her anti-fascist daughter that the Führer had asked after 'Little D'.[6]

Having met Hitler again, Lady Redesdale now openly admired him and the 'marvellous' things he was doing in Germany.[7] Throughout her life she had always conveniently developed blind spots about anything unpleasant; it meant she saw what she wanted to see and edited out the negative parts. She had done this in her private life – now she did it in her politics. As someone who primarily saw the world in simple black and white terms and through the prism of how it affected her family, it was characteristic of her that she liked a man who was so supportive of her most vulnerable daughter. Back in England, she was determined to do further research, reading political books which Debo parodied as *Stalin: My Father, Mussolini: The Man, Hitler: My Brother's Uncle*, or *I Was in Spain* and *The Jews: By One Who Knows Them*.[8]

The fact Hitler's charm offensive worked on a fundamentally naïve woman like Lady Redesdale is not surprising; the Führer was able to win over more worldly political animals than her. In September 1936, former prime minister David Lloyd George visited Germany. After a carefully curated tour, which included visits to immaculate model farms, land reclamation projects and motorways, he met Hitler, who flattered the elder statesman. Afterwards, Lloyd George wrote a controversial article for the *Daily Express*. Calling Hitler a 'born leader', he compared him to George Washington and described his 'magnetic, dynamic personality with a single-minded purpose, a resolute will and dauntless heart'.[9] If the man who had led Britain to victory during the First World War could not see through Hitler, there was little hope a woman who had lived as rarified an existence as Muv would do so.

While Lady Redesdale became increasingly supportive of Hitler, it would be incorrect to view her as becoming as fanatical as Unity, because politics was just part of her life. When, after Sydney's death, Jessica found her engagements diary for 1937, 'Tea with Führer' was listed as just another event alongside births of calves and foals, staff holidays, dinner parties and dances.[10] Although she began to write to the newspapers about politics, she continued to pursue her own personal preoccupations. She still sent letters on her favourite topics, opposing strict rules about the tuberculosis testing of cows and promoting the health benefits of wholemeal bread.[11]

Sydney's granddaughter, Constancia Romilly, like many members of Lady Redesdale's family, has pondered why her grandmother supported Nazi Germany. She comments:

> It's really impossible for me to explain how or why anybody would be a fascist or supporter of the Nazis except in so far as [...] a lot of it is, I think social, who you're spending time with. We all tend to live in silos where everybody that we know is on the same wavelength to everybody else.[12]

Since the 1920s, at Conservative meetings, Lady Redesdale had heard of the threat communists and socialists posed to the established order. The idea of there being a bulwark against these forces became attractive. Lady Redesdale's granddaughter-in-law Charlotte Mosley explains: 'She was passionately anti-communist, that was why she took the other side. At that time, you were either in one camp or the other. There wasn't a middle ground.'[13] Sydney was one of a substantial number of women who made the move from the Conservative party to a more extreme political stance. Some women were members of the Tory party and more right-wing groups simultaneously. Others were totally disillusioned with traditional politics. Dorothy, Viscountess Downe, a wealthy Norfolk landowner and friend of Queen Mary, had been a pillar of her local Conservative Association for years, but she abandoned her old party to join the BUF and became a parliamentary candidate for Mosley's organisation. Like Lady Redesdale, she had visited Germany and admired what she saw.[14] She became a friend of Diana and later Sydney.

In his study of the family, Jonathan Guinness emphasises that his grandmother was never 'emotionally captivated' by Nazism. However, she was impressed by her visits to Germany and thought that Hitler was doing more for the Germans than the democratic system was doing for people in Britain. He explained, 'By a route of her own, she came round to a view close to that of Mosley, based on her father's vision of England's manifest destiny on the seas.'[15] Understanding Muv's political upbringing helps to explain her attitude to Nazi Germany. Thomas Bowles believed in a country being led by a strong man who could change the fortunes of a nation. Strategically, her father argued that Britain's success relied on the country being a strong naval power which did not get involved in continental land wars in Europe. Hitler talked about Anglo-German friendship, which left Britain's Empire intact if Germany was given a free hand on the continent of Europe. Jonathan emphasises Thomas's influence on Sydney. She inherited his independence of mind, but as Jonathan explains, 'it is a bitter paradox that this independence was to lead Sydney into an admiration for, of all people, Hitler'.[16]

When Lady Redesdale returned to England after her tour of Europe, her home was no longer a grand country house. In 1936 her husband had sold Swinbrook and the surrounding estate, partly for financial reasons but also because Tom was not interested in ever living there. His tastes were more like his mother's side of the family than his father's, as he enjoyed cultural rather than country pursuits.[17] Farve had sold during a slump in agricultural prices, so they did not make the most money possible from the sale.[18] Poignantly, as well as the Hepplewhite furniture, Jacobean tapestries and Persian rugs were sold, and Muv's Bechstein grand piano was also auctioned.[19] Instead of their large mansion, they now lived in either a small fishing cottage at Swinbrook or Old Mill Cottage at High Wycombe – when they were not in London. Their daughters charted the decline of the family fortune in the refrain: 'From Batsford Mansion to Asthall Manor to Swinbrook House to Old Mill Cottage.'[20] The Redesdales were not the only aristocrats to be downwardly mobile. Since the First World War one quarter of the land in England had changed hands, which was the largest transfer of estates in the country since the Norman Conquest.[21] As one historian writes, Farve was the 'classic case of the alienated peer'.[22] These disenchanted landowners, who had lost both economic and political power, were ripe for recruitment by more extreme right-wing groups.

It was the end of an era, but Muv made the best of the situation. While staying at the cottage at Swinbrook, she described it as 'perfect': they were able to swim in the river while Farve fished.[23] With fewer staff to do the chores, Lord and Lady Redesdale kept telling Debo how much they enjoyed housework. Despite them both making the best of the situation, the same old problems between the couple soon surfaced, and Debo described the atmosphere as like being in a Russian novel. Lord Redesdale had painstakingly chosen items for the house which he hoped his wife would like, but she loathed them and spent her time removing them. When she came across particularly tasteless lampshades decorated with stars in her bedroom, she immediately pointed out that she had not chosen them. Farve looked totally crestfallen.[24]

Dividing her time between their country cottage and London town house, Muv took Debo to several dances a week. Lady Redesdale enjoyed the parties, writing particularly enthusiastically about one glamorous ball where the new king and queen, George VI and Elizabeth, joined the partygoers. She described the king as looking like a changed man, who was much happier and more alert, but the queen looked more serious.[25] Knowing how much her youngest daughter enjoyed horse racing, Sydney took Debo to the races at Ascot. During their day out together, Debo was amused by Lady Redesdale's surreal comments. All the Mitford girls joked with each other about their mother's unintentional quips. As one of Muv's nicknames was 'the Fem', Debo said that she wrote them down in a notebook dedicated to 'Femmerism'. At Ascot, Lady Redesdale had suggested that it would have been better to walk around on stilts and hop over the crowds. Having reported her amusing anecdote to her sisters, Debo admitted that these one-liners did not look as funny when written down because they needed to be spoken in Muv's distinctive drawl.[26]

The following year, when Debo came out as a debutante, Sydney was chaperone for the sixth and final time. Debo was described by the press as one of the loveliest debutantes of the year, who promised to be a great beauty.[27] In March, the dance given for her at Rutland Gate was done in Sydney's own inimitable style. Four cooks worked in the Redesdales' home for four days to produce a delicious supper of hot salmon kedgeree and game pie followed by black cherries and Devonshire clotted cream. The 300 guests ate off the Redesdales' exquisite eighteenth-century Berlin porcelain, decorated with birds, moths and butterflies.[28] The decoration in the ballroom was described as 'unusual' by the press, as large bouquets of mixed flowers were glued onto two tall mirrors. Showing family solidarity, Diana and Unity came to support their sister. Debo looked stunning in a simple white faille dress, worn with no jewels, with just three small white orchids tucked into her halter-neck collar.[29]

During the season, Debo became friends with the new American Ambassador Joseph Kennedy's daughter, Kathleen, known as Kick. She also met her new friend's handsome brother, Jack. Lady Redesdale was very interested in the Kennedys and particularly admired their matriarch, Rose Kennedy, who with nine children had an even larger family than Sydney. Showing a remarkable eye for talent-spotting, Lady Redesdale commented, after watching Jack, that she would not be surprised if the charming young man became President of the United States one day.[30] At the debutante parties, Debo met Andrew Cavendish, the younger son of the tenth Duke of Devonshire. They fell in love, but as they were both only eighteen, they were considered too young to marry, so they secretly got engaged. In her memoirs, Debo recalls a rare occasion when her mother was angry with her. At one of the balls, she had broken the unwritten rule that a deb should not dance more than two dances with the same partner. Instead, because Andrew was not there, and Debo was missing him, she danced all evening with her friend Mark Howard. In the taxi home, Muv was furious. It was so unusual for her to tell Debo off that it made a lasting impression. No doubt part of Sydney's reaction was because she was tired after staying up until 5 a.m. while her daughter partied.[31]

Lady Redesdale's daughters took for granted all she did for them. She never reminded them of her self-sacrifice, and only once suggested that launching yet another daughter in society might be a chore. As she set off for yet another round of dances, she wrote to Jessica from Swinbrook, 'It is lovely now in the garden here and I rather hate going to London in this lovely weather.'[32] Whether her children wanted it or not, her love and support was there at every stage in their lives. When Jessica and Esmond returned to England in autumn 1937, Muv tried to do everything possible to help them. Showing her embarrassment about the timing of Jessica's pregnancy, Lady Redesdale had kept it secret from everyone except Farve, not even telling her other daughters. Her attempts at concealment did not work, because as the young couple were returning, they all soon knew about it. To the girls' amusement, trying to disguise the fact that the baby was conceived out of wedlock, Sydney encouraged her daughters to tell people that the child was due in the spring rather than January.[33] Muv offered the expectant mother Old Mill Cottage, or suggested she helped her find a nursing home for the birth. But, fiercely independent, Jessica and Esmond preferred to do their own thing.[34] They moved into a rented house in Rotherhithe Street, East London. Jessica was in a difficult position. Her husband did not approve of her seeing any of her family except Tom, but she wanted to see her mother and favourite sisters. When Esmond was out, Muv and Unity used to visit Jessica. Occasionally, Lady Redesdale had dinner with her son-in-law and daughter in a restaurant, but there was too much bitterness on both sides for these occasions to be relaxed.[35]

On 20 December 1937, Jessica gave birth to her daughter Julia. Three days afterwards, Muv and Unity came to see the newborn baby, bringing Christmas presents. Sydney worried that Julia was too thin and offered to send Nanny Blor to help, but Jessica was determined to manage on her own. Tragedy struck when Julia was just five months old. There was a measles epidemic and, unlike most women her age, Jessica had never had the illness, nor had she been inoculated against it because Muv disapproved of vaccines. Without any immunity, when both mother and child caught measles, they became seriously ill. Julia then developed pneumonia and died in May 1938.[36] Jessica had learned from Sydney how to hide her true feelings and put on a brave face. Jessica and Esmond just wanted to get away from the sympathy of their family and friends and be together. The day after Julia's funeral they left for Corsica, where they remained out of communication for three months.

11

Causing Controversy

In Europe, tensions were mounting due to German belligerence. Rather than observing from the sidelines, the Mitford family were determined to be involved. Thanks to Diana, Nancy, Jessica and Unity's actions, the Redesdales found themselves frequently in the newspapers. Muv said that every time she saw the headline 'peer's daughter' in the papers she feared it was about one of her children. However, by the late 1930s, Lord and Lady Redesdale were causing controversy themselves as they increasingly aligned themselves with Germany. Emotions were running high in Britain as it became clear that war was on the horizon. Prime Minister Neville Chamberlain continued to follow his policy of appeasement, while Winston Churchill warned of the threat the Nazi regime posed to the civilised world. It was a time when people were taking sides, and those choices mattered.

In March 1938, Hitler's troops marched into Austria to incorporate Austria into the German Reich, in what was known as the Anschluss. In the House of Lords, the red benches were full, as an unusually large number of peers attended to debate Germany's actions. Ambassadors, keen to hear Britain's reaction, were among the visitors. According to the newspapers, Lord Redesdale made one of the 'most remarkable' speeches of the debate. He claimed that Hitler was entitled to gratitude for avoiding a catastrophic civil war without bloodshed, and declared that the Führer had been welcomed by the Austrians as 'a saviour and not an unwanted tyrant'.[1] He added that he hoped, when the present excitement had died down, the government would not postpone friendly conversations with the German administration for too long.[2] After his speech, a sharp retort came from the Conservative peer Lord Cecil, who said that Lord Redesdale would not have talked of a bloodless operation if he had happened to be a liberal, or a Catholic, or a Jew in Austria.[3]

Controversial as his view was, Farve was not alone. The Archbishop of Canterbury, Cosmo Lang, also supported the absorption of Austria by Germany. Lord Tavistock wrote a supportive article in the *New English Weekly*, while Lord Londonderry blamed Britain for failing to be friendly enough to Germany.[4] However, approval of Hitler's regime was now increasingly confined to a dwindling group of 'enthusiasts'. The Anglo-German Fellowship's Council did not approve of Germany's action, and wrote to Ribbentrop criticising it.[5] Most newspapers also disapproved, with *The Times* running as its headline 'The Rape of Austria' above an article on Germany's brutal methods.[6]

For a man who had rarely seemed particularly interested in politics, Lord Redesdale became more politically active than he had ever been before. He became a member of the Link, a controversial organisation founded by Admiral Sir Barry Domvile, a former Director of Naval Intelligence, who was an antisemite believing in outlandish Jewish conspiracy theories. Like the Anglo-German Fellowship before it, the Link promoted friendship and understanding with Germany, but it was more openly pro-Nazi and less respectable than its predecessor.[7] Although not an overtly fascist organisation, some of its members supported fascism in Britain.[8] As well as Lord Redesdale, the Link's aristocratic membership later also included the Duke of Westminster. Despite having supporters among the upper echelons, unlike the Anglo-German Fellowship, it aimed to be a populist organisation, which extended its reach beyond the elite to sign up people from different classes across the country. The group published a magazine and held meetings. Among its visiting speakers were young Nazis on holiday in Britain. Lady Redesdale was involved in fostering similar links, because she hosted a luncheon party for forty-five visiting Hitler Youth members in the ballroom at Rutland Gate. When the event took place, she was rather disappointed by the young men. Instead of handsome boys of seventeen or eighteen, most of them were aged about thirty and rather dreary and unattractive. She wrote that she thought it was very sensible of Hitler to put them into uniforms as it made them look much better.[9]

Politics still only filled a fraction of Sydney's time because, as always, her daughters came first – and with so much happening in their lives, there was no respite for their mother. She was constantly needed by one or other of them. In the summer of 1938, Unity was taken ill with pneumonia at Bayreuth. Hitler made sure she received the best care; he sent his personal doctor to look after her and said that any bills should be sent to him. Once Lady Redesdale heard how ill Unity was, she rushed out to Germany to be with her. Finding her daughter in a private clinic under the care of Dr Theodor Morell, Hitler's physician, Sydney was dismayed to discover he was giving Unity up to fifteen injections each day. In her memoir of Unity, she wrote critically of the infamous doctor, but as he was there on the Führer's orders, for once she did not dare to interfere with the medical treatment. Sydney read the patient novels by Thomas Hardy and Rudyard Kipling to soothe her.[10] Unity was very grateful to have Muv with her, and she wrote to Diana saying how much she appreciated her coming.[11] After Lord Redesdale arrived, his wife briefly returned to England because Nancy was having a threatened miscarriage and needed her.[12] Nancy had been trying to get pregnant for years and losing the baby was a great disappointment. As usual, Sydney was practising triage, trying to be there for whichever one of her daughters needed her most.

When Unity was well enough, she went with her father to Berlin, where they lunched with Hitler. Farve insisted on reimbursing the Führer for the bills he had paid for his daughter's healthcare. Once again, Lord Redesdale fell totally under the dictator's spell. Afterwards, Unity persuaded her father to send the Führer a Japanese statue of a life-size bronze eagle landing on a rock as a present.[13] In September, Lady Redesdale returned to Germany to join her husband and daughter at the Nuremberg Parteitag. The ancient medieval town was packed; even international diplomats found it hard to get a hotel room. The Redesdales stayed at the Grand Hotel, the most fashionable hotel in the area. Usually there were more international visitors present, but this year the French had withdrawn and there were fewer English people than normal staying. The English contingent was mainly made up of aristocrats who supported an Anglo-German alliance or backed Mosley's BUF.[14] Included in the fifty-three British visitors invited to attend as guests of honour were Lord Brocket and the Redesdales.[15]

According to the journalist Virginia Cowles, Lord and Lady Redesdale seemed rather bemused by it all. She wrote that they 'treated the whole affair as though it were as detached from their lives, or the future of their country, as a bizarre operetta'. The couple behaved as though they were characters from a P.G. Wodehouse novel. Lord Redesdale wandered around as if he was at a strange house party, where no one could speak any English. Muv sat in a corner of the lobby, doing her embroidery. When she lost her needle, Farve got down on his hands and knees to search for it, while the jack-booted Stormtroopers and SS men marched past him in all directions.[16] When Lady Redesdale later read Virginia's description of her as a 'small retiring woman', she was very amused, telling Jessica, 'I don't know myself quite as this!'[17]

The Redesdales were treated as honoured guests by the Nazis. Given prime seats in the front row of the stadium, they watched as immaculately uniformed, tall, blond, young men marched to the rousing tunes of military hymns, beneath thousands of fluttering red, white and black swastika flags.[18] When Hitler spoke, the crowd fell silent. Then, once he had finished, they began chanting '*Sieg Heil*' over and over again in a 'frenzy of delirium'. It was the ultimate display of German militarism and encapsulated the spirit of Nazi Germany.[19]

Reflecting their special relationship with Hitler, Unity and her parents were invited to a party given for foreign visitors in the Führer's rooms. The guest list, which included Göring, Himmler, Goebbels and Hess, was limited to only seventy people, so it was a highly prized invitation. With the fate of Czechoslovakia in the balance and the prospect of war on the horizon, the German leader had seemed preoccupied all week. He refused to receive foreign diplomats or talk to his own advisers. Nonetheless, when he spotted Unity, his face lit up and he gave her the Nazi salute.[20] After the reception, he spent half an hour alone with Unity and her parents in his suite. He only left them when he had to address the adoring masses. He politely explained: 'I must go now. This tyrant must show himself.'

In retrospect, Lady Redesdale regretted not taking this opportunity to talk to Hitler about the danger of war. Instead, she discussed it with one of his generals. When he asked her if the English were likely to fight, she told him they would, and if necessary for ten years at sea.[21] It was Sydney's chance to feel she was a powerbroker in world affairs, when really she was just a pawn. Nancy claimed that her parents had been won over by Hitler's flattery, because for the first time in their lives they were treated as important players. She believed that this was due to the Nazis' lack of understanding of how British politics worked; they placed too great an emphasis on the influence wielded by the aristocracy.[22]

In fact, according to eminent historian Simon Heffer, in Britain most of the political class did not give the Redesdales a second thought. Diana had become problematic when she married Mosley, and Unity was an embarrassment, but, as a whole, the family had no political significance.[23] Leading historian Richard Toye also doubts that anyone took Lord and Lady Redesdale enormously seriously. People on the left would probably have seen them as sinister, while those on the right might have regarded them as 'silly, naïve or simply a bit of a nuisance'.[24] Lord and Lady Redesdale were not the only aristocrats to be seduced by Hitler's flattering attention. Lord Brocket was also wooed by the Führer at Nuremberg. Like the Redesdales, the peer developed grandiose ideas, deluding himself that he was an essential link between Hitler and Chamberlain. In fact, rather than being a major player, James Lees-Milne summed him up as 'a fundamentally nice man' but stupid.[25]

Hitler's relationship with Unity was on another level from his strategic courtship of other British aristocrats. The Führer met and talked to her on 140 days in less than five years. The debate continues about whether they were ever more than friends. Rumours had begun to circulate that Hitler was considering marrying Unity. Lord Redesdale quashed the story, telling a newspaper that, 'There is not, nor has there ever been any question of an engagement between my daughter and Herr Hitler. The Führer lives only for his country and has no time for marriage.'[26] According to Unity's biographer, David Pryce-Jones, Nancy told him that Unity had reached the point of discussing marriage with Hitler, but after his staff had checked her out, he told her that he could not marry her.[27] However, Jonathan Guinness states categorically that they did not have a love affair.[28] According to Jonathan's mother, Diana Mosley, Hitler was not particularly interested in sex. Diana was certain her sister never slept with Hitler, but she believed that if the Führer had asked her to do so, Unity would have agreed.[29] In her memoir of her daughter, Sydney emphasised that Unity was aware of Hitler's relationship with Eva Braun and was never jealous of his mistress. She described Eva as friendly and well dressed.[30] Whatever its exact nature, Hitler's relationship with Unity seemed to be important to them both. She amused him, and they laughed a great deal together. To entertain her, he used to do imitations of his colleagues, Göring, Goebbels and Himmler, but she liked his impersonation of Mussolini best. She claimed that if he was not Führer, he would make a hundred thousand dollars a year on the vaudeville stage.[31] Unlike most people around him, she was not in awe of him and said what she thought.[32]

Shortly after the Nuremberg rally, there was an international crisis. Having invaded Austria, Hitler now had his sights set on Czechoslovakia. In a bid to prevent war, Prime Minister Neville Chamberlain travelled to Germany to negotiate with Hitler. At the end of September, Germany, Italy, Britain and France signed the Munich Agreement, which let Germany annexe the Sudetenland in Czechoslovakia. During the first ten days of October, German troops occupied this area.[33] At an Anglo-German Fellowship dinner held at Claridges, 300 guests, including the Redesdales and Lord Brocket, celebrated Chamberlain's 'triumph' at Munich. The chairman of the society, Lord Mount Temple, claimed that even though the two countries had come 'within an ace of war', the fellowship had never met 'under fairer circumstances'. Toasts were then drunk to the King and the Führer.[34]

Lord Redesdale also celebrated the agreement in an article for the *Anglo-German Review*, written jointly with the Duke of Wellington and

Sir Ernest Bennett, a Member of Parliament. They praised Hitler and Chamberlain for supporting a policy which put right the faults of the Treaty of Versailles.[35] Joining other members of the Link, he also signed a letter to *The Times* strongly deprecating 'the attempt which is being made to sabotage an Anglo-German rapprochement by distorting the facts of the Czechoslovak Agreement'. The signatories congratulated Chamberlain for 'courageously' pursuing the policy which promised 'a new era compared to which the tragic years that have gone since the War will seem like a bad dream'.[36]

This pro-German attitude certainly did not represent the whole country. Public opinion was divided: some people were just relieved not to be going to war, but others were disappointed to see Britain give in to a dictator. The Redesdale family were more divided than most on this issue. While the Mosleys promoted the slogan 'Mind Britain's Business' and wanted their country not to interfere in central Europe,[37] Aunt Weenie's husband Percy Bailey was ready to go to Czechoslovakia to fight Hitler. To Sydney's disapproval, her son Tom was opposed to the peace deal and was close to joining what she described as 'the war party'.[38]

In November, Lady Redesdale wrote to Prime Minister Neville Chamberlain.* She had never met him, but she wanted to congratulate him for his recent 'magnificent action' in Munich and set out her pro-German views. With breathtaking naïvety, she wrote about Hitler as if he was some sensitive family friend who had been offended at a cocktail party, not a brutal dictator who persecuted people and threatened the stability of the world. She suggested that the Führer was 'most deeply hurt' by how the Munich agreement had been received in Britain. She explained:

> Hitler, whom I know personally, is above all a person of heart. And that you and he made real friends was evident, and he meant from

---

* The letter was dated 11 November 1938, just after Kristallnacht. We cannot know how much Lady Redesdale knew about the horrors of Kristallnacht, but extensive reports had appeared in *The Times* on 11 November 1938.

his heart what he wrote on that paper – as you did. What a tragically hurtful disappointment that his open gesture is received in England in hostility and suspicion. When a man feels hurt he generally hits out.

This letter shows that although Sydney had been involved in Conservative politics at constituency level for years, she had a complete lack of understanding of realpolitik. She was as simplistic about the developing international situation as she had been about history, when she taught her children from *Our Island Story*. She prided herself on doing her own research and forming her own opinions, but she came across as being as unworldly as her daughters claimed when she suggested that a social occasion should be arranged with Hitler, Neville Chamberlain and his wife, and the foreign secretary, Lord Halifax, and his wife. She added:

> Germany feels that no friendly notice is ever taken of her, she is left out of all the social doings between the countries. Their joy at receiving you was partly owing to the feeling that at last a great Englishman was visiting their beloved Führer for the first time very nearly.

According to Munich Crisis expert Professor Richard Toye, what stands out in this letter is Lady Redesdale's 'misreading of Hitler's attitude and her belief in his sincerity – an interpretation that contradicts what we know of his true motivations'. He adds, 'it is fascinating to see how she projected her own views on him'.[39] Like her belief that her opinions on medicine trumped doctors' expertise, ignoring any evidence to the contrary, Lady Redesdale was adamant that her analysis was right. Never had she been more her father's daughter as, like Thomas, she emphasised that she knew best, concluding: 'I do not apologise much for putting before you what I know is true, so great faith have I that you want to make friendship between the countries.'[40]

Lady Redesdale was not the only person to write to Chamberlain congratulating him after the Munich Settlement. In the following weeks, he was sent more than 20,000 letters and telegrams and many gifts; a large proportion were from women.[41] Many were from mothers and wives, relieved to think that their sons and husbands would not be going to war. They came from across the country and from people of different backgrounds and ages. Among the prominent women, who expressed their gratitude to the prime minister for preserving the peace, were Lady Londonderry, Lady Desborough and the author Enid Blyton.[42] Like Lady Redesdale, few showed much understanding of the complexity of foreign affairs. However, Sydney differed from most of her fellow correspondents in championing Hitler. It seems that Chamberlain was flattered and reassured by these letters, mentioning in broadcasts and speeches that he had the support of the women of Britain.[43]

In the German Reich, the persecution of Jewish people went to a new level when on 9–10 November 1938, Nazi leaders unleashed a series of pogroms against the Jewish population throughout Germany and Austria. Known as Kristallnacht, or the Night of Broken Glass, that night Jewish businesses, homes and synagogues were attacked. More than 30,000 Jewish men were taken to concentration camps and nearly a hundred Jews were murdered. German officials concealed the organised nature of the violence, instead claiming that it was a spontaneous and justified reaction from the German population towards the assassination of a German diplomat in Paris. In fact, the perpetrators of Kristallnacht were Brownshirts and SS men. They dressed in civilian clothing in order to support Goebbels's propaganda that Kristallnacht was triggered by popular anger against the Jews.[44] Shortly after Kristallnacht, it was agreed that German Jews would be forbidden from working in most professions or running businesses. These shocking events caused international outrage.[45] Even people who had previously been supportive of Germany now changed their minds. The diarist and Conservative MP, Chips Channon, wrote, 'Are they (the Nazis) mad? The Jewish persecutions carried to such a fiendish degree are short-sighted, cruel and unnecessary.'[46]

In the following months, Chamberlain continued his policy of appeasement. Despite being 'horrified' by Kristallnacht, he did not want to provoke Hitler by taking definitive action against Germany or changing his strategy. In light of the recent horrific events, other people who had previously enthusiastically supported friendship between the two countries reconsidered their position. The Anglo-German Fellowship experienced 'an existential crisis' after Kristallnacht when faced with the reality of German antisemitism. The chairman of the organisation, Lord Mount Temple, resigned in protest at the persecution of the Jews. A formal notice from the group's council was published in newspapers and sent to each member, stating their deep regret at recent events which had 'set back the development of better understanding between our two nations'.[47] Within weeks, the fellowship lost many members, leaving it with 'only a lot of useless fanatics', according to one informant. Sponsorship was withdrawn and prominent hosts and hostesses refused to support its events.[48]

The Redesdales remained as stalwarts of the organisation, and at Christmas, when Unity came back from Germany, they attended the Anglo-German Fellowship's party with their daughter. A photograph of Unity and Muv with Captain Fitz Randolph of the German Embassy appeared in the *Daily Express*.[49] To remain pro-German after the recent events was deeply controversial, but the Redesdales very publicly tied their colours to the mast. In February 1939, Lord Redesdale was one of three well-known British men mentioned in a German newspaper as being in favour of Germany's former colonies being returned to the Fatherland. His name was mentioned with Professor William Dawson of Oxford University and Sir Ernest Bennett. Lord Redesdale was quoted as saying:

It is high time for an agreement by which Germany receives back her colonial possessions. It was absurd to take them away from her. This should never have happened. Germany's claims must be satisfied. I should be pleased if my home country would undertake a step voluntarily and independently of other countries.[50]

Even though Lord Redesdale's quotes were genuine, they were not quite what they seemed. When questioned by British journalists, he told them he had not made the statement to the newspaper, but that it was based on the speech he had given in the House of Lords two years earlier. When the German newspaper asked him whether his views had altered, he told them that they had not and that he was happy for them to quote him.[51]

In March 1939, an article by Unity was published in the *Daily Mirror*, setting out 'What Miss Mitford Would Like to See'. Some of her arguments would have delighted her grandfather, Thomas Bowles. She explained that, as Germany had signed an agreement with Britain in 1935 to keep German naval power to 35 per cent of the Royal Navy, Hitler had demonstrated he did not want to go to war with Britain again. She added: 'Every German knows that the future of the Reich lies, not in a large overseas colonial empire, but in an entirely different direction [...] in which there is no reason at all why she should come into conflict with British interests.' She concluded that a world war could be averted if Germany became the greatest continental power while Britain was the most powerful colonial one.[52]

Her arguments were discredited before the article was published, because shortly before it appeared, the Germans marched into Prague and took control of Czechoslovakia. This action left only the most extreme British enthusiasts supporting Germany.[53] It demonstrated that Hitler was determined to take territory which was not inhabited by Germans. It emphasised the futility of Chamberlain's attempts to negotiate with an aggressive dictator, not to mention Sydney's naivety to think he could be treated like a piqued house guest.[54] After Prague, politicians who had admired Hitler no longer supported a policy of appeasement.[55] Previously pro-German, Lord Lothian, Britain's incoming ambassador in Washington, explained that Hitler had shown himself to be 'a fanatical gangster who will stop at nothing to beat down all possibility of resistance'.[56] Yet, although Lady Redesdale was at first upset when Germany marched into Czechoslovakia, she still believed that Britain should keep out of Eastern European affairs. Her argument was that the Führer did not interfere in India, so Britain should leave him to his own devices on the Continent.[57] Essentially, it was an updated version of her father Thomas's philosophy and in line with Unity's argument.

Other members of her family saw the situation differently; they were more interventionist and did not think Eastern Europe was just a faraway place of which they knew little. Jessica was furious about what the Nazis were doing. She blamed her parents and many of their class for supporting the Germans, arguing that their acceptance would inevitably lead to war. Hating what they saw happening in Europe, early in 1939, Jessica and Esmond left to start a new life in America.[58] Ironically, they were only able to emigrate because of Sydney's frugal foresight. When each of her children was born, Lady Redesdale had opened a savings account for them. Each week she had contributed a small amount to these funds which would be made available to each child on their twenty-first birthday. When Jessica came of age, Sydney met her for lunch and gave her the £100 trust fund. It was this windfall which funded the Romillys' transatlantic trip.[59]

Nancy also opposed the fascists' aggression across Europe. In May 1939, she joined her husband Peter in Perpignan, France, where half a million refugees from the Spanish Civil War had gathered to escape from Franco's regime. She helped them to find food, accommodation, clothes and asylum abroad.[60] After witnessing the plight of the mothers and babies, she angrily pointed out to her mother that if she had also seen the consequences of fascism, she might be less keen to see the swastika flag fly in Europe. She attacked Sydney's argument that Germany was encircled, stating other countries were not encircling the Nazi regime but protecting themselves from Hitler's aggression. Like her mother, she did not want war because her husband would have to fight, but she blamed the Nazis, not the British, for the increasingly bellicose situation.[61]

It was not just the younger generation who disagreed with Sydney's stance. Her oldest friend, Violet Hammersley, held very different political beliefs from Muv. Dubbing the Mitford girls the 'horror sisters',[62] she wrote to Diana that she and her siblings seemed to love dictators, but she certainly did not. Despite her disapproval, Violet overlooked the political divide and remained a loyal friend to the family.[63] Even Sydney's brother George disagreed with his sister. Since fighting in the First World War, anything German was anathema to him. In recent years, he had read of German rearmament and the persecution of the Jews and did not approve. He was horrified when he heard that his goddaughter Diana had married Oswald Mosley in a ceremony in Goebbels's flat, and even more shocked that his usually sensible sister was also taken in by Hitler.[64] Yet, despite her abhorrent views, he loved Sydney, and so he just treated it as another of her foibles.

In June 1939, as negotiations continued between Britain and Russia to sign a military pact, Lady Redesdale wrote an article in the *Daily Sketch* disagreeing with people who argued that there was nothing to choose between Bolshevism and fascism. Instead, she claimed that the differences went 'deep into every department of life'. Demonstrating her fundamental belief that the Church and State should support each other, she argued that while Bolshevik Russia was a 'Godless State', in Germany the State financed the Evangelical and Roman Catholic Churches. She added that in Germany, 'in spite of all one hears to the contrary' religion was freely practised, and the churches were full. She admitted that the clergy were not allowed to preach against the state, 'but otherwise in the practice of religion there is complete freedom'.[65] Once again she was wilfully ignoring the reality. In the mid-1930s, the head of the Gestapo and the SS Security Service, Reinhard Heydrich, had persecuted clergy in the Catholic Church. He concocted evidence and then prosecuted hundreds of priests for alleged paedophilia. His aim had been to discredit one of the only remaining institutions that did not owe its allegiance to Hitler.[66] Hundreds of Protestant pastors, who tried to defend their church against state interference, had also been persecuted.[67] The previous year, the plight of Pastor Niemoller, who continued to be imprisoned without trial, had led to adverse publicity in the British press.

As the stakes became higher, Lady Redesdale openly supported the BUF. In July she went with Diana and Tom to hear Mosley speak at a 'demonstration for peace' in Earls Court Exhibition Hall. Beneath a backdrop of an enormous Union Jack, Mosley gave the fascist salute and then addressed the audience of 20,000 people. He argued that Hitler should be allowed a free hand to move eastwards because then he would not wish to fight Britain. It was the largest rally he had ever held. Afterwards, Sydney, Tom and Diana joined Mosley for dinner with his mother.[68] As Sydney now openly supported Diana's beloved husband and his politics, mother and daughter's relationship was transformed. The two women became closer than they had ever been before: Diana's previously lukewarm affection changed into a lasting affinity.[69]

The Mitfords were now described in newspapers as 'the first family of fascism' in Britain. During the late spring or summer, Lord

Redesdale joined a new secret society, the Right Club, becoming one of sixteen 'wardens' of the organisation.[70] It was founded in May 1939 by Conservative Member of Parliament Archibald Ramsay, who was an obsessive antisemite and pro-Nazi.[71] The group opposed communism and war against Germany, but Ramsay later explained that his main objective was to 'oppose and expose the activities of Organised Jewry'.[72] The names of the members were kept strictly secret, but it has been revealed that a large number of prominent people were on the list, including aristocrats and a dozen MPs.[73] Not all members joined it for antisemitic reasons; some were anti-Bolshevist and anti-war, but most must have been aware of Ramsay's extreme views and this did not deter them from joining the movement.[74,75]

While Lord Redesdale's membership of the Right Club remained secret, his involvement in the Link was public knowledge and becoming increasingly controversial. In August 1939 an article appeared in the *Daily Mirror*, naming Lord Redesdale as a member of the Link's council. The organisation had become a focus of attention because the Home Secretary, Sir Samuel Hoare, had described it in the House of Commons as 'an instrument of the German propaganda service' and stated that one of its organisers had received money from the Nazis. The Chairman of the Link, Admiral Sir Barry Domvile, denied that his group was subsidised by Germany or that it was a pro-Nazi organisation, although he admitted that some members held those views.[76]

Shortly afterwards, Lord Redesdale was one of 'Hitler's Friends' targeted in 'a warning' published in the *Sunday Mirror*. The article criticised the prominent people of 'wealth, influence and title', including the members of the House of Lords, who were associated with the Anglo-German Fellowship. Among the peers named were Lord Brocket, Lord Londonderry and Lord Redesdale. In its attack on Lord Redesdale, the newspaper reminded readers of his support for the return of Germany's former colonies. Simon Haxey, the author of a new book on Conservative politicians, explained that only these colonies remained to symbolise Britain's victory in the First World War, but Lord Redesdale had expressed a wish to see even these surrendered. He added, 'Who ever before heard Conservative members of the British House of Lords and House of Commons advocate the cession to the enemy of territory won by force of arms? This is something new in British politics.'[77]

The article acknowledged that some of the characters mentioned had been duped by the Nazis and were innocently helping them, but it added, 'these people – or many of them – have unwittingly transformed themselves into terrifyingly useful weapons for Herr Hitler and his propaganda chiefs'. Issuing an uncompromising warning to them, the newspaper stated, 'In our opinion too, their activities, however innocent or misguided they may be – have inspired a wave of deep resentment and suspicion throughout the country.' As the nation prepared to defend itself, it asked the people mentioned to consider a final question: 'Are the men and women of Britain in a mood to tolerate this kind of thing?'[78]

As this negative publicity raged around them, the Redesdales tried to carry on with their normal lives as though nothing was happening. In the early summer, Unity returned home for a month. Family gatherings with the aunts and uncles were awkward because many of them did not approve of Unity's politics. Undeterred by their reaction, Muv remained staunchly loyal to Unity and, reflecting their shared interest in political ideas, mother and daughter attended a series of lectures together on world affairs at the Conservative College at Ashridge.[*]

In the late summer the Redesdales went to stay at their new home in Scotland. The previous year, they had bought Inch Kenneth, a remote island in the Inner Hebrides. Lord Redesdale heard from a fellow member at the Marlborough Club that the island was for sale, and when they visited, both Farve and Muv fell in love with the place.

---

[*] Guinness, *The House of Mitford*, p. 424. Established in 1929, the institution had been set up in response to the intellectual projects of the Left. Its aim was to act as a school for right-wing intellectuals, or 'Conservative Fabians'. Based in a stately home in Hertfordshire, it was a 'College of Citizenship', which offered a series of weekend, weekly and fortnightly courses on a wide variety of topics, including social service, the place of the countryside in national life and the future of the Empire. Clarisse Berthezene, 'Training Minds for the War of Ideas: Ashridge College, the Conservative Party and the Cultural Politics of Britain, 1929–54', *Twentieth Century British History*, Vol. 27, Issue 1, March 2016.

Inch Kenneth took its name from Kenneth, a missionary from Iona, and until the Reformation it was inhabited by monks who had built a chapel on the site. In the eighteenth century, Dr Johnson and Boswell had stayed on the island. It was reputed to be haunted: at midnight, Boswell went to the chapel to say his prayers but speedily returned because he was frightened by a ghost.[79]

Travelling to the island was a challenge. It involved taking the overnight sleeper train from London to Oban, then a ferry for several hours to the Isle of Mull. After a fifteen-minute drive across Mull to Gribun, the final leg of the journey was a short boat trip to Inch Kenneth. If the weather was bad, a visitor could be marooned on the island for days. The only buildings were a large three-storey house, a cottage and a ruined chapel. There were two permanent employees: a wife, who helped Sydney in the house, and her husband, who cared for the land and livestock and maintained the boat *The Puffin*, which ferried guests from Mull. With her usual skill, Sydney turned the house into an elegant but comfortable home. She moved in family furniture, including a grand piano, and bought china, glass and kitchenware from Peter Jones's department store in London. Her eye for a bargain meant she managed to furnish the whole house for just over £500.[80] The furniture was transported by removal van and then steamer from Glasgow to Inch Kenneth.[81]

The Redesdales enjoyed a simple life in Scotland. Like on their trips to Canada, they relished doing practical work. Lady Redesdale planted a kitchen garden to produce vegetables and kept chickens and cows. The food was fresh and delicious; locally caught lobster, crab and mackerel were frequently on the menu for others, while groceries and meat were transported by boat from Mull. Lord Redesdale had always wanted to live on an island where he would not have to worry about neighbours or many visitors. Now, more than ever, he needed to get away from it all. He joked that he wanted a large noticeboard to be put up on the jetty with a one-word message in 20ft letters printed on it: 'OUT'.[82] During that last summer before the war the weather was glorious, but the Redesdales could not shut the world out for long: a tidal wave of tragedies was about to engulf them.

12

Unity's War

As the war drew closer, Unity wrote to Sydney from Germany saying that she planned to go to the mountains in the Tyrol if hostilities began. She told her siblings a different story, explaining to Diana that she would not live if the two countries she loved fought each other.[1] Once war seemed inevitable, Lord Redesdale was so worried about his daughter that he sent her extra money for emergencies and a message begging her to come home.[2] On 3 September the British consulate contacted her and told her they had a telegram for her. When she arrived, they explained that Britain had declared war, and they appealed to her to leave while she still could. Instead, she ignored their warnings and wrote a final letter to her parents saying goodbye. She told them that she hoped when the war was over that there would be the friendship between Germany and England, which they had all wished for. She added that hopefully they would see Hitler again.[3] Now war between Germany and Britain was declared, Unity knew what she must do. She went to the Englischer Garten in Munich, took out her mother-of-pearl-handled pistol and shot herself through the right temple.[4]

Hundreds of miles away on their remote Scottish island, Lord and Lady Redesdale had no idea what had happened. Faced with a feeling of uneasiness but no news, they carried on as though nothing had changed. George and Madeleine Bowles, with their children Julia and Tom, came to stay. Looking to the future, on one sunny day the grown-ups planted sacks of daffodil bulbs, ready to bloom in the spring. There were motor-boat trips to Iona, Fingal's Cave and MacKinnon's Cave on Mull. Days were spent pottering around the island, exploring the shell cove with its kaleidoscope of coloured shells and white sand. On wet afternoons there would be impromptu concerts: Farve chose Gilbert and Sullivan operettas or Sousa's Marches, while Debo preferred playing the popular songs *Three Little Fishes* and *My Very Good Friend the Milkman* on the radiogram. Sometimes Muv would play Chopin or Beethoven's *Moonlight Sonata* on the grand piano in the drawing room for her guests. The Bowles children had a magical time, hardly aware of the pressures their aunt and uncle were under, but the adults were full of apprehension about what the future would bring.[5]

Characteristically, Lady Redesdale buried her emotions and just kept calm and carried on. She wrote to Jessica, from Inch Kenneth, that it was so heavenly on the island they never wanted to leave. She added that she was very glad to have children staying and she had wanted to take some evacuees, but she had been told the island was too remote.[6] In her unpublished memoir of Unity, Sydney claimed that she did not feel particularly anxious about her daughter at this time because she knew that Unity would be cared for in Germany.[7] It seems she was following her usual technique of blocking out negative thoughts. For someone who was in many ways so honest, she could be a mistress of self-deception, shutting out whatever did not fit her chosen narrative.[8] She practised this on both a personal and political level, and in both the public and private sphere it proved problematic, isolating her from those close to her who refused to deny what was really happening.

At times, even Muv could not maintain her sangfroid. When war was declared, Nancy was staying with her mother and inevitably, as they were never compatible, the two women clashed. Increasingly alienated from Sydney, Nancy turned to Violet Hammersley as a surrogate mother figure and confidante.[9] Her letters to Mrs Hammersley often portrayed Muv in an unflattering light. Perhaps partly to shock but also to amuse her mother's oldest friend, she sometimes embellished what happened to make a good story.[10] Nancy told Mrs Hammersley that she thought Muv had finally gone 'off her head' and seemed to view Hitler as her favourite son-in-law.[11] Apparently, when Sydney was driving her daughter to the Oban ferry to return to London, Nancy made a disparaging comment about Hitler which made Lady Redesdale so furious she ordered her daughter to shut up or get out of the car and walk.[12] Nancy was incredibly angry about Sydney's stance, particularly as her husband Peter was about to join up. She wrote to Mrs Hammersley that she found her mother impossible because Muv hoped Britain would lose the war.[13] Once back in London, Nancy could not resist commenting sarcastically to Debo that, knowing how much her mother hated the communists, she supposed Sydney was pleased to have the Russians on her side, since they had signed the German–Soviet Pact of Non-Aggression the month before.[14] Unlike her mother, Nancy thought there was nothing to choose between the fascists and communists; they were both 'fiends'.[15]

Nancy also vented her anger in her latest novel, *Pigeon Pie*, which was published in 1940. The heroine, Sophia, talks about her 'grudge' against her pro-German husband Luke, claiming that the war was due to people like him going off to Germany and suggesting to the Nazis that England would put up with anything. When he returned to Britain, he praised Hitler and von Ribbentrop, describing them as bulwarks against Bolshevism. Luke is portrayed as naïve, thinking that he was fostering good relations between the two countries. He was taken in by the Nazis' flattery and the red-carpet treatment they offered, enjoying the free rides in Mercedes. Sophia's lover Rudolph is less judgemental and does not think people like Luke can be blamed for the war. He believes that Luke was susceptible to the Germans because he 'never cut any ice' in England. When the Nazis treated him like minor royalty, he was totally taken in. Even though by promoting German propaganda he had harmed his country, he had not realised what he was doing, and he was decent at heart.[16]

Not only was Lady Redesdale's relationship with her daughter threatened by her extreme views, but her marriage was fatally undermined by her political beliefs. Although Farve had also been taken in by the Führer, once war was declared, he patriotically turned against the Nazis and supported his country. He was not the only aristocrat to do a similar volte-face. In September 1939, Bendor, the Duke of Westminster, had made a statement opposing the war against Germany and calling for immediate peace. However, after his friend Winston Churchill wrote to him, he finally did his patriotic duty, doing everything he could to help Britain win the war.[17] As Jessica explained in her memoir *Hons and Rebels*, 'the upper classes, even the most pro-Hitler of them, would now swing into line to do their duty to King and Empire, and would no doubt find themselves in their ordained role of leadership'.[18] In Nancy's novel *The Pursuit of Love*, she captured her father's attitude in her description of Uncle Matthew's love of his country. She wrote that he considered the idea of England as sacred. If his homeland was threatened, he would never leave to save himself because he was inextricably bound to the land.[19]

To clarify his position, on 5 September Lord Redesdale made his change of opinion known in the *Daily Mirror*. He explained, 'I am a very sad man. All I ever worked for was friendship, but the King's enemies are now the enemies of every honest Englishman. I made a mistake.'[20] Nancy joked that her father had recanted 'like Latimer', but her mother did not do the same.[21] Muv's admiration for Hitler before his invasion of Czechoslovakia was not unusual among her contemporaries, but the fact she remained anti-war once it was declared was more shocking. It was to be the biggest act of defiance of her life, revealing beneath the conventional facade she was as great a rebel as any of her daughters.

As well as representing her stubbornly held political beliefs, perhaps this rebellion also reflected the strain she was under. For several weeks, Lord and Lady Redesdale had no news of Unity and did not know if she was alive or dead. There were rumours that she was in a concentration camp or had been killed by the Germans. At the end of September, Muv received a letter from Unity, dated 1 September. In it, she asked her mother to thank Jessica for a birthday present but did not provide the all-important information of what she intended to do. As Jessica was living in a neutral country at the time, letters between the USA and Germany could still get through, so Lady Redesdale asked her daughter if she could try to get news about Unity.[22]

On 2 October, Sydney received a letter from a family friend, Teddy von Almasy, who was in Hungary, informing her that Unity had been ill and was in hospital in Munich. At this stage the family did not know exactly what had happened or what state she was in. They sent a telegram to Teddy begging for more news and received a reply that Unity was improving.[23] Shortly afterwards another telegram arrived stating there was further progress, and their letters were forwarded.[24] After this limited communication, the Redesdales only slowly received more information. Lady Redesdale tried everything within her power to get in touch with Unity. As Switzerland was a neutral country, she sent letters to Geneva. She admitted to Jessica that it was 'so very hateful not to be able to get any news [...] We don't even know if she is still in hospital. How I do wish she could come home and come here which is such a perfect and heavenly place.'[25]

At the end of October, Lady Redesdale and Debo returned to London, while Farve remained at Inch Kenneth. Sydney found the capital greatly changed: the restaurants and night clubs were still full, but many people had left the city. Businesses had shut down and even her beloved Harrods seemed empty. There were few cars on the road, and every night the blackout was imposed. Rather than live in the main house, Lady Redesdale stayed in the mews, which they called 'the garage'. Their only employee was their maid, Mabel, because most young women were filling the jobs men had left when they joined up. As old-fashioned as her father and husband about female roles, Muv did not approve. She wrote, 'It seems unnecessary with all the unemployed and it is so bad for girls to overstrain themselves.'[26] After moving out of the main house, the Redesdales put all their furniture into storage in the Pantechnicon, a furniture store behind Lowndes Square. Unfortunately, there was a fire, and the store burnt down. Luckily, only one van containing their belongings was destroyed. Sydney kept the loss in perspective, writing, 'Actually, "things" don't seem to much matter when one thinks of the terrible world conflagration.'[27]

As the weeks dragged on Lady Redesdale still did not know what had happened to Unity. In early November she heard through the US Embassy that Unity was in hospital in Munich and making a good recovery from an attempted suicide.[28] Unable to be with her sick daughter, she tried to remain positive, but she told Jessica, 'It is a terrible and a continual worry. [...] One cannot bear to think of what terrible agonies of mind she must have been through, as she never believed a war could happen between the two countries.'[29]Inevitably, the newspapers speculated on Unity's fate. In the middle of the night a journalist phoned Lady Redesdale asking for confirmation of a story that Unity was dead.[30] Sydney told Jessica, 'I didn't believe it though it was very horrid hearing it like that.' She then contacted some British journalists and the Foreign Office, who thought it was probably not true. Other sources informed her that Unity was well and had left hospital a few weeks earlier. The sister of a nurse in Unity's hospital claimed that she was in good hands and was now staying on a farm. Knowing Jessica would be worried about her sister, Lady Redesdale immediately contacted her, telling her to ignore stories of Unity's death if she saw them in the American papers.[31] A month later, in December, rumours about Unity's fate circulated in the British press. As Sydney walked through London, she could not avoid seeing the lurid headlines on the billboards, but she tried to ignore them. She told Jessica, 'I pay no attention as I know she is all right. But I think quite probably she isn't really well yet or I believe she would have managed to get a letter through.'[32]

On Christmas Eve, the Redesdales received a phone call from Unity, who was in Bern, Switzerland. She had been brought there from Germany in an ambulance train, accompanied by a nun who had nursed her in a Munich hospital. Desperate to come home, she asked Muv when she was coming to get her.[33] At last Sydney knew where her daughter was and that she was safe. When she finally heard the full story, she learnt that Unity had shot herself in the temple and the bullet had lodged in her skull. Immediately taken to hospital, Unity had nearly died and was unconscious for several weeks. Hitler was informed during the campaign in Poland; he then telephoned the hospital for news and paid the bills for her care. In November, he made a trip from the Polish front to visit her. When he asked whether she wanted to stay in Germany or return to England, she replied that she wanted to go home, so as soon as she was well enough, he arranged it.

After the months of anxiety, Lady Redesdale could not wait to be with her daughter. Leaving England just after Christmas, travelling across a war-torn Europe with Debo, Muv went to collect her seriously ill daughter. Sydney dreaded the state she would find Unity in, but when they were reunited she described them as just being so happy to be together.[34] She wrote to Jessica, 'It was wonderful to see her after four months and after all the dreadful rumours. She lay in bed and seemed all eyes, she was as excited to see us as we were.' Despite trying to be positive, Muv admitted that Unity looked terribly ill: her hair was matted with dried blood and cut short, and she was very thin.[35] When she spoke, she got words wrong, saying chocolate when she meant sugar.[36] Debo was also shocked by the transformation; with her vacant smile her sister seemed like a different person.[37]

When Unity was well enough to leave Switzerland, Lady Redesdale, Debo and Unity had a difficult journey back to England. It took four days instead of two, and at times Sydney wondered if her fragile daughter would survive. When they arrived at Calais, they had missed the boat train, so they had to stay for two nights in a hotel. Journalists discovered where they were and then pestered Lady Redesdale for an interview with her daughter. She firmly told them that Unity had been very ill but was much better. She added that her daughter had received the greatest possible care while in Germany.[38] Before they could set sail customs officers went through Unity's fourteen pieces of luggage. Finding some white pills in her handbag, they insisted that they were cocaine, and accused Unity of being an addict. Furious, Lady Redesdale insisted that they analysed the tablets – they turned out to be pills for her dog.[39]

As Unity was a member of Hitler's inner circle, when she was due to arrive in Folkestone, MI5 gave orders that a tight security perimeter should be constructed around the area. She was supposed to be searched, and a doctor was meant to make a full assessment of her medical condition. There was an assumption by the security services that she might be accused of treason and face internment. However, the Home Office intervened and many of the measures were bypassed. There was no medical examination, and the Mitford party were treated as ordinary passengers. This change of plan led to a high-level debate. Sir Guy Liddell, head of counterespionage for MI5, thought Unity should be thoroughly examined and probably interned, but Sir Alexander Maxwell, the permanent Undersecretary of State at the Home Office, refused his request, and the Home Secretary supported his decision. Sir Guy Liddell wrote that if Unity had been a member of the public rather than the aristocracy 'the probability was that we should not be arguing the case'. He added that the Home Office decided not to intern Unity because they had not taken action against members of the Anglo-German Fellowship or the Link, despite the fact that both groups had organised visits to Germany and established close links with Hitler's regime.[40]

Finally across the Channel, Unity, wrapped in a blanket, was taken off the boat on a stretcher. At Folkestone, Lord Redesdale was waiting for his wife and daughters with an ambulance. After only a few miles the vehicle broke down, so the family had to book into a hotel for the night. Once again, they were mobbed by journalists who wanted interviews. Photographers took pictures of a frail Unity walking into the hotel clinging onto her father's arm. Trying to protect her daughter, Lady Redesdale asked them, 'Are you all quite mad?'[41] Reports in the newspapers of Unity's return described her as 'Hitler's Jew-baiting little friend'. Suggesting she had friends in high places in Britain as well as Germany, and was given special treatment by the British authorities, the *Daily Mirror* complained:

All that was lacking was the red carpet and the military band and the drinks all round. Let the Tommies who come back wounded from France get the welcome of military guards and special trains. They serve this country a little better than this hysterical associate of Nazi bullies, braggarts and blackmailing trigger-men.[42]

The day after she landed in England, Unity was taken by ambulance to Old Mill Cottage in High Wycombe. When the family arrived, they were given police protection because the hostile publicity had stirred up public hatred and there were fears that Unity might be attacked.[43]

The Master Mariner, Thomas Gibson Bowles. (Chronicle/ Alamy Stock Photo)

Sydney in her sailor suit aboard the *Nereid*. (From Thomas Gibson Bowles, *The Log of the Nereid* (London: Simpkin, Marshall and Co., 1889))

Ready for romance: Sydney as a young woman.
(From Julia M. Budworth, *Never Forget: George
F.S. Bowles: A Biography* (privately published, 2001))

Henning Grenander, Sydney's first love.
(History and Art Collection/Alamy
Stock Photo)

A confident woman: Sydney in her prime.
(Chronicle/Alamy Stock Photo)

atsford House. (Foto-zone/Alamy Stock Photo)

Asthall Manor. (Luise Berg-Ehlers/Alamy Stock Photo)

Swinbrook House. (Tim Graham/Alamy Stock Photo)

Learning to read: Unity and Jessica in the garden at Asthall Manor. (TopFoto)

Photo of Sydney looking bored with her husband and Nancy as a toddler. (The Devonshire Collections, Chatsworth; reproduced by permission of Chatsworth Settlement Trustees)

Sydney relaxed and laughing on the beach. (From Budworth, *Never Forget*)

The golden years: the family together. (Pictorial Press Ltd/Alamy Stock Photo)

Ready to leave: Diana and Nancy.
(Chronicle/Alamy Stock Photo)

A restless spirit: Unity as a teenager.
(Chronicle/Alamy Stock Photo)

Happy at home: Debo with her dogs. (Chronicle/Alamy Stock Photo)

...scaping: Diana marries Bryan Guinness. (Chronicle/Alamy Stock Photo)

...Bright Young Thing: Nancy the writer.
...hronicle/Alamy Stock Photo)

The glamorous Mrs Guinness: Diana as a young married woman. (Chronicle/Alamy Stock Photo)

Bored: Jessica as a moody teenager. (Chronicle/Alamy Stock Photo)

Sydney with Unity and a friend. (Smith Archive/Alamy Stock Photo)

Pamela with Lord Redesdale. (Chronicle/Alamy Stock Photo)

The Mitford girls together. From left: Jessica, Nancy, Diana, Unity and Pamela. (Pictorial Press Ltd/Alamy Stock Photo)

Oswald Mosley addressing a
Blackshirt meeting in the East
End of London. (Heritage Image
Partnership Ltd/Alamy Stock Photo

The Redesdales' only son, Tom.
(Archive PL/Alamy Stock Photo)

Jessica and Esmond Romilly working together in a bar. (© SZ Photo/Scherl/Bridgeman Images)

Unity with Hitler. (Pictorial Press Ltd/Alamy Stock Photo)

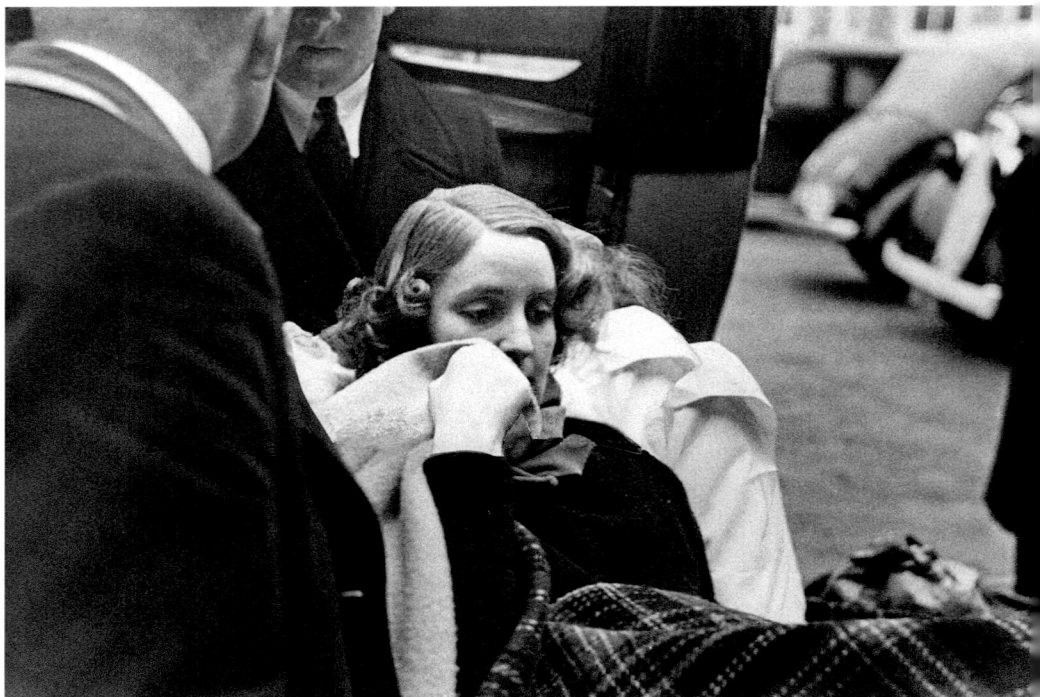

Unity arrives in Folkestone from Germany after shooting herself. (Trinity Mirror/Mirrorpix/Alamy Stock Photo)

Debo with her husband, Andrew Cavendish. (Chronicle/Alamy Stock Photo)

Nancy, the successful writer with her barbed pen. (Chronicle/ Alamy Stock Photo)

Sydney in her boat at Inch Kenneth. (From Budworth, *Never Forget*)

Inch Kenneth, Sydney's final home. (Mike Read/Alamy Stock Photo)

Swinbrook Church. (Andrew Roland /Alamy Stock Photo)

The press coverage of Unity's return was controversial. A letter appeared in *The Times* from Raymond Savage, a literary and film agent, who protested about a newsreel made by Paramount News Service which was shown in cinemas throughout the country. Describing the film as an outrage against common decency, he accused the filmmakers of concocting a fake film of Unity's arrival accompanied by a 'ribald and degrading commentary in verse'. He added, 'they have spared no one – even the tragic face of Lord Redesdale and close-ups of the girl herself are given.' Apparently, they also took cuts from films of the army, navy and Royal Air Force to make it appear that Unity was protected by the authorities and that a guard of honour was waiting for her at Folkestone.[44] The matter was also raised in the House of Lords, where Lord Denman complained that the film's running commentary had made 'rather cheap jokes' at the expense of Lord Redesdale and his daughter.[45] Dubbing it 'The Mitford Scandal', 'Cassandra' in the *Daily Mirror* retaliated by asking, 'What do we have to do when Hitler's friends return here – hold our tongues and give the Nazi salute?' Mentioning other Nazi sympathisers who the *Mirror* considered had been interned for less, the article added, 'The Mitford girl who has openly been consorting with the King's enemies (surely a treasonable offence?) goes scot-free. Why? God and the House of Lords only know.'[46] The public scrutiny continued in the House of Commons when a socialist Member of Parliament, Joseph Henderson, asked the Home Secretary, Sir John Anderson, whether he intended to keep Unity in a home or hospital under supervision until she was well enough to be detained.[47] Labour Member of Parliament Herbert Morrison also challenged the decision not to intern Unity.[48]

Few people knew the full extent of Unity's brain damage. At first, Lady Redesdale found it hard to face the truth. Playing it down, she told a reporter that her daughter was 'recovering well [...] My daughter must not be made into one of history's tragic women.'[49] Despite the positive spin Muv put on the situation in public, in private she was more honest, admitting to Jessica that in some ways Unity seemed like a completely different person and that her recovery would take a very long time. She convinced herself that her daughter's brain damage was like concussion and would eventually resolve itself.[50]

From now on, Lady Redesdale's life would be dedicated to caring for Unity. When they first got back to England, the Redesdales and their daughter lived in the cottage at High Wycombe. The family rallied around. Nancy came to stay, and Debo was often with them. Nanny Blor arrived to help Muv with the nursing Unity required. Gradually, Unity got better, but she never completely recovered. The bullet was still lodged in her skull and the surgeons had to decide whether they should try to remove it. She was treated by the eminent brain surgeon Professor Sir Hugh Cairns in a hospital in Oxford.[51] While Unity was under observation for several weeks, Muv did not leave her side; she had a bed in Unity's room and watched over her at night as if she was a baby. Unity had a series of tests and X-rays to assess her condition. With all the medical equipment around them, Sydney described the room as more like a battleship than a hospital.[52] Both mother and daughter were relieved when the surgeon decided not to operate because, according to Muv, 'the good body' had made a type of protective envelope around the bullet which isolated it from affecting her brain.

Once again, Sydney was annoyed by the negative newspaper coverage. Journalists claimed that Unity had secretly gone into hospital and there was a private detective to protect her. According to her mother, she had no special protection and they had come perfectly openly. As friends and family knew where Unity was, letters and flowers were delivered to the hospital in her name.[53] Rumours about Unity's condition on her return to England have persisted until the present day. In 2007, a Channel 4 documentary, *Hitler's British Girl*, claimed Unity may have secretly given birth to a child in a small nursing home in Wigginton, Oxfordshire, shortly after her return from Germany. In the programme, a member of the public claimed her aunt had acted as midwife at Hill View Cottage in the village when Unity gave birth to Hitler's baby and then the infant was given up for adoption. Another woman, who had lived in Wigginton at the time, claimed to have seen Unity at the nursing home, but recalled that she was there to recover from a nervous breakdown, not to give birth.[54] Neither of these accounts tally with Lady Redesdale's reports in her letters to Jessica.

As the months went by, Unity began to seem more like her old self, sometimes laughing at jokes and talking cheerfully to friends and family. Despite the improvement, her brain damage left her with the mental age of an eleven-year-old. She suffered from mood swings, and she looked completely different, as she had lost 2 stone in weight. Caring for Unity took most of Sydney's time and energy, as her life was dedicated to helping her daughter get better. It was like having a small child again, but this time the hands-on work was done by Sydney and not a nanny. When Unity came home, Muv slept in her room to make sure that she was all right during the night. As Unity was doubly incontinent, Sydney had to wash her sheets every day in the small kitchen sink and then hang them out to dry.[55] When Unity was too weak to get out of the bath by herself, her mother helped her. At first Unity could not read more than a few lines, so Sydney employed a tutor once a week, and afterwards worked on reading exercises with her. The brain-damaged young woman also found it hard to write, because for a time her right hand had been completely paralysed, so they worked on that too. To combat Unity's depression, Muv tried to keep her occupied, but it was hard work because she had a short attention span. As her daughter suffered from occasional blackouts, which lasted a few seconds, she was unable to go out on her own, so Lady Redesdale usually went with her. The highlight of their week was going to WH Smith. It was not just Unity's blackouts that worried Muv: when they were out shopping, she was concerned that her daughter would be recognised and attacked.[56]

Unlike his wife, Lord Redesdale could not cope with his daughter's condition or the political backlash against his family. Nor could he any longer tolerate Unity's or Sydney's views. The arguments between Muv and Farve became more heated and prolonged. Listening to the news on the wireless every evening triggered more quarrelling.[57] The reports about his daughters' politics in the press, which inevitably mentioned him, led to Farve receiving a flood of anonymous abusive letters. He was hurt by the attacks and wanted to put the record straight. Helped by his brother-in-law, George, who had been instrumental in making him realise that he had been wrong about Hitler, Lord Redesdale wrote a letter to *The Times*.[58] He explained, 'My only crime, if it be a crime, so far as I know, is that I was one of many thousands in this country who thought that our best interests would be served by a friendly understanding with Germany. In this, though now proved to be wrong, I was at any rate in good company.' He added that many people had changed their minds since Munich, and that 'certainly today my only desire is to see the earliest possible victory for the Allies'. He concluded the letter by stating how wounded he was to be described as a fascist, writing, 'Now, I am not, never have been, and am not likely to become a fascist.'[59]

Lady Redesdale did not agree with her husband, and she stood her ground. She thought it was a disaster for Britain and Germany to go to war with each other and she refused to stop admiring Hitler.[60] Ignoring all evidence to the contrary, it seems she still saw the brutal dictator as misunderstood. In her eyes he remained the polite man who had invited her to tea and cared for Unity when she was ill.[61] Her misplaced loyalty prevented her from recognising that her daughter's obsession with the Führer had ruined her life. Rather than blaming Hitler, Sydney regarded Winston Churchill as one of the architects of the conflict.[62] Although Sydney was critical of Britain's leaders, she supported the country's troops.* She was proud of her son Tom and her nephews and sons-in-law who were fighting in the war, and described 'our fighters' as 'most wonderfully brave'.[63]

---

* In a letter to Jessica on 6 January 1941, she wrote that 'everyone here is much heartened by the news from Libya'. The Allied forces had just won the Battle of Bardia, which allowed them to continue their advance into Libya. Sydney Redesdale to Jessica Mitford, 6 January 1941. Jessica Mitford Correspondence, Ohio State University, Special and Rare Manuscripts, OC89, Box 203, Folder 6.

As the months passed, the political divide between the Redesdales became more entrenched. Nancy wrote to Mrs Hammersley in March 1940 that her father was now more violently opposed to Germany than anyone and he was against any form of peace until Britain had won the war.[64] Sydney annoyed him by taking the opposite position, telling him that when the Germans had won everything would be wonderful. She added that they would treat the British much better than 'those wretched beastly Poles'.[65] Her comment suggests that she agreed with Diana and Oswald Mosley, who argued for a negotiated peace. At the beginning of the war, Mosley claimed England had nothing to gain and everything to lose by fighting Germany on behalf of Poland, and that the only reason to go to war should be to defend Britain or the Empire.[66] He declared that members of his party should do all that the law required of them and they would fight if Britain was threatened, but he was not offering to fight in 'the quarrel of Jewish finance'.[67] A desire for peace was not uncommon at the beginning of the war, but people's reasons for seeking it differed. While some pro-peace campaigners were high-minded pacifists, others were motivated by extreme attitudes which saw Jews and communists as the greatest threat and Hitler still as the bulwark against it.[68]

Divided by their attitude to the war and their feelings towards their sick daughter, Nancy told Mrs Hammersley that she thought her parents really hated each other now.[69] Debo also described the toxic atmosphere: her father was always cross and for the first time her mother was genuinely angry.[70] It got to a point where it seemed best to live separately. At first, they were very annoyed with each other, but it seems that as time passed the Redesdales' separation was more in sadness than anger. It was very painful for both Sydney and David because they still loved each other, but they could not find the common ground to live together anymore. For the rest of their lives, they still wrote to each other almost every day.[71] When Lord Redesdale visited London, Muv tried to see him, but sometimes she could not leave Unity.[72] She particularly hated not being with her husband at Christmas, but she hoped that one day they would be able to live together again.[73] For their family, Sydney and David's parting came as a shock. Jonathan Guinness remembers finding it inconceivable that they should separate because until then they had done everything together. He considered it to be 'a great tragedy'.[74]

The decision to put her daughter before her husband was largely forced upon Muv; while Farve could walk away from Unity, she would never have abandoned her vulnerable child. However, the ideological element of their quarrel was through choice. The reason Lord Redesdale no longer wanted to live with his wife and daughter was political as much as personal. In some ways, it was surprising that Lady Redesdale did not back down, because in the past she had always aligned herself with either her father's or her husband's political stance. According to Debo, her mother's generation of women was brought up to accept their husband's decisions and to make the best of their circumstances.[75] On this occasion she refused to do so. For those who knew her well, her reaction was incomprehensible. They expected ideological fervour from her daughters, but not from her. Sydney's niece, Julia Budworth, explained her aunt was usually 'so calm, so intelligent, and well balanced, so unfitted to adopt any kind of wild fanaticism, much less one that alienated her dearly loved and loving husband'.[76] Julia concluded that Sydney was suffering from 'severe political myopia'.[77] The obstinacy and steeliness which had always been part of her character now came to the fore. As Jonathan explained, 'Sydney always took longer to make up her mind than David, but when made up, no force outside herself would change it.'[78]

For the rest of the war Lord Redesdale spent most of his time at Inch Kenneth. At first the family had thought the remote island, far away from public scrutiny, would be an ideal place for Unity to recuperate. This plan was ruled out because Lady Redesdale and Unity were not granted permission to go there, as Inch Kenneth was within a protected zone under defence regulations and Unity was seen as a security risk. Once again, the family found themselves at the centre of a political controversy, as the matter was discussed in the House of Commons. The Home Secretary, Sir John Anderson, explained that privately owned islands on the West Coast of Scotland were being kept under police supervision to prevent them being used by pro-Nazi sympathisers. After his statement, a Scottish Labour Member of Parliament told the House that the fact that Lord Redesdale had been on the island recently, entirely unsupervised, was causing 'great perturbation' in the north of Scotland.[79] He added that local people were concerned that associates of well-known fascists could visit the islands while perfectly loyal men and women could not visit their relatives who lived there.[80]

When Lady Redesdale heard they were banned, she remarked sarcastically, 'In case we might be signalling to those dear Russians.'[81] In contrast, Lord Redesdale did not question the decision, but he was upset by the insinuations against him. On his return to London from Scotland, he told reporters, 'I have always been most bitterly opposed to any form of fascism and can only suppose that I am believed to be a fascist because my daughter is married to Sir Oswald Mosley.' He then explained that he did not know his son-in-law and had never attended any of his meetings. He added, 'I certainly blame no man who at this moment does or says anything which he believes on the information he has, to be in the interests of the safety of the country. But I am very anxious indeed to make it quite plain once and for all that this charge against me is in fact completely untrue.'[82] In private, he blamed his wife for the situation, believing they might have been permitted to go if she had been more open about the extent of Unity's disabilities and less blatant in her support of Hitler.[83]

Left alone together, Sydney and Unity rented the old fishing cottage next to The Swan pub at Swinbrook. Lady Redesdale had minimal help – just Mrs Stobie, her loyal cook. She kept chickens and goats, which helped to occupy Unity and supplemented their food rations. Describing herself as an ageing milkmaid, Lady Redesdale milked the goats and then made cheese, selling what was left over in the neighbouring town of Burford. Debo described her mother's milking technique in a letter to Diana. As she milked the goat, Sydney would shut her eyes or gaze into the middle distance, so the milk went everywhere but into the bucket.[84] Inevitably, caring for her temperamental and incontinent daughter was physically and mentally exhausting. Sydney relaxed by swimming in the millpond every day. With the physical work she was doing and food rationing, Muv became thin, but she was rather pleased with her svelte figure and felt very well.[85]

Occasionally guests visited, including Nanny Blor and Muv's old governess, Thomas's mistress, Tello. When they needed a change of scene, Unity and Sydney went to stay with Pam at Rignell House in Berkshire, taking their three dogs and a goat in their car with them.[86] Many of the neighbours at Swinbrook refused to mix with Unity, nor did some members of the family wish to socialise with Hitler's special friend. Aunt Weenie, whose sons were fighting in the war, hated her niece and refused to see her.[87] If they had met up there would have been rows, because Aunt Weenie's husband Colonel Bailey was fiercely patriotic, putting up a notice in his home which read, 'In this house we are not interested in talk of defeat.'[88] Sydney's brother George remained in touch, but while making his position clear, he did not bother quarrelling with his sister because he knew how stubborn she was.[89]

The authorities were suspicious of Sydney as well as Unity, so, other than a few exceptions, servicemen and women in uniform were banned from visiting her.[90] The villagers who had known Lady Redesdale and her daughter for years remained protective of them. Gradually, Sydney and Unity once again got involved in village life. Sydney said she wished they still had a big house, but only so that she would be able to take in evacuees.[91] Although she was no longer the lady of the manor, Muv did her bit in the community. She hosted a tea party for evacuees from London and Unity helped to serve school dinners to the village children. At Christmas, Unity dressed up as Father Christmas and handed out presents, bought by Muv, to the local children in the village hall.[92] Comparing herself to a character in an Elizabeth Gaskell novel, Lady Redesdale admitted to Jessica that her routine was dull as it comprised of 'goats, chickens and funny little tea parties with neighbours in Cranford style'.[93]

The atmosphere in the cottage was not always as serene as Lady Redesdale portrayed it. Debo found it claustrophobic living with her mother and sister, and they both got on her nerves.[94] Unity was jealous of her and resentful, and flew into a rage if her youngest sister annoyed her, calling Debo 'a bloody fool'.[95] Debo wrote to Jessica saying that

Muv was wonderful with Unity, never losing her temper with her or becoming impatient, even when she was infuriating.[96] There were occasions when Unity behaved inappropriately. Her doctor advised Lady Redesdale to encourage Unity to be more independent, so she sometimes took the bus into Oxford on her own, but on the journey she occasionally asked the other passengers for money.[97] Her obsessive nature now focused on religion, which led her to explore one denomination after another. For a time, a Christian Scientist practitioner visited her regularly.[98] Her religious obsession could be difficult to handle. If Debo dared to say 'damn', Unity turned on her and told her it was wicked to swear.[99]

Muv treated her daughter's challenging behaviour as just another one of her family's foibles. She was used to her relatives being eccentric. During the war, her brother Geoffrey went around in a siren suit (like Winston Churchill), wearing a bowler hat and carrying a furled umbrella. Every day he went to *The Lady*'s office and placed an uncooked herring on each desk for the staff. It was one of his healthy eating fads and he claimed to live on nothing but herrings himself throughout the war.[100] Cocooned within the family, Unity could be treated as just another cranky character, but it was harder when she ventured into the outside world.

13

War On Many Fronts

U nity was not the only member of the family whose life was completely transformed by the war. None of Lady Redesdale's children would come through the conflict unscarred by the experience. As each daughter faced her own problems, Muv dashed from one to another, trying to be there for whoever was most in need. The situation was not helped by the family being so divided on politics; it took all Sydney's diplomatic skills to keep the six Mitford girls talking to her, as they were certainly not all 'on speakers' with each other.

In May 1940, a month after Diana had given birth to her fourth son Max, her husband was arrested. Having campaigned for peace before the war, Mosley now wanted a negotiated settlement. He stated that the BUF was at the disposal of the armed forces and its members were expected to resist if Germany invaded.[1] His statement did not prevent him from being seen as a particular threat to national security. Under the Emergency Powers Act, Defence Regulation 18b (1a), the Home Secretary was able to detain any person who was a leader or member of any organisation presumed to be 'subject to foreign influence or control' or of which the leaders 'have or have had associations with persons concerned in the government of, or sympathetic with the system of government of, any power with which His Majesty is at war'.[2] The emergency powers allowed the suspension of *habeas corpus*, so a person could be held indefinitely without trial.[3] As fear of a German invasion swept the country, Winston Churchill's new national government arrested nearly 2,000 people, many of whom were members of the BUF. As leader of the BUF, Mosley was considered by Churchill to be the most likely contender to become a puppet dictator, taking orders from the Nazis if the Germans invaded, so he was imprisoned. As the net tightened, Nancy told Debo that people constantly asked her if her parents had been interned yet for their support of Hitler.[4] The Redesdales were safe because being a member of the Anglo-German Fellowship or the Link was not in itself considered grounds for detention. However, some of these organisations' leaders were arrested, including Sir Barry Domvile and C.E. Carroll, the secretary of the Link and editor of the *Anglo-German Review*.[5]

When Lady Redesdale heard what had happened to her son-in-law on the nine o'clock news on the wireless, she immediately phoned Diana to say that she thought Mosley's arrest was disgraceful. Over the following weeks, knowing how upset Diana was, Sydney and Unity visited Diana often, travelling by bus to be with her.[6] Shortly afterwards, the War Office commandeered Diana's home. Once again, she turned to her mother for advice. Sydney suggested she should take her children and stay with Pam at her large home, Rignell House, in Berkshire.[7] On 29 June, Diana was also arrested and imprisoned in Holloway prison. As a friend of Hitler's, she was thought to be just as dangerous as her husband.[8] Taking her cue from her mother, Diana repressed her emotions during her detention. In her autobiography she explained that her upbringing had trained her never to show weakness and she was determined not to let anyone see she was 'crushed'.[9]

Diana was still breastfeeding her baby son; she had to leave him and his two-year-old brother with their nanny at Pam's home. Lady Redesdale would have taken them in herself, but she was fully stretched looking after Unity.[10] Later, Muv arranged for the boys to move in with the family who had bought Swinbrook House. Once they were living in the village, she could visit her grandsons every day.[11] Sydney also had Diana's older children, Jonathan and Desmond, to stay with her in the school holidays. Jonathan describes her as 'an exceptional grandmother'. He was very fond of her, adding, 'she was wonderful, always and she was a rock'. She looked after him and his siblings throughout this difficult time. Unlike some of her children and other grandchildren, he found her warm and enjoyed being with her.[12]

Lady Redesdale was one of the few people who was there for Diana in her hour of need. It took between four and six hours travelling by bus and train from Swinbrook to Holloway, at a time when she was exhausted by caring for Unity, but Muv visited Diana nearly every week. She told Jessica that she found the journey 'frightful' because she often had to stand all the way on the train.[13] She did not completely lose her sense of humour and was amused when the bus conductor called out, 'Holloway gaol! Lady Mosley's suite!'[14] Once she had arrived at the prison, Lady Redesdale waited an hour in a cold, damp room. On one visit she was so disgusted by the filthy visitors' lavatory that she wrote on the wall, 'This lavatory is a disgrace to H M Prisons'.[15] Eventually, she had a quarter of an hour with her daughter. During her visits, Sydney updated Diana on the latest family news and brought her gifts of fresh food. Their meetings were listened to by a wardress, who then reported what was said to the authorities. There were some amusing mistakes where she misheard their conversations: Esmond Romilly became 'Desmond Donelly' and Decca was changed to 'Betty'.[16] Diana relied on these brief encounters, describing them to her sisters as 'a joy', but she was ashamed that her mother had to make such a long journey in the blackout.[17] She would never forget Muv's actions. Her daughter-in-law Charlotte Mosley explains, 'I think her loyalty to Diana during the war meant a great deal to her.'[18]

Referring to Diana as 'Mrs Quisling', Nancy was not so loyal.[19] Shortly before Diana was arrested, Nancy had denounced her sister to the authorities. She also informed on Pam and Pam's husband Derek, explaining that she thought they should be kept under observation because they were antisemitic, anti-democratic and defeatist.[20] Nancy was determined to make it plain that she did not support the fascist views of some of her relatives. Instead, she wanted to do her bit for the war effort. When Lord Redesdale handed over their Rutland Gate house to be used to accommodate east-enders who had been bombed out of their homes, Nancy prepared the house to receive them. She invited a few friends to help, and a cook was provided by the Women's Voluntary Services to prepare three meals a day for the evacuees. Nancy found it rewarding but tiring work.

About fifty of the new residents were Jewish. Under the headline 'Lord Redesdale's Guests', newspapers ran the story with a photograph of the east-enders playing skittles in their new home.[21] Farve told a reporter, 'All I have done is to lend the house, which is no more than a man with an empty house should do.'[22] When Lady Redesdale visited, she was upset to see her home in a mess. Apparently, she told Nancy that she would never want to use it again after Jewish people had lived there.[23] Nancy complained to Mrs Hammersley that her mother hated people who were poor or suffering from misfortune.[24] When Muv saw the evacuees, some sympathy for their plight mixed with her prejudice, but she still made an abhorrent antisemitic comment. She wrote to Jessica, 'I could wish they were Cockneys I must say, but one can't help being sorry for the poor creatures, only they are so ugly poor things.' Lady Redesdale added that she was glad that they were now well fed and had a room for each family rather than having to live in a school or town hall.[25] She was also concerned that Rutland Gate was not comfortable for them as there was hardly any furniture and just straw mattresses, blankets, pillows and only a few chairs.[26] As she was worried Nancy was working too hard, she was willing to swap places with her and look after the evacuees while her daughter had a rest at Swinbrook.[27] When Nancy got flu, Lady Redesdale took over for a fortnight and described it as just like housekeeping for a large house, only on double the scale.[28]

One of the few rays of sunshine during this bleak time was Debo's wedding to Andrew Cavendish, the second son of the Duke of Devonshire, in April 1941. Nearly 200 guests accepted an invite to the wedding because everyone wanted a good party to cheer themselves up. Relatives, friends and the family's old retainers including Nanny Blor, Mabel, the parlour maid and Mrs Stobie the housekeeper were invited. Lady Redesdale wanted to show her staff how much she valued their long-term support. She wrote to Jessica that they were a great comfort to her, and she felt lucky to have them.[29] It was a gathering of the clan, and even Sydney's reclusive brother Geoffrey was there. When his niece

Julia met him lugging crates of champagne around, he introduced him-self saying, 'Hullo, I'm your cracked Uncle Geoff.'[30]

Organising a wartime wedding was a challenge, but Sydney drew on her ingenuity and creativity. Two nights before the wedding day, London experienced one of the heaviest air raids of the war. Two houses in Rutland Gate were destroyed in the bombing and every window in the Redesdales' house was blown out. After the broken glass was swept up, Muv improvised to make sure the ballroom looked as attractive as possible for the reception. The curtains, which had been torn to shreds, were replaced with mock brocade curtains which Lady Redesdale made from rolls of grey and gold wallpaper.[31] Lacking paintings, as they were in storage, Sydney decorated the room by filling enormous wash basins with dozens of red camellias sent from Chatsworth, the Duke and Duchess of Devonshire's estate. The reception then went on as though nothing had happened.[32] Due to food rationing, there could be no icing on the wedding cake, but it was put in white cardboard casing, which looked reasonably realistic. The wedding was a happy day for the family, but the sight of Lord Redesdale giving his youngest daughter away in his Home Guard uniform was poignant. He looked a broken man, much older than in his sixties; the family crises and damage to his reputation had been too much for him. After Unity was seen at the wedding, outwardly looking a normal young woman, questions were asked in Parliament about whether she was well enough to be interned. The Home Secretary, Herbert Morrison, rebuffed them, stating there was no indication that she was a threat to national security.[33]

Throughout the war the family lurched from one crisis to another. At the end of the year, Debo gave birth to a stillborn child. Muv was with her throughout the traumatic experience. Afterwards, depressed by the loss, her youngest daughter needed support, so Lady Redesdale sent Unity off to stay with friends while she concentrated on comfort-ing Debo at the cottage.[34] Fortunately, after the stillbirth, Debo's next pregnancy went well, and nearly a year and half later she gave birth to her daughter Emma. Around the same time as Debo lost her baby, Nancy had an ectopic pregnancy. Sadly, the surgeons had to remove her fallopian tubes, which meant she would never have the child she longed for.[35] As Lady Redesdale rushed from one daughter to another, trying to help them, even Nancy had to admit her mother was superb, as, rather bewildered, she supported both her daughters. When Nancy's condition was explained to her, she said that she had thought ovaries were like caviar, meaning women had hundreds of them. When Nancy said she could not stand the thought of a huge scar on her stomach, Muv just questioned who would ever see it.[36] As usual, Nancy's positive feelings towards her mother did not last long. Apparently, the surgeon who operated on her for the ectopic pregnancy asked if she had ever been in contact with syphilis. When Nancy asked her mother, Sydney thought a nurserymaid might have been infected. From then on Nancy blamed Muv for her childlessness.[37]

Jessica was the one daughter Lady Redesdale could not help because she was determined to keep well away from her family in America. On 9 February 1941, Esmond and Jessica's daughter Constancia (known as Dinky) was born. Sydney was delighted with the news: when Unity opened the telegram and told her, Muv cried.[38] Lady Redesdale wrote to Jessica, 'Well what an excitement and joy I felt when I heard it and this is the only bit of real good news and real happiness we have any of us had for ages.'[39] Disappointed not to be able to see her new grand-daughter, Lady Redesdale had to make do with a photograph of mother and child. Frank as ever, Muv wrote to Jessica that the baby looked 'wonderful', but the picture of Jessica was 'horrible beyond words'.[40]

Once his uncle, Winston Churchill, became prime minister, Esmond signed up to join the Canadian Royal Air Force. He then dedicated himself to the defeat of fascism, believing that life would not be worth living unless the Nazis were beaten.[41] Tragically, in November 1941, he was killed on a mission to Bremen when his plane went down over the North Sea. He was only twenty-three years old when he died. On 2 December, Jessica received a telegram saying Esmond was 'missing in action'. Unable to accept her soulmate was dead, at first Jessica clung onto the belief that he was still alive and would be found. When the reality sunk in, although her mother wrote to her asking her to come home, she refused. Having lost her husband in the war she felt even more animosity towards those members of her family who had supported Hitler, telling her American friends that she would not go back to her 'filthy fascist family'.[42]

Unable to communicate easily with her daughter, Sydney kept in touch with Virginia Durr, a great friend of Jessica's, who had taken Jessica into her home once Esmond joined up. After Esmond's death, Virginia secretly approached Lady Redesdale because she was so concerned about Jessica's situation as 'a stranger in a strange land'. After much hesitation, Virginia had decided it was the right thing to do, because she knew from what Jessica told her how loyal Muv was to her children and her strength of purpose.[43] Sydney replied by telling Virginia how grateful she was to her for looking after her daughter. She wrote, 'It seemed impossible to help or advise, I could only feel deeply thankful she was with you and not alone. If she should ever think of coming home, it would be our greatest joy but of course she will decide.'[44] Virginia was very aware of Jessica's ambivalent feelings towards her family. She wrote to Muv, 'She has in her heart an affection for you and her sisters that nothing can erase. I have listened by the hour while she has told me of your life together and there seems to be an intense family feeling still.'[45] She added that she had never met anyone who had more strength of spirit than Jessica and, from what she had heard, her friend must have inherited her strength from Sydney.[46]

Both women were very worried about the young widow and her baby daughter. Virginia wrote that she had never known anyone who so hated being beholden to other people, but Jessica needed help. She wondered if Sydney could support her in a way that would make her feel it was her right, not just a gift.[47] Muv asked her bank to send her allowance of £10 a month to Jessica. Knowing her daughter might reject her financial support, Muv wrote to her, 'I do hope darling this is not wrong, you can quickly stop it if you don't want it sent.'[48]

Determined to support herself, Jessica remained in America and built a new life for herself. She got a job in the Office of Price Administration (OPA), a federal agency established to prevent wartime inflation. She told her mother she loved the job but could not resist complaining that she would be doing even better if she had been able to go to university.[49] Without telling her mother beforehand, in 1943 she married her second husband Robert (known as Bob) Treuhaft, a left-wing Harvard-educated attorney, whom she had met while working for the OPA. Bob's family had come to America as Jewish refugees from Hungary, where they had escaped a pogrom. Together, Bob and Jessica dedicated their lives to fighting fascism, and the year after their marriage Jessica joined the American Communist Party.[50] Although Jessica remained in touch with her mother, their relationship was conditional. Politics still came between them. Jessica explained that 'all our ideas and beliefs are so tremendously different and opposed that it would be impossible now to go back to ordinary family life'. Softening a little, she added, 'I don't think any more, as I once did, that this means one can't be on written, or even speakers, if close enough!'[51]

Lady Redesdale trod a fine line between her estranged daughters. She wanted to remain in contact with Jessica, but she was more in tune, both emotionally and politically, with Diana. Since their imprisonment, Lady Redesdale had done everything she could to get her daughter and son-in-law released. She used all her political skills in the campaign and launched a crusade which was reminiscent of her father's tactics. Her dedicated work for the Mosleys suggests what an effective politician she could have been. Jessica later commented, 'Goodness she was a good organiser.'[52] Sydney lobbied the Lord Chancellor and the editor of *The Times*, as well as various peers, Members of Parliament and ministers, on her daughter and son-in-law's behalf.[53] When the water supply at Holloway was cut off due to a bombing, Sydney contacted her local MP to get it restored. She also drew up a scheme for how the 18b prisoners should be treated. Knowing how much Diana relied on Mosley, she fought for husbands and wives to be interned together. Eventually, once Winston Churchill intervened with the Home Secretary, this demand was met, and Diana was able to live with Mosley in Holloway.[54] Sydney also asked why the 18b prisoners could not be treated in the same way as the interned German, Austrian and Italian 'enemy aliens' who had come to Britain in search of political asylum but were now housed on the Isle of Man. She argued that, surely, the Mosleys could be allowed to live outside prison under supervision. From June 1941 most women internees, though not Diana, were moved from Holloway to the Isle of Man.[55]

Rather than focus on just the Mosleys as individuals, Lady Redesdale turned this into a campaign about wider principles, claiming she was defending the ancient liberties of the individual in Britain. Drawing on the history she had learned from her father and then passed on to her daughters in their history lessons, she referred to the law of *habeas corpus* enshrined in the Magna Carta, that no English man or woman should be imprisoned without a fair trial by their peers. She suggested that the interned prisoners should be tried in a court of law. Then, if they were found guilty of treason, they should be shot, but if they were judged to be innocent, they should be set free. As the years went by, her letters became increasingly angry. She considered the poster declaring 'Freedom in Danger' comic and claimed that she was witnessing the death of English liberty.[56] Every time there was an article in the newspaper, a debate in Parliament or a broadcast on the wireless, she contacted the participants and made her point. The irony of Lady Redesdale, who was a known supporter of Hitler, setting herself up as a defender of British freedom seems to have not been lost on her recipients. At times in the correspondence, you can sense their exasperation with Lady Redesdale's arguments. Lord Cranborne, the minister for the Dominions, pointed out to her that rather than being an attack on liberty, the internments were essential for the preservation of liberty in Britain.[57] When Sydney wrote to the Lord Chancellor, Lord Simon, putting the 18b internments on a par with Hitler's abuse of legal powers, he replied that there was no comparison between what the British government was doing and what went on in Germany.[58] In a recent BBC broadcast he had said, 'Whoever heard of anybody in a German concentration camp applying for a writ of Habeas corpus? [...] The simple truth is that 80 or 90 million Germans are living as slaves because there is no German law to protect them and because there is no German court that would dare to interfere with the edicts of the bullies in power.'[59]

While Diana was in prison, her mother was her envoy to the outside world. Lady Redesdale kept in touch with some women members of the BUF, exchanging letters with Viscountess Downe, who was very supportive of her daughter. She also made a substantial donation to the charity which was set up to help detainees and their families.

When Oswald Mosley's health was deteriorating due to phlebitis, Diana asked her mother to contact Clementine Churchill, who had been her bridesmaid four decades earlier, to try to persuade her to appeal to Winston. Sydney did not want to as she hated asking a favour from the Churchills, but she swallowed her pride for the sake of her daughter. The meeting between the two opinionated matriarchs did not go well. Clementine was unsympathetic, saying the Mosleys were safer in prison because if they were released the fury of the public would be unleashed on them. Sydney was irritated by her response and coldly replied that they were willing to take that risk.[60]

In April 1943, Sydney wrote to Winston complaining that Diana had been kept in prison for nearly three years. Appealing to the man she knew, she wrote, 'that they should remain shut in prison year after year after year without charge and without trial is so entirely contrary to English justice that I feel completely sure that you are not in favour of this procedure for it is alien to all I know of you.'[61] Whether Lady Redesdale's intervention influenced the prime minister cannot be proven, but in November, Winston sent a secret memorandum to the Home Secretary, Herbert Morrison, stating:

I am convinced 18B should be completely abolished as the national emergency no longer justifies abrogation of individual rights of habeas corpus and trial by jury on definite charges. [...] There are of course a number of totalitarian-minded people who like to keep their political opponents in prison on lettres de cachet, but I do not think they constitute a majority.

He added that he had already spoken in Parliament about his 'distaste for these exceptional powers' and his hope that 'success and security would enable us to dispense with them', but as the Home Secretary took a different stance, he had not pressed his view.[62]

Winston had given a clear steer, which was followed. In November, the Mosleys were released from prison on compassionate grounds. There were many restrictions governing where they could live, but with Sydney's help, they moved into a former pub, the Shaven Crown at

Shipton-under-Wychwood, which was near Swinbrook. On Christmas Day the Mosleys and their children joined Muv and Unity at their cottage. Lady Redesdale tactfully did not mention it in her letters to Jessica, who was now working for the Joint Anti-Fascist Refugee Committee.[63] Her antennae finely tuned, Jessica guessed her mother was not telling her the full story and so she did not write to her for several months. She had been furious when Diana and Oswald Mosley were released from prison because she saw them as dangerous enemies. She described their release as 'a real act of treachery against everybody who is fighting', and wrote to Churchill to protest. She agreed with the people who demonstrated against it.[64] Appearing to want her mother to choose between her and Diana, Jessica warned her mother that she would stop writing completely if she put the Mosleys up in her house.[65] She wrote, 'It actually makes me feel like a traitor to write to anyone who has anything to do with them.' Tempering her anger, she conceded that the situation was difficult for Muv and it was not her fault.[66]

Life seemed to be gradually getting back to normal for Sydney. In April 1944, she received some good news: Debo's first son, Peregrine, was born. Shortly afterwards, she heard that Jessica had also given birth to a baby boy, Nicholas. It was the opportunity for a partial reconciliation between Farve and his estranged daughter. He sent her a letter sending his good wishes and love to her and his new grandson, adding that when the war was over, he hoped to see them.[67]

Although Muv still looked after Unity, she had respites as her daughter was now well enough to stay with other people. From 1942 it had been arranged for Unity to stay as the guest of the Reverend and Mrs Sewell-Corby in the vicarage at Hillmorton. Mrs Sewell-Corby slept in the same room as Unity and acted as her nurse through the night. In the summer of 1944, Unity applied for permission to live at Inch Kenneth. The Home Secretary granted approval after considering special reports from the military intelligence, Special Branch and Scotland Yard.[68]

Finally, Sydney could return to her remote home, but her first visit to the island in four years was strained. During the war, Lord Redesdale had become very thin and frail. He tired easily and his eyesight had deteriorated so much he feared he was going blind. The previous year he had undergone successful cataract operations on both his eyes which had restored his sight, but he was still fragile. Unable to live alone but unwilling to live permanently with his wife and daughter, Farve had been looked after on the island by his housekeeper, the Redesdales' former parlour maid, Margaret Wright, who was a trained nurse. When Lady Redesdale visited the island in May 1944, she felt that she was treated like a guest rather than mistress of the house. She was annoyed by Margaret's proprietorial attitude to her husband and felt that the younger woman had usurped her role. Sydney thought Margaret was bossy and tactless and gave herself airs, but if she complained Farve took his housekeeper's side.[69] During Muv's visit, bad weather set in, and they were cut off from the mainland by rough seas for several days. Being isolated on a small island increased the pressure. Their only contact with the outside world was through the news on the wireless. Muv was worried about Tom, who was fighting in Italy. The D-Day landings were about to be launched, and as Sydney wrote to Jessica, 'everyone's thoughts are on the coming so called Second Front and in expectation'.[70]

In July, there was another family reunion. Unity went with her mother to Inch Kenneth, and Tom joined them while he was on leave. Debo came too, but to Muv's fury, her daughter was not allowed to bring her baby with her because Margaret did not want the extra work children would involve. Everyone was given chores to do. While Farve and Tom tended to the livestock, Muv did the cleaning, and Unity helped Margaret in the kitchen.[71] Thrown together on the island with few distractions, the atmosphere was so strained no one could relax. Debo described their summer holiday as 'a kind of hell'.[72] Unity behaved eccentrically, playing out her religious obsession. Pretending to be a clergyman, she made a cassock out of a sheet and then insisted that her mother and sister came to the ruined chapel while she held a service. When she forgot the words for the 'jubilate' and '*Te Deum*' she became frustrated and angry with herself and her congregation.[73] The clash between Margaret and Lady Redesdale also came to a head. When the news came on the wireless, Muv refused to listen with Farve and his companion because Margaret insisted on making banal comments.[74]

At mealtimes Muv and Farve hardly spoke to each other, then after dinner Lord Redesdale helped Margaret in the kitchen rather than sit with his family in the drawing room.[75] Debo now came to the same conclusion as Nancy had at the start of the war: that Farve seemed to hate Muv.[76]

The Redesdales' children realised the situation could not continue because it was making their mother deeply unhappy. Tom spoke to his father, and he also gave his mother advice, suggesting that she should just stay on the island and make it so awkward for Margaret that she would have to leave.[77] Trying to resolve the situation, Sydney invited her brother George to Inch Kenneth to mediate. He advised his sister that, rather than show her irritation, she should lavish Margaret with thanks for looking after Farve because this would prevent Lord Redesdale from stepping in to defend her rival.[78] None of their suggestions worked. Typically, after five years, Farve had become bored with living on the island and was ready for his next move. He decided to go to Redesdale Cottage in Northumberland, taking Margaret with him. Planning for the future, Lord Redesdale had decided to make the island over to his son. Lady Redesdale agreed to move to the island with Unity for part of the year and manage the farm while Tom was away. She was happy to do it as she enjoyed the work and loved living by the sea.

Staying on at Inch Kenneth into the autumn, Sydney felt settled enough to begin to look back over the past few years. She updated the detailed photo album of the family she meticulously kept throughout her life. The tome spanned eighty years, going back to her father, Tom Gibson Bowles, and her father-in-law, Bertie Redesdale. As she put in the photos of her latest grandchildren, she admitted that making it had given her a great deal of pleasure.[79] Over the winter, she continued to revel in nostalgia, amusing herself by writing a memoir of her childhood and youth for her grandchildren.[80] Later, her completed autobiography, entitled *Five Houses*, was typed by George and privately published for only her family.[81]

Unfortunately, the wartime chapter in Sydney's life was not yet finished, and before the conflict came to an end the family was to suffer their greatest tragedy. As the end of the war approached and the Allied troops advanced through Europe, Tom asked to be posted to the Far East. He did not wish to be part of the force marching into Germany because he did not want to kill German civilians, whom he liked.[82] Before leaving, Tom had driven down to Swinbrook with his old friend James Lees-Milne to see Muv and Unity. His sister was on good form and made him laugh. During his visit, she spoke of Hitler, which she rarely did, other than in private with her mother. She talked about the Führer as if she still admired him and complained about the enthusiasm with which the British newspapers reported the bombing of German cities.[83] After a few days, Tom said goodbye. Sydney was brave about it even though she knew that she might not see her son for three years.[84]

Shortly afterwards, Tom went out to Burma as a Brigade Major. Rather than be in a relatively safe staff post, he asked to join a fighting battalion at the front near Mandalay. On 24 March, shortly after he arrived, he led some of his troop against a small group of Japanese soldiers. Sheltering behind some corrugated iron, he was shot in the neck and shoulders by a Japanese sniper. The bullet penetrated his spine and left him paralysed but still conscious. After being taken to the main dressing station in a Jeep, he thought that he was getting better and was cheerful, but he developed pneumonia. Six days later, on Good Friday, he died. He was just thirty-six years old.

When the Redesdales received the news, Farve was in the Mews in London and Muv at Inch Kenneth. On 2 April, Lord Redesdale received a telegram saying Tom was wounded. Five days later, he was informed that his son had died of his wounds. He immediately sent a telegram to his wife in Scotland, which began, 'I do not know how to tell you this'.[85] Lady Redesdale wrote to Jessica, 'As the days passed, we grew so hopeful and the shock was so bad when it came.' At first the sea was too rough for her to cross to the mainland. She recalled, 'I nearly went mad being so far away at Inch Kenneth.'[86] As soon as the weather permitted, Sydney took the next train down to London because she did not want her husband to be alone.

Joining their parents in London, Nancy, Unity, Debo and Diana tried to console each other. According to Nancy, Lady Redesdale was the bravest of them all and seemed almost cheerful. At this bleak time,

Unity unintentionally amused them by saying that she thought Tom was lucky to die on Good Friday. She added that she envied him because he would be having stimulating arguments with Dr Johnson now.[87] The family could tap into their irrepressible sense of humour, which never completely left them, but there was no escaping their overwhelming grief. Tom was the one member of the family all the sisters and both parents had always got on with well. His loss was immense for each one of them. Muv wrote to Jessica: 'You can just imagine what it is to us both and in fact I know to all of you to lose Tom, he was actually the best of sons and brothers, and I think we relied so much on him.'[88] Charlotte Mosley emphasises, 'You could never underestimate the blow of Tom's death. What Sydney went through during the war, most of us would have been flattened.'[89] Displaying her usual stoicism, Lady Redesdale did not say much about it, but friends and family thought she never got over this loss. She admitted to Tom's old school friend James Lees-Milne that she was 'sadly heartbroken'.[90]

The dozens of letters she received from Tom's friends comforted her. They praised his courage as a soldier and mourned the great loss he was to his country. Like at the beginning of the war when Unity shot herself, at first Sydney had minimal information about what had happened. She hated to think her son had not been with good friends, and she had terrible visions of him being left unattended when he was ill. She told James Lees-Milne that she wished that she could hear from someone who had been with him.[91] Through her grief, she found some solace in believing in an afterlife. She told Jessica, 'I do feel so very certain they [Tom and his comrades] are all together somewhere and it will not be very long before I at any rate shall know what it is all about.'[92]

The war had begun for the Mitford family with Unity shooting herself and ended with Tom's death. As well as losing her only son, Sydney lost two nephews, as her sister Weenie's sons Christopher and Anthony were also killed during the conflict.[93] Whether Lady Redesdale's experiences had changed her view of Hitler and the Nazis was not clear, even to those closest to her. On receiving the terrible news about her brother, Jessica explained to Muv that she had found it hard to write anything comforting to her at first because: 'To me it seems that anyone who was killed in this war has died for the most magnificent cause in history – but I didn't know if you would agree. Since getting your letter, I think that at last you do agree, and that you see that it would be better for all of us to be wiped out than to live in the same world with the Nazis.'[94]

Perhaps because she knew how divisive politics was within her surviving family, Lady Redesdale kept her thoughts to herself or tailored what she said to appease her listener. Nancy told Jessica that Muv never mentioned the war or politics to her, but she feared that she was still 'very unsound at heart'.[95] For once, being enigmatic was the best policy, and it was safest to remain vague rather than alienate any of her remaining children. However, although Sydney and her daughters were not united on the cause of the catastrophe, they did agree on how to cope with adversity. Lady Redesdale was determined to be brave, and when she wrote to Jessica, who had suffered the loss of her great love during the conflict, she knew that she would understand. Muv explained:

Alas of course we are only one of thousands all over the world. What a terrible world it has become, all black and dark. But we must not grieve too much but take up life with what courage we can. I have to learn from you darling for your great courage was an example for anyone, but you were always such a brave Little D.[96]

Keeping the Family Together

A photograph of Lady Redesdale in her rowing boat at Inch Kenneth, taken shortly after the war, reveals the toll the last few years had taken on her. She looks gaunt and grim. The down-turned set of her eyes and mouth make her appear even more severe. Her clenched hand, displaying one piece of jewellery, her wedding ring, suggests she was just managing to cling on. When Debo visited her mother on the island in October 1945, she wrote to Diana saying that at first Muv tried to be cheerful, but during her visit she seemed very sad, and she became increasingly silent. Lady Redesdale had lost so much in the war that she had to build a new life for herself and what remained of her family, but it was not easy. Unity was like a child, never leaving Sydney alone and constantly demanding her attention.[1] To fill the long days together, mother and daughter used to go out in the boat and row around the island for hours.[2]

The Redesdales' world had changed beyond recognition. Once the conflict was over, 26 Rutland Gate and much of the family furniture was sold.[3] Sydney divided her time between Inch Kenneth, the mews house in London, and visits to her daughters. She never lived with her husband again, which was his choice, not hers. Instead, he stayed in the small cottage at Redesdale in Northumberland with Margaret Wright. Whether Lord Redesdale and his housekeeper had a romantic relationship is open to question; Jessica thought they were more than just employer and employee. However, most of the family disagreed, and his increasing infirmity made a liaison less likely.[4] The once upright, handsome man had become a shadow of his former self. James Lees-Milne described the pathos of seeing 'a bent figure with a shrunken, twisted face, wearing round, thick spectacles, looking like a piano tuner'.[5]

Farve developed rheumatoid arthritis, which limited his mobility and caused him a great deal of pain.[6] Increasingly, he relied on Margaret as his carer, as well as his companion. His daughters did not like the woman who had usurped their mother. Debo felt that she was critical of the sisters and was only interested in Farve. She complained about his companion's 'prissy voice' and conventional outlook. Despite his family thinking Margaret was boring company, Lord Redesdale enjoyed being with her more than with his wife.[7] Nancy joked that he had become 'a good time boy' as they went to cocktail parties every evening with their neighbours.[8] When Nancy saw Margaret in Paris, she noted that Farve phoned her or wrote to her every day. Nancy told Diana that she thought it was 'wonderful' that her father had found someone that he really liked because he never received much love from Muv. She added that she did not think Sydney had even particularly liked him, although she did not blame her mother.[9] As usual with Nancy there were elements of truth in her observation, but it painted Sydney in the most negative light. The bond between Lord and Lady Redesdale remained deep and, even though they could not live together, they were occasionally reunited at family occasions. Husband and wife wrote to each other regularly, and the tone was always affectionate. They addressed each other as 'darling' and signed off 'all love'.[10]

Unlike in their childhood, Sydney's daughters were now closer to their mother than their father. They felt it was unfair that Lord Redesdale did nothing to help with Unity. Lady Redesdale and her daughter spent half the year at Inch Kenneth, living a rarified life, diluted by visits from relatives and friends. As someone who loved the whole family and had known them in their heyday, James Lees-Milne found it sad to see them so diminished. He wrote that he saw no future for Unity except 'a gradually dissolving fantasy existence'.[11]

Although Unity was able to live a more independent life than when she first returned from Germany, she was still incontinent and volatile. Sydney worried about who would look after her daughter after she died. Diana and Pam both reassured their mother that they would step in, but Sydney was still anxious about it and thought that she alone was the right person to care for Unity.[12]

After Tom's death, Lady Redesdale admitted to Jessica that she found it difficult to take much interest in anything because it all seemed so pointless and dull. Rather than admit the full effect of their personal tragedies on her, she focused on world events. She wrote, 'The future appears in a mist of uncertainty, I think it is the effect of the atom bomb – it may be the end of the world, who knows?'[13] She felt negative, but she refused to completely give in to despondency and fought back by turning away from the past towards the future. Having her grandchildren and their friends on the island cheered her up.[14] In August 1947, Diana and her four sons, accompanied by her cook and nanny, spent a month with Sydney and Unity on Inch Kenneth. The children loved it. When Lady Mosley told her youngest boys not to fight too much, they reassured her that Granny Muv was becoming so deaf she would not know if they were fighting or not.[15] The weather was so hot they swam in the sea every day, and then, in the evenings, climbed the island's hills, the Humpies, to watch the sunset over a panoramic view of the Inner Hebrides.[16] During their holidays on the island, Sydney's relationship with her eldest grandson Jonathan grew deeper as she spent a great deal of time with him. He recalls, 'at Inch Kenneth, she was the boss – but not in a bossy way.' As he grew older, he did not think of her as a confidante, but any advice she gave was good. She was able to cope with any situation that arose and thus set him an excellent example. She also passed on her love of the sea to him.[17]

The loss of Tom had unintended financial consequences for his parents. As Lord Redesdale had made Inch Kenneth over to his only son, when Tom died leaving no will, under Scottish law, the island was inherited by his sisters rather than his parents. Each of the Mitford girls had a sixth share of the inheritance. All the sisters except Jessica agreed that their mother should be able to live on the island for her lifetime. Instead of supporting the majority decision, Jessica insisted on making a political point by giving her sixth share to the British Communist Party. There was talk of the island having to be sold. In fact, the British Communist Party was not interested in a remote outpost, so Jessica suggested that she would sell her share to her sisters. They were all furious with her for putting their mother through more stress, but Sydney kept her calm and found out for her daughter that her sixth was worth £500. Eventually, Jessica decided to keep her portion while her sisters gave Muv a life tenancy.[18]

Jessica tried to explain her actions to her mother. Emphasising that she did not want any of the money from the island for herself, she explained that she was using it as a political weapon. She was determined that her share should go to 'undo some of the harm that our family have done, particularly the Mosleys and Farve when he was in the House of Lords'. Still unsure of her mother's political position she added:

> I don't know whether developments in the last ten years have yet proved to you what a criminal thing it was to have supported Hitler and an appeasement policy for England, but you do know what I think about it, so therefore you can see the logic of my trying to do everything possible in the other direction – including using the money from the island in this way.[19]

Rather than complain about the effect it had on her, Muv just appeased her daughter, fearing that a confrontation might end their relationship.

It seems that, as Jessica suspected, Lady Redesdale had not learnt the error of her ways. Jonathan wrote that she never changed her political views. She continued to believe isolationism would have been the best policy and that it would have been wiser if Britain had kept out of the war and just let Germany and Russia fight each other.[20] She believed the war had ended Britain's hope to prevent the country sliding into decline and, rather than seeing Churchill as a hero or a villain, she saw him as a tragic figure. She remained a supporter of her son-in-law, Oswald Mosley, and hated the postwar settlement of Europe.[21] Most of the family were as perplexed as ever by her views. On a visit to her aunt shortly after the war, Julia Budworth recalled that they were warned not to say anything 'derogatory about the Nazis as Sydney might get furious'. Her niece added, 'this was a situation as puzzling as it was appalling. In all other ways Sydney was sanity itself.'[22] To this day, her relatives cannot explain her contradictions. Her granddaughter, Constancia, says:

You ask how the same inclinations could exist in one person. Well, I think the famous example of that is Diana. Everybody that knew Diana loved Diana, I heard nothing but positive statements about her, but obviously she never overthrew her endorsement of the Nazis.[23]

To understand why Sydney remained so intransigent, it helps to study Diana's attitudes. Her daughter-in-law, Charlotte Mosley, emphasises that it was hard to reconcile the contradictions in Diana's character. She writes:

The latent anti-Semitism and racism of pre-war Britain, assumptions that she never questioned, were at odds with her innately empathetic nature. Her admiration for a barbaric regime, whose essential characteristic was dehumanising its opponents, jarred with the qualities of generosity and tolerance that led her family and many friends to cherish her.[24]

Like her mother, Diana prided herself on her 'intellectual honesty', but as one of her biographers writes, at times it morphed into 'wilfully blind disingenuousness'.[25] Even after the war she remained loyal to her friendship with Hitler, describing him as a charming character.[26] Near the end of Lady Mosley's life, when an interviewer asked her what her reaction was to seeing film footage of the concentration camps, she told him that she felt horror and revulsion against the people who did it, but she could not blank out from her memory her experience of Hitler before the war. She admitted that her feelings were complicated, and she could not really relate the two things to each other.[27]

Diana's daughter-in-law suggests that Diana continued to hold her views partly because of her love for her husband, Oswald Mosley.

Diana had sacrificed so much due to her politics that she could not recant without having to admit that the losses she had experienced were for no purpose.[28] She had been brought up to block out anything which was too painful, so she continued to do that now.[29] It seems probable that her mother's postwar reaction was for similar reasons. If Sydney had admitted she was wrong, she would have had to face the truth about Tom's death, Unity's brain damage and the breakdown of her marriage, and admit that Hitler, not Churchill, was to blame for ruining her life. Faced with chaotic situations, she had always carefully constructed her own parallel world; it might have destroyed her to deconstruct it now.

A leading historian of this era, Professor Richard Toye, considers that Sydney's refusal to revise her opinions was not unusual. He explains, 'People have a natural instinct for self-justification and often find ways to rationalize their actions, even in changed circumstances. They may admit minor mistakes, while convincing themselves that they were fundamentally correct.' After the war there was a cohort of individuals, including some supporters of Mosley and aristocrats with links to Nazi Germany, who did not publicly express regret for their beliefs.[30] According to Andrew Lownie, biographer of Edward VIII, the views of the Duke and Duchess of Windsor did not really change either. They continued to believe fascism was a bulwark against communism, which remained a perceived threat.[31]

Living together on the isolated island for much of the year, Sydney and Unity reinforced each other's attitudes. Rather than trying to erase evidence of their relationship with the Führer, mementos were carefully preserved. Unity's records of Nazi songs 'Horst-Wessel-Lied' and 'Die Wacht am Rhein'[32] were kept in the drawing room alongside Wagner's The Ring Cycle, which was a gift from Hitler, complete with a friendly inscription.[33] For the rest of her life, Muv played the music Unity had brought home from Germany on the grand piano, including 'Als die goldne Abendsonne,' a propaganda song about Nazi troops marching into a German town.[34] Even in old age, Sydney's fascination with the Führer persisted. When an employee at the BBC asked Lady Redesdale if she would like to listen to any material in their archive, she requested Hitler's speeches.[35]

When David Pryce-Jones was researching his biography of Unity, he visited Inch Kenneth. Although it was under new ownership, he found books left by mother and daughter on the bookshelves. Among them was Louis Golding's *The Jewish Problem*, E.O. Lorimer's *What Hitler Wants* and M.G. Murchin's *Britain's Jewish Problem*. Some of the books had detailed annotations in the margins setting out the reader's reaction.[36] During his research, Pryce-Jones also saw a copy of the inflammatory antisemitic *The Protocols of the Elders of Zion*. This was a fabricated volume of claims promoting a conspiracy theory that the Jews were seeking world domination. According to him, its pages were often underlined or scored in the margin with exclamations like 'Too true!' and 'I always said so' in a hand which he took to be Lady Redesdale's.[37] Whether these notes were made before or after the war we cannot know, but if they were written by Sydney, they expressed views that were in line with her brother Geoffrey's opinions. In November 1946 he wrote to a newspaper stating, 'It does not matter who wrote or forged or plagiarized (kidnapped) the "Protocols of the Elders of Zion." [...] The one thing that does matter is that the predictions in the Protocols have come true up to now. What can prevent the remaining predictions from also coming true?'[38] Such hateful views were unacceptable after the Holocaust. Simon Heffer explains, 'Most sane people were so appalled by what they learned Hitler had done to the Jews that they held back their expressions of prejudice towards them. But from what little I know of Lady Redesdale she was exceptionally stupid, which perhaps explains her persistence in her attitudes.'[39] Sydney was not stupid; it was her judgement not her intelligence which was at fault. Her obstinate refusal to reassess situations in the light of incontrovertible evidence, alongside her entrenched prejudices and her misguided loyalty, made her hold onto pernicious attitudes which had proved catastrophic on both a global and personal scale. As so often in her life, she only saw what she wanted to see and tightly shut her eyes to anything which might contradict her worldview. In other situations, this could be excusable, but in this case her blind spot indicates an indefensible moral failure. Rather than being actively involved in politics, Muv's life was dedicated to caring for Unity. As she had always done, she pandered to her daughter's needs; she tried to build a social life for her. Shortly after the war ended, Lady Redesdale invited locals from Gribun to a dance for Unity's birthday held in the drawing room at Inch Kenneth. Everyone danced reels until 3.30 a.m. and then Mr MacGillivray, the boatman, sang mournful songs in Gaelic to entertain the guests.[40] When friends came to stay, in the evenings, Unity enjoyed playing the card game Racing Demon with them. Treating her daughter as she had when she was a child, Lady Redesdale whispered to a guest that she always let Unity win because she might mind if she lost.[41] As Unity liked singing, she would perform a solo while Muv accompanied her on the piano. A great favourite for both of them was *The Grace Darling Song*, which rekindled memories for Sydney of her father, as it had been sung by the Aldeburgh sailors.[42]

Unable to attend church when they were on the island, Unity held services for family and friends outside Inch Kenneth's ruined chapel. Her cousin, Julia Budworth, remembered on one visit Unity pretended to be a vicar, dressing herself in a sheet. She then preached a sermon opposing the use of the atom bomb before going to the churchyard gate to shake hands with her congregation.[43] According to Nancy, one Sunday when Unity was holding an improvised service with just her mother, a stranger joined them. Lady Redesdale saw him first and whispered to her daughter to look. A man with a small moustache and dark flattened hair, dressed in a raincoat was with them in the ruined chapel. By the end of the service, he had disappeared. Lady Redesdale tried to find out who the Hitler lookalike was. She wondered whether it was a reporter trying to entrap them into talking, but the boatman told them that no one had travelled to the island that day. The identity of the figure remained a mystery.[44]

Unity longed to have a husband and children like her sisters. One friend said that she used to spend hours with Unity looking through *The Matrimonial Times* for potential partners for her and roaring with laughter at what they found.[45] She told another friend that she was going to have six sons; the eldest would be called Adolf and all the rest John.[46] Lady Redesdale later recalled, 'she did love children and was at her best with them for they liked her too.'[47] Her frustrated desires could cause problems. In 1946, Aunt Weenie told Nancy that Mosley had tried to seduce Unity. Apparently, the story had originally come from Unity, but Diana blamed her aunt for spreading it. She was furious about the accusation, telling Nancy that the rumour existed because her husband was one of the few people who had tried to be kind to Unity.[48] Even Nancy, who always enjoyed a tease, thought it was a fantasy because she did not believe Mosley would have been interested in her 'pathetic' sister. To silence the gossip, she suggested Diana should discuss the matter with Muv.[49] The Mosleys were not the only members of the family who found it hard to deal with Unity. Debo invited her mother and sister to spend their first Christmas at Edensor in Derbyshire with them. Pre-empting problems, Debo's husband Andrew was realistic and refused to have the Christmas tree party for the village children while they were staying because he did not want Unity to meet their local vicar. He thought it would be embarrassing because she always asked clergymen intrusive questions, such as whether they enjoyed sleeping with their wives.[50]

Everyone realised the strain caring for her brain-damaged daughter put on Sydney, who was now in her late sixties, but no one had a solution. Aunt Weenie remained as protective of her older sister as ever and when she visited Nancy in Paris, she gave her niece a lecture on not doing enough for her mother. According to her, Sydney was very unhappy, even suicidal.[51] Diana thought this was an exaggeration, but when Nancy visited Muv in England she realised that Muv was depressed.[52] The sisters discussed what could be done to improve the situation, including paying for Unity to live in a separate cottage with a carer so Lady Redesdale could have some space.[53] It was arranged for Unity to sometimes stay with friends and family so that Muv had more respites.

Although Unity was the centre of her world, Sydney never neglected any of her daughters. In the postwar era, Lady Redesdale was the linchpin who kept her family together. She did everything she could to rebuild relationships with her surviving daughters. The Mitford girls were scattered around the world. Jessica's life was in America, while Nancy moved to Paris. France was Nancy's spiritual home, and this was

Nancy's time. Like her sisters, she had been looking for a hero to worship and she finally found him in General de Gaulle's righthand man during the war, Gaston Palewski. He was a fighter in the Resistance, who Nancy had met in England towards the end of the war. He became the love of her life, but he would never commit to marrying her.[54] Nancy wondered how her mother would react to her being Palewski's mistress. When Nancy's husband, Peter Rodd, wanted a divorce, Nancy was nervous about telling her mother. She asked Diana if she thought Muv would mind.[55] However, Sydney had moved with the times and was far less judgemental than before the war. When Nancy introduced her mother to her lover, Palewski thought there was an 'unnatural quietness' about Muv, but Nancy told him that was usual. Lady Redesdale made no comment about what she thought of him.[56] More forthcoming in a letter to Jessica, she described him as a cross between Maurice Chevalier and a florid-faced hunting squire like Weenie's husband Colonel Bailey.[57]

In the postwar era, Nancy achieved the literary success she craved with her novel *The Pursuit of Love*. Written in the final months of the war and published later that year, it was a fictionalised version of her childhood. In this book and its sequel, *Love in a Cold Climate*, Aunt Sadie, the innocuous aristocrat who ineffectually floats around doing nothing much, was based on Muv, while Farve was recreated in the blustering, hilarious Uncle Matthew. Lord Redesdale was amused and rather delighted with his caricature. He wrote to his wife, saying Nancy's writing showed how savage he must have been without knowing it.[58] Lady Redesdale was more critical of her daughter's novel. She wrote to Diana that a friend had sent a publisher's notice for the book which said, 'Everywhere in Europe men lost their heads when the beautiful, elegant Mitford sisters dominated the salons, Oh dear what nonsense.'[59] In many ways, Nancy had created affectionate portraits of her family, ironing out the more difficult political beliefs which divided them. However, by downplaying Sydney's politics, the portrayal of Aunt Sadie loses the essence of who Sydney really was. It creates a more one-dimensional character, albeit a more politically acceptable one. Perhaps it was Nancy's way, like her mother, of seeing the world as she would like it to be rather than as it really was. Certainly, her novel helped to change public perception of her family, making them known more for their amusing eccentricities than their controversial views.[60]

In the real world, politics could not be so easily eradicated. Jessica and Diana remained estranged from each other because of their very different ideologies. Trying not to get caught in the crossfire, their mother was determined to keep in touch with them both. Sydney went to great lengths both physically and emotionally to build bridges. Missing Jessica after their years of separation, shortly after the war Sydney wrote to her, 'Some day I shall get into an aeroplane and arrive at your house, seven years is too long. You probably won't know who it is when I do arrive.'[61] Since she had last seen her daughter, Jessica had given birth to three children; the latest addition was her second son Benjamin, who was born in 1947. Lady Redesdale wrote a letter to America most weeks and sent presents for Christmas and birthdays, which reminded Jessica of her childhood. Muv hand-knitted jumpers for her grandchildren and sent them favourite children's books and card games, including Old Maid and Happy Families.[62] Contact purely by post was never enough for her. When Jessica's seven-year-old daughter Constancia (Dinky) sent a letter asking her grandmother if she would visit them in America, Sydney immediately agreed. Even though it involved a long journey, Lady Redesdale dropped everything and flew out to San Francisco. Sydney was very sick during the fifty-hour journey and her daughters worried about the strain it would put on her heart, but she was just pleased to finally arrive and see Jessica and her family.[63]

Jessica was touched that her mother was making the effort to see her, but nervous about their reunion. When Sydney got off the aeroplane, looking exhausted and more vulnerable than her daughter remembered, Jessica's attitude towards her became more sympathetic. She could tell immediately that her mother was determined to be on good terms with her.[64] For a seven-year-old little girl, dressed in her best outfit, the experience was rather different. Constancia Romilly recalls her first meeting with Granny Muv:

Here comes this imposing figure with this hazy accent that I'd never heard before, and I think I was basically intimidated. I don't think

I had much of an ability to have a spontaneous reaction. And then of course Dec [Jessica] and Bob were tense, it was not an easy visit for them.[65]

Constancia's behaviour was like Jessica's at her age. She was very independent and used to pack her case and threaten to run away if she was told off for misbehaving. Jessica told her mother, 'We think she has running away blood in her, and is bound to really do it one day.'[66] While they were driving back from the airport there was an uncomfortable silence, which was broken by Constancia asking her grandmother, 'Granny Muv, when are you going to scold Decca for running away?' Her question made everyone laugh so much they all relaxed.[67]

During Lady Redesdale's visit, Constancia remembers observing as her mother and grandmother talked to each other:

It was just a little tableau. Imagine a child playing with dolls and here's a doll that is Lady Redesdale, just sitting there on the sofa trying to make sense of it all. One thing is, I had a hard time understanding what they were saying because of their accents. In those situations, it was me watching a tennis match as an observer.[68]

Inevitably, there were some tense moments, but it was an opportunity to work through long-held resentments. Jessica reminded her mother about how much she had wanted to go to school. As she told Muv, all the old fury and frustration welled up in her and she burst into tears. Their discussion revealed that Sydney had spent time analysing where she went wrong in her children's upbringing. She finally admitted that it had been a mistake not to let Jessica go to school, explaining, 'At the time, you see, all my worries were about the older children; you and Bobo and Debo seemed quite safe and happy in the schoolroom.'[69]

The visit went much better than Jessica could have hoped. Lady Redesdale got on very well with Jessica's husband, Bob, who found her 'directness and lack of guile were baffling and a constant source of wonder'.[70] Jessica had money in her Drummonds bank account in London which had not been transferred to her in America because of currency restrictions. She asked her mother to see if she could persuade the bank manager to release the funds. When he asked Lady Redesdale why Jessica required the money, she was completely honest and told him her daughter would probably give the money to the Communist Party. Shocked, Drummonds' manager refused the request.[71] On a less important matter, Bob was also surprised when his mother-in-law was equally blunt after Jessica put on her glasses. Muv asked, 'Why are you wearing those hideous spectacles, Little D?'[72] Rather than taking it the wrong way, Jessica realised that Sydney was just saying what she thought, not meaning to be critical. Muv relished being with her daughter's family. She taught Constancia how to knit and was amused by Nicholas saying 'Okay' to everything she asked him.

Looking back on her grandmother's visit decades later, Constancia thinks coming to America must have been a strange experience for Sydney. She explains, 'The circumstances in which we were living were so unrelated to anything Muv had probably ever experienced before. We grew up in a lower-middle-class neighbourhood in Oakland. We had one car, my mother was working for the Civil Rights Congress.'[73] To everyone's surprise, Lady Redesdale embraced her daughter's new life with enthusiasm. She thought Oakland was like a musical comedy set and she praised everything and everyone she met.[74] She did not care that the house was untidy or that there was no wardrobe in her bedroom for her clothes, so she had to put them on the piano. She even enjoyed visiting a supermarket, and approved of it so much that, on her return to England, she wrote to *The Times* suggesting that similar stores should be introduced in England.[75] Having read Evelyn Waugh's novel *The Loved One*, a satirical look at the funeral business in Los Angeles, Muv wanted to see an American funeral parlour.[76] Jessica did what she requested but when she told her friends where she had taken her mother sight-seeing, they were 'horrified'.[77]

Even mother and daughter's very different politics did not prove to be a problem. Working for the Civil Rights Congress, which had been created by communist leaders after the war to establish civil liberties for black people in America, Jessica was dedicating much of her time to fighting against racial prejudice.[78] Although it was a world away from

Muv's beliefs, to Jessica's surprise, her right-wing mother got on exceptionally well with her communist friends.

Lady Redesdale was delighted with how the trip had gone. When she got back to England, she met up with Nanny Blor and told her all about her visit. Loyal as ever to her former employer, Blor wrote to Jessica, 'Don't you think it was splendid of her to fly out to see you? I thought she looked so well when she came back and very delighted to have been with you.'[79] After the visit, Jessica revised her opinion of her mother. She wrote, 'My fondness for Muv, and my appreciation of her remarkable qualities dated from this visit to Oakland.'[80] She told Sydney that they had all enjoyed having her tremendously. She added that the children 'still talk constantly about Grandma Redesdale and how you weren't the mad English type after all'.[81]

Shortly after her return from America, Sydney was faced with another family crisis. In May 1948, while mother and daughter were staying at Inch Kenneth, Unity developed a feverish cold. There was no telephone on the island and rough seas prevented a doctor from reaching them for several days. By the time he arrived Unity was worse, suffering from a severe headache and sickness. One morning she woke up and said, 'I'm coming,' which worried her mother. Despite medication, her temperature did not come down and the scar from her bullet wound on her temple became tender. When she was diagnosed with meningitis, there was a desperate dash to the mainland involving a nightmare journey which Sydney would never talk about afterwards. When they arrived at the cottage hospital in Oban, Unity was given penicillin, but it was too late. The doctors could not save her.[82] She died on 28 May 1948, aged thirty-three.

Lord Redesdale immediately travelled up to Scotland to support his wife. The couple returned together on the sleeper train, accompanying the coffin down to Swinbrook. On a bright late spring day, the Redesdales and their family gathered at the ancient village church.[83] One of Unity's favourite pastimes had been planning her own funeral, pondering which hymns she would like and changing them according to her mood.[84] Muv followed her wishes and during the service the family favourite, 'Holy, Holy, Holy, Lord God Almighty' was sung.

Diana described it as the saddest day of her life.[85] Rather than face the reality of her sorrow, Lady Redesdale remained defiant, making it sound as though her daughter was a heroine who had died fighting the good fight. For Unity's tombstone, Sydney chose a line from the Victorian poet Arthur Hugh Clough, 'Say not the struggle naught availeth.'[86] Perhaps she was trying to convince herself that it had all been worthwhile.

Even when she was in the depths of grief, Sydney still defended her daughter. On 2 June a letter from her was published in the *Daily Mail*, challenging an obituary the newspaper had run on Unity. She emphasised that her daughter should not be seen as a tragic figure. According to her, at the start of the war it was untrue that Unity had contacted Hitler and he had refused to see her. The reason her daughter had tried to kill herself was not personal; it was because the idea of war between the two countries she loved was intolerable to her. When Hitler visited her in hospital, he had offered to give her German nationality, but she turned it down. Lady Redesdale wrote, 'she never renounced her nation or her family, and was never cast off by anyone.'[87]

Diana believed that Unity was probably Muv's favourite child.[88] Having looked after her daughter for eight years, Unity's death left a huge gap in Lady Redesdale's life. Nanny Blor wrote to Jessica, 'I'm afraid she is terribly shattered now by the death of Bobo and that she will miss her for a long time. She has been simply wonderful in her devotion and in trying to make her life as happy as possible.'[89] Lady Redesdale had expected to die before her daughter, so the loss came as a shock. She told Jessica, 'Just now I feel completely at a loose end and my life seems wonderfully useless.'[90] She hoped her dead daughter and only son were reunited. She wrote to James Lees-Milne, 'If there is anywhere they can be together she must be with Tom now and her other good friends.' She also took comfort in something Unity had said to her when she was ill: 'No one ever had such a happy young life as I did up to the war.'[91]

15

The Last Goodbye

After Unity's death, Jessica was concerned that her mother would be lonely, but characteristically Sydney coped well.[1] Once her initial grief passed, there was relief that she no longer had to worry about who would look after her daughter when she died.[2] She also finally had the peace which had eluded her while Unity was alive. Nanny Blor was aware of the pressure it had put on Lady Redesdale; she wrote to Jessica about Unity, 'One is thankful that she is at rest for one never knew where her restlessness might lead her.'[3] In her final years, descriptions of Sydney usually describe her as relaxed and laughing. The unsmiling figure of the past had been transformed and most of her daughters believed she had mellowed. Perhaps only now, at the end of her life, could she really relax, because she no longer felt responsible for all the demanding characters in her family who had taken up so much of her time and energy. Finally, she could just think of her own needs, without having to withdraw emotionally to protect her inner peace.

As her daughters were living around the world, Muv kept in contact with them through occasional visits and regular letters. Lady Redesdale's letters were carefully written to avoid offending whichever daughter she was writing to. As Jessica explained, her mother exhibited 'that impartial loyalty to all her children that was to become a salient characteristic of her old age'.[4] The woman who had never cared what people thought of her had become the ultimate

people-pleaser within her family. She knew her children well enough
to give each one what they wanted from her. When Jessica regaled
her with stories of her civil rights campaigning, she just listened
and never criticised. She handled them all so skilfully that each of
her daughters thought she approved of what they were doing. Both
Diana and Jessica also believed that their mother loved and admired
their husbands, although the right-wing Oswald Mosley and the left-
wing Bob Treuhaft could not have been more different ideologically.[5]
To a degree, it was true: she did like her sons-in-law, but as Sydney's
grandson Jonathan explained, being polite and supportive did not
imply a surrender of her own views.[6] She had just learnt when it was
best to keep her real opinions to herself.

Constancia wonders how accurate a reflection of her grandmother
her correspondence really is. She explains:

> If you read these letters the writer falls into a certain style, a conven-
> tion of letter writing, and I don't know how much one can deduce
> of the true feeling of the person behind them. After all she was the
> Mum of these five girls and she wanted a relationship, we all want to
> maintain a relationship with our children when they are grown up no
> matter how different they may turn out from us.[7]

Physical distance helped to improve the relationship between Jessica
and Lady Redesdale. Now Jessica had an independent life in America,
the balance of power had changed between them and so they met
on totally different terms.[8] Later, after her mother's death, Jessica
wrote to Nancy, 'After re-getting to know her after 1955, I became
immensely fond of her, really rather adored her. Therefore, in my
memory she turns into two people; I'm sure she didn't change much
because people don't except for a certain mellowing with the onset of
old age.' Rather than her mother altering, Jessica thought she herself
had changed.[9] The woman who comes across in Lady Redesdale's letters is unrecognisable from the cold, vague parent Jessica remembered
from her childhood. Sydney's tone with her daughter was supportive
and loving. Relating to each other as adults and fellow mothers, they

became great friends. Constancia explains, 'I think Muv was very reserved, but once people were gone, in the letters, she was able to lose some of that reserve.'[10]

Finally, Sydney was able to admit what she had really felt. Rather than the detachment which made her daughters feel she did not care as they were growing up, a different picture emerges; Sydney's cool exterior was masking her constant anxiety about them. She told Jessica, 'Children are the most awful worry – at least to me. You are lucky not to worry much.'[11] In another letter she explained further, writing, 'I do think one goes through times of such great worry with one's children. And especially when they are just growing up. [...] What they do then may probably influence the rest of their lives.' Over the years she had reflected deeply on what went wrong in their relationships. She added, 'All our anxieties at that time were for Nancy and Diana, and poor you and Debo seemed safe for some time to come. Parents of course never do know what is going on in their children's minds, and that makes it all still more difficult.'[12]

During the 1950s, the Cold War era in America, Jessica faced worries of her own. As communists and civil rights campaigners during the McCarthyite era in America, Bob and Jessica were particularly vulnerable. In 1951, Jessica helped organise a campaign to save a black truck driver who had been condemned to death for raping a white woman in Mississippi. Due to the Treuhafts' involvement in this case, they were subpoenaed by the House Committee on Un-American Activities, and Joseph McCarthy described Bob as one of the most subversive lawyers in America.[13] Jessica and Bob feared they might be imprisoned for their political activities. When her son-in-law warned Sydney of the situation, she replied laconically that it would be a shame, but then of course she was used to seeing her daughters put in prison.[14]

As well as political challenges, the Treuhafts experienced personal tragedy. In February 1955, Jessica's ten-year-old son Nicholas was killed in an accident. He was a paper boy and, one afternoon, he was struck by a bus while riding his bike home. Jessica coped with the tragedy in the same way as her mother: she repressed her emotions and just carried on. In the immediate aftermath, she reassured Muv that she was all right and her other children, Dinky and Ben, made it bearable.[15] Like Sydney, she could not cope with sympathy.[16] She did not refer to her son's death in her letters to her sisters or her memoirs.[17] Lady Redesdale understood her daughter, and when she wrote to her, she did not say much because there was nothing to say. Having lost two children herself, she knew what her daughter was going through. Repeating the same phrase she had used when she wrote to Jessica after Esmond's untimely death, she wrote, 'You are very brave, but I always knew you were that.'[18]

Shortly after the tragedy, Jessica returned to England for the first time since before the war, with her husband and daughter. Jessica and Bob had wanted to visit five years beforehand, but they had been unable to travel because they had difficulty obtaining passports due to their membership of the Communist Party. Jessica had wanted her mother to appeal to Winston Churchill about it, but Lady Redesdale refused to ask him for favours.[19] Once she was allowed to travel, Jessica was keen to see her mother and certain members of her family. During her 1955 visit, she stayed with Sydney at Inch Kenneth and in London. Meeting her mother on home territory, Jessica saw Muv from a different perspective and, for the first time, she felt sorry for her. She later told Nancy, 'I could see what an incredibly thin time she had had, on the whole, in life.'[20] However, her relationship with her mother and sisters was always better when it was conducted through letters rather than in person. Constancia recalls the encounters, 'There was always some level of tension when my mother was with her family. I picked up on the tension. Again, my memories of that are a pretty stiff situation between Dec [Jessica] and Muv.'

As a teenager Constancia, like her mother, did not feel she had much in common with her grandmother and her English family. She realises how different her mother's upbringing was from her own. 'I grew up in such a totally different environment than my mother and cousins. [...] Their lives seemed like a novel or a fairytale, I couldn't really comprehend it.' Describing her mother and herself as 'prickly', Constancia says, 'Everybody was trying to be very nice to me, but I was critical of their class. I fancied myself a rebellious revolutionary working for justice in the United States and these people were about as far removed from that as it was possible to be.'[21] During their stay, there was a heated argument, when Jessica noticed on Sydney's engagement pad that she had arranged a lunch with the Mosleys the following week. Furious, Jessica said she would not eat with 'murderers', while Lady Redesdale retorted that she should not call her sister a murderer.[22] With the Atlantic between them they were compatible; in the same country they were not. Even though her grandmother had written enthusiastically about wanting to see her, Constancia never found Granny Muv to be a warm character. She explains, 'My image of Muv is this kind of remote matriarch but, again, that's in the context of this uneasy tension between her and my mother, so I imagine that if I had spent more time with her, I would have seen the caring, nurturing side of her.' Instead, she witnessed the more uncompromising aspect of her grandmother's personality. When they were staying in Lady Redesdale's London mews house in Rutland Gate, one day the three women were supposed to go on an outing together. Constancia went out for a walk and arrived back at the house five minutes after the designated time. Her mother and grandmother had left and locked the front door, so, as Constancia did not have a key, she decided to sit and wait for several hours until they came back. When Jessica returned, she told her daughter, 'When Muv says twelve o clock she means twelve o clock, not a minute past.'[23] Lady Redesdale's memories of the visit were more positive than her granddaughter's. She described it as 'one of the happy moments of my life'.[24] Her other daughters knew just how much she had looked forward to it.[25] When Jessica and Constancia had gone home, she wrote to them, 'Oh dear I do miss you both, it is quiet and dull and no chatting or "SCRABBLE." [...] We did have a lovely time when you and Dinky were here.'[26]

Sadly, Jessica did not see her father during her trip to England. They had not met since her elopement nearly two decades earlier. Sydney acted as go-between, but neither side seemed able to make the compromises necessary to put the past completely behind them. When Jessica told Sydney she would only see her father if he agreed not 'to roar at' her husband and daughter, Lady Redesdale replied that if she was going to lay down conditions it would be better that she did not see Farve.[27] It was the last opportunity for a reconciliation and it was missed.

Lord Redesdale's health was deteriorating, and his arthritis was making him increasingly immobile. When Sydney saw him, she asked, 'Oh dear, I hope you are not in pain?' He replied, 'Oh no, I am under drugs,' which horrified his wife, who disapproved of most medicines. Luckily it was not as bad as she thought: when she quizzed him about what he was taking, he said, 'I've been taking an aspirin,' which put her mind at rest.[28] Lady Redesdale still found it inexplicable that her husband should choose to live in a small cottage with Margaret rather than at Inch Kenneth with her. She complained to Nancy that his Northumberland home did not seem comfortable, and she did not think Farve got enough to eat. Whatever his wife thought, Lord Redesdale never complained, and if there was any criticism of Margaret he defended her.[29] When it was Lord and Lady Redesdale's golden wedding, Aunt Weenie contacted her nieces, ordering them to come to London to celebrate. Nancy refused thinking it was a ridiculous idea, joking to Diana that it must be at least his silver anniversary with Margaret.[30]

Lord Redesdale always treated his wife with respect even though he did not wish to live with her again. She still received an allowance from him, but in the mid-1950s there was a discussion between them about whether he could still afford to pay her it. He reassured her that no change would be made if he could possibly avoid it, although it would depend on rises in income tax and surtax. He promised that, if necessary, he would sell off some of the family diamonds to make sure he could continue financing her.[31] Her letter to him shows how dependent her financial position was on other people. Rather than complain, she asked her husband to give her as much notice as possible if he had to cut her allowance so that she could leave the island. She added that she was very grateful to him and the children for allowing her to live on Inch Kenneth for so many years. As for the family diamonds, she knew that as soon as her husband died, they would pass to his heir, his brother Tommy. Even her diamond ring, brooch and two small clips were not her own.[32] It was a humbling position for such an independent woman to be in after she had dedicated her life to the Mitford family, but it was due to archaic aristocratic rules of inheritance rather than the fault of her husband.*

Shortly before Lord Redesdale died, Sydney visited him with Diana and Debo to celebrate his eightieth birthday. He had become very fragile and could hardly get out of bed, but he was delighted to see them.[33] Diana wrote about witnessing her father's joy at seeing her mother. Together for the last time, all their disagreements were forgotten and it was as if they had gone back two decades to the happy times before tragedies tore the family apart.[34] The elderly couple spent hours together, with their two daughters popping in and out. It was a poignant meeting for Sydney. She wrote, 'He was quite like his old self, and we had a most happy day, he was really so pleased to see us and said some funny things and we all laughed.' Before she left to travel up to Inch Kenneth, his final words to her were, 'Are you going to Oban?' When she said yes, he replied, 'Oh! – Remember me to the Hall Porter.' Three days later, on 17 March 1958, Lord Redesdale died. After his cremation in Northumberland, his ashes were buried in Swinbrook churchyard. Following the service, the woman who had been his wife for more than half a century wrote, 'All is much changed, and all the family. It was so sad. But Farve was terribly weary and tired and had no interest left in life.'[35]

When Farve's will did not leave anything to Jessica, because he was concerned that she might give it to the Communist Party, Muv was worried that her daughter would be upset. She was relieved when Jessica reassured her that she did not mind.[36] Nancy also felt her father's will was unfair, so she decided to try to redress the balance by giving her share of Inch Kenneth to Jessica.[37] She joked to her mother that Jessica would probably use the island to build an Atom Bomb Base and they would see the Russian leader, Nikita Khrushchev, visiting soon, but she

---

* In fact, Lady Redesdale had more money than this exchange of letters suggests. In her will she left £750,000 in today's money. Once again, Lord and Lady Redesdale seem to have underestimated their wealth. Email from Charlotte Mosley, 22 January 2025.

was willing to take the risk.[38] Lord Redesdale's death left his wife worse off financially. As the Redesdales' only son was dead and their daughters could not inherit the title, family heirlooms, including jewellery and antique furniture, now passed to Farve's heir, Tommy. Auctioneers came to the mews house and Inch Kenneth to price up several pieces of the French furniture.[39] Fortunately, prudent as ever, Sydney had been putting aside a little money each year for when she was widowed. To increase her income, whenever she went away, Muv rented out the mews house.[40] For a time, she wondered if she could afford to continue living on Inch Kenneth. To put her mother's mind at rest, Jessica came to the rescue: she had inherited some money from the Romilly family and told Sydney that she would gladly share her fortune with her.[41] She knew how much her mother loved the island and believed that Muv would just 'fade away' if she ever had to leave.[42] In 1959, she bought out her sisters' shares of Inch Kenneth and let Muv live there rent-free for the rest of her life.[43] Diana and Debo only agreed to the arrangement for their mother's sake.[44]

16

The Final Voyage

In her final years, Sydney was on good terms with all her children, but remnants of the old dynamics remained. Nancy identified with her father and his side of the family more than her mother and her relatives. She admitted that she had some of her grandfather Tommy Bowles's blood in her veins; she never minded people attacking her books because it was good for sales, but she wished she was less like him.[1] She told Diana that she hated their Bowles relatives and wished she did not have any of their acidic blood running through her. She made an exception about her mother but added that even she could be unpleasant.[2] Diana agreed about Grandfather Bowles, writing that she also did not care for him, although she remembered from her childhood that he had been highly intelligent and good company. Unlike Nancy, she added that she loved his descendants.[3]

Occasionally, Nancy would lash out at Muv, bringing up the past to attack her. When it was taking Nancy a long time to finish an essay, she told Diana to tell their mother it was because she had not given her any education.[4] These remarks did not upset Lady Redesdale much because she was used to Nancy's barbs, and when Nancy was unpleasant Sydney just commented that her eldest daughter was 'a very curious character'.[5] She added that there was always 'a small knife concealed somewhere' in each of her letters.[6]

Sydney could also be sharp-tongued, and she was more critical of her eldest daughter than her other children. When, in May 1958, General de Gaulle became leader of France, Lady Redesdale wrote, 'Nancy is in Seventh Heaven over de Gaulle and has become almost like Bobo [Unity]. Odd how my children admire and love dictators.'[7] Nor did she always approve of her daughter's writing. When there was a furore over Nancy's essay on the English aristocracy, which claimed the upper classes were defined by their use of language, and she labelled a word either 'U', if it was upper class or 'Non-U' if it was lower class. Lady Redesdale described it scathingly as 'nonsense'.[8] Sydney subtly had a dig at her snobbish daughter in one of her letters by using the words 'writing paper', then correcting herself to 'notepaper' because, as she pointed out, that was more appropriate language for her as she was of middle-class, not upper-class, origins.[9] Nor did she approve when Nancy claimed in an interview to hate America and Americans. Her daughter's comments made her laugh, but Lady Redesdale thought she was being absurd and unkind. She told Jessica, 'I don't know any Americans except all of you, and you I happen to like.'[10]

Although Jessica and Sydney's relationship had drastically improved, old resentments also occasionally re-emerged. Following in Nancy's footsteps, Jessica wrote a memoir of her childhood, *Hons and Rebels*, which explains why she became so estranged from her family. When Jessica showed Lady Redesdale the book before it was published, she was nervous. To her relief, Muv seemed positive about it and only made a few corrections. She asked Jessica to remove a few points which might be hurtful and information which was inaccurate. She explained that the governess was paid £120 a year, not £100, and she did not want to be quoted as saying the Conservative Member of Parliament in Oxfordshire had been 'such a dull little man' in case it upset him.[11] She was also unhappy that Tom's nickname 'Tuddemy' was included because in her daughters' slang it meant adultery. She did not like anything that showed her beloved son in a bad light. She also pointed out that the 'unheard of treatment' given to Jessica during an illness by her eccentric parent was now recognised and often used in modern medical treatments.[12] Lady Redesdale offered some suggestions which she thought would improve the book. She disliked the title, thinking *Hons and Rebels* sounded snobbish (although 'Hons' was because of the family's hens, not their titles 'the honourables'). Instead, she suggested that the memoir should be called *Red Sheep*. Jessica tactfully told her mother that she agreed with her, but it was too late, and her publishers refused to change it.[13]

When Sydney saw the final version, she told Jessica, 'It is very funny and my laughs were loud and long.' Nonetheless, she was annoyed that her daughter had not taken out the part about the Redesdales being lent a chauffeur-driven Mercedes by Hitler when they were in Germany. She emphasised that they never travelled in anyone's car but their own. As she explained, 'You wouldn't catch Farve in anything but his own Morris.'[14] She was also protective of her late husband, claiming not to recall the silences during meals and adding, 'the picture of him always in a rage is also not a bit true. But it does make a funny book.'[15]

When the book was reviewed, it caused a major row in the family. Most reviews commented on the 'splendid upper-class eccentricities' of the Redesdales. When one critic called Sydney a formidable, self-confessed eccentric, she roared with laughter: she was surprised by the description, adding, 'I always thought I was quite normal.'[16] A few reviewers went much further and attacked Farve and Muv for their inadequate parenting.[17] *The Observer*'s critic described them as 'two very singular parents' and suggested that if they had been 'at the other end of the social scale they might well have been thought unfit to look after their own children'.[18] The *Times Literary Supplement* was even more critical, claiming that Jessica's book described a childhood environment of 'almost incredible aridity – tasteless, stupid, wasteful and idiosyncratic only in its scorn of all intellectual and aesthetic values'. It continued its attack, describing Lord and Lady Redesdale as coming across as 'supremely unpleasant' and 'monsters of arrogance and dullness, whose neglect, in all but a material sense, of their children might well have resulted [...] in alcoholism or the analyst's couch'. It ended by asking whether Jessica connected Farve and Muv's 'egoism, discourtesy and self-satisfaction with the fate of her sisters Unity and Diana'.[19]

Diana was so incensed by the review she wrote a reply to the *Times Literary Supplement* the following week, describing the portraits of her parents as 'grotesque'. She pointed out that there had been plenty of culture available to them, as their childhood was filled with classical music and they had access to 'an exceptionally well-chosen library'.[20] Mrs Hammersley also entered the fray to defend her oldest friend. She called the descriptions of Farve and Muv in the review 'a complete travesty of the truth'. The Mitford children had 'a charming home and, on the face of it, all that the heart could desire'. However, she admitted that Lord and Lady Redesdale were 'sui generis, not to say eccentric', and she put this down to Sydney's upbringing by Tommy Bowles. She concluded that 'the vagaries of the Mitford sisters were due more to heredity than to parental oppression'.[21]

Although she tried to see the funny side of the situation, signing off her next letter to Jessica 'All love Arrogant MUV (dull)', Sydney was upset.[22] She told her daughter that she thought it was 'a horrid review' by someone who seemed to have 'a hearty dislike of Farve and me'.[23] It was not just the reviewer who had hurt her. She resented being portrayed as a snob by Jessica and believed that she had been turned into a laughing stock. It made her feel that all her years of bringing up her family and doing everything that she could for them was treated as just a joke. Suppressing her true feelings, she did not have a row with Jessica about it because she was afraid her daughter would ostracise her.[24] Her failure to confront either of her author daughters directly when their writing upset her lulled them into a false sense of security. It let them think they could continue their 'gently malicious mockery' of her with no consequences.[25] Therefore, it came as a surprise to them when a few years later Sydney finally had enough.

In 1962, a short piece by Nancy about her nanny Blor's strengths and her mother's shortcomings was the last straw. In the essay, which appeared in the Sunday Times and a book, The Water Beetle, Nancy wrote critically about Sydney being an 'abnormally detached' mother, even by the standards of the era. She suggested that Muv did nothing around the house and was unaware of what was going on in the nursery. Adding to the insults, she described her as being badly read and disliking society.[26] Charlotte Mosley, who has edited Nancy's letters, explains the author's motivation: 'I think she had a very unhappy life in a way, and I think her mother was a scapegoat.'[27] However, the essay expressed Nancy's firmly held opinion. A few years later, after Lady Redesdale's death, Nancy told Jessica that she respected her mother and enjoyed her company and jokes, but she had not loved her because she believed Sydney never loved her. In later life, Nancy felt that her mother disliked her and was sarcastic and cold towards her.[28]

When Lady Redesdale read the essay, she was deeply wounded. She wrote that it seemed everything she had done for her children had backfired. This was an awful thought but it could not be put right now.[29] Finally expressing the hurt which had built up over the years, Sydney told both Jessica and Nancy exactly what she thought: her one wish was that they would no longer include her in their books. They could write what they liked after she died, but she resented reading her mad portrayal while she was alive.[30] Nancy tried to excuse herself by saying she thought her mother would find her article funny. She told Deborah that she had always seen her life as 'a hilarious joke', while Sydney had become sentimental about the past.[31]

The other sisters had also had enough. When Nancy and Jessica met up with Pam and moaned about their miserable childhood, Pam flushed and began to cry, telling them that it was simply not true.[32] Diana and Debo agreed with her. They felt very protective of Muv and thought their siblings should not be so cruel now their mother was elderly. Later, Diana explained that she considered her sister's attacks were particularly unfair because, as Nancy was a popular writer of humorous books, the public naturally believed Nancy, while Sydney was unknown to them.[33] Aunt Weenie was also outraged on her elder sister's behalf. When she met Jessica for tea at the mews house, during one of her visits to England, Weenie ignored her niece. But before she left, she demanded a word with her. As they walked to the door, Weenie told Jessica exactly what she thought of her. Calling her 'a filthy little cad', her ageing aunt explained that she would never forgive Jessica for the cruel way she had treated her parents when she eloped. She then berated her for writing a book which was critical of Sydney.[34]

Unlike Nancy and Jessica, Debo always emphasised the positive legacy she had inherited from Muv. She explained that when she became Duchess of Devonshire and chatelaine of Chatsworth, she was inspired by her mother's example to decorate the house herself. As a child, she had watched Sydney transform their homes without interior designers and with less money than many of her friends. She was determined to bring touches of her mother's impeccable taste to the Devonshires' vast house. When Lord Redesdale sold a large dinner service at Sotheby's, which had been bought by a Mitford ancestor from Warren Hastings, Debo had fond memories of her mother using the exquisite china at their debutante dances, so she persuaded her husband to buy it for the Cavendish collection.[35] It was not just china Debo inherited from her mother. Sydney's entrepreneurial spirit was passed on to the next generation, and helped to make the Duchess of Devonshire an impressive businesswoman.

Jessica believed that Debo was their mother's favourite child. She told her youngest sister about how Muv's face lit up when letters from her arrived.[36] The Duchess of Devonshire appreciated her mother's honesty, describing her as the only genuinely truthful person she knew. If she asked her mother for advice, she knew that her answer would be interesting, or at least real.[37] Showing her love and admiration, Debo named her youngest daughter Sophia Louise Sydney after her mother.* Lady Redesdale was so delighted she always insisted on calling her new granddaughter by her full name.[38] Debo included her mother in her life as much as possible, and Sydney thoroughly enjoyed being kept up-to-date by her youngest daughter. A fan of Elvis Presley, Debo asked Muv if she would like to go to a Rock and Roll session. The seventy-eight-year-old leapt at the chance; Muv wrote to Jessica, 'I long to see what it is like, just a good dance I expect.' She approved of the craze because it fitted into her lifelong belief that people should pursue a healthy lifestyle.[39]

Having known the Kennedy family since she was a debutante, Debo became a close friend of Jack Kennedy during his presidency. As Lady Redesdale had talent-spotted Jack in his youth, prophesying that he would become president, she enjoyed hearing about their friendship.

---

* Born March 1957.

In January 1961, Debo and her husband Andrew were invited to attend Kennedy's inauguration. They received a warm reception in Washington, staying at the British Embassy and attending many parties. During the inauguration Debo was invited by the president to sit next to him during the march-past, while Jackie Kennedy had gone for a rest.[40] When a photograph of Debo and the president sitting together appeared in *Life* magazine, Sydney admitted to Jessica that her youngest daughter looked 'half frozen' because she did not realise the whole event would be outside and she had not brought enough warm clothes with her from England.[41]

Diana was also devoted to her mother. Like Jessica, her attitude to Sydney had changed over the years. She told her cousin that in her youth they had sometimes been at odds, but what her mother had meant to her since the war no one would ever know.[42] Diana's son Jonathan thinks his mother and grandmother were very similar. He explains, 'People were often slightly intimidated by them. They had presence and could sometimes come across as cold to people who didn't know them well.' He adds that the older they got the closer they became, and they visited each other as often as possible.[43] When they were both in London, Diana tried to see her mother every day. Lady Redesdale used to meet up with Diana and Debo at Harrods bank. The two sisters would sit either side of her on the sofa, shouting out the latest gossip to amuse her.[44] Diana's husband Oswald Mosley also got on very well with his mother-in-law, and she was his favourite out of all his wife's family.[45] Sydney continued to admire him politically. When Mosley stood for Parliament as a Union Movement candidate in North Kensington in 1959, calling for restrictions on black immigration, Sydney loyally attended his meetings.[46]

Whether they acknowledged it or not, Sydney passed on many of her characteristics to her descendants. As Diana's daughter-in-law Charlotte says, 'All of them had terrific courage, and faced up to the things life threw at them, or the things that they had created in their lives. None of the sisters were complainers. I think that came from her.'[47] Jessica's son Ben Treuhaft has found some of the family traits less positive. He explains, 'Muv was supposed to be quite distant from the children. I always figured my inability to be intimate with people comes from my Mum. It's in my blood, I think it's genetic.' Ben used to enjoy spending time with his friend's family because it was so different from his own home. He adds, 'They were just so loving and demonstrative and so relaxed basically. Unlike my family that was not relaxed.'[48]

In her last years, Lady Redesdale was happiest at Inch Kenneth. Her daughters felt that the island had become part of her.[49] Despite knowing how essential her Scottish home was to her wellbeing, they were worried it was becoming too much for her and suggested she should move back to a house in Swinbrook. Lady Redesdale responded by quoting her father, Thomas. When Sydney prepared a comfortable lodge on their estate for him to live in, he had rejected it explaining: 'Two voices there are. One is of the mountains, one the sea, each a mighty voice. The "lodge" has neither. I cannot live there.' His daughter felt the same.[50]

Living in the rambling house and keeping cattle, sheep and goats, she would arrive on the island in the spring when the daffodils were coming out. She enjoyed being surrounded by animals, but she stopped keeping bullocks because she hated seeing them sent off to be killed and instead started a stud of Shetland ponies.[51] The only other people on the island were Mr and Mrs MacGillivray, the boatman and his wife; Mr and Mrs Campbell, the gardener and cook; and Betty, the parlourmaid.[52] During the months when Lady Redesdale did not have guests staying, she sometimes felt lonely. If she spotted, through her binoculars, day-trippers coming across to the island, she would often invite them in for tea. It was a lottery what they were like, but she seemed to enjoy the gamble.[53] The long evenings were spent playing Scrabble by herself, listening to the news on the wireless, or reading the latest books. She liked history and biographies best but admitted that she found books about the war hard to read.[54] Alone with her thoughts, she was surrounded by memories of the past, from the familiar furniture she had brought from Swinbrook to the scrapbooks she kept chronicling family events.[55]

Her children and grandchildren tried to see her as often as possible. As the house had ten bedrooms and four bathrooms, there was plenty of room for her ever-expanding family, which now also included great-grandchildren.[56] Furnished in her favourite eighteenth-century French style, it was run like a luxurious country house hotel. The linen was sent by train to be laundered at Harrods, and groceries from the store's Food Hall supplemented the delicious local produce. Even Sydney's library books came from London.[57] Pamela believed that the true charm of the island completely depended on Muv; the way she organised it created a quiet peace where nothing seemed to go wrong, and nothing mattered providing everyone was happy and enjoying themselves.[58]

For all the comfort on offer, not everyone was willing to make the long journey to Scotland. Sydney admitted that going by sleeper train from London to Oban was 'truly terrible' as in the winter the heating sometimes did not work.[59] Blunt as ever, her sister Weenie described travelling to the island as 'like marriage [...] not to be taken in hand lightly or wantonly [...] but [...] advisedly, soberly and in the fear of God'.[60] Nor did Nancy enjoy her Scottish holidays. The chic, Dior-clad writer dismissed her mother's remote home as 'Wuthering Heights'. She loathed the unpredictable weather and rugged landscape.[61] She also usually ended up having a row with Muv about politics as Lady Redesdale still made pro-German comments.[62] Lady Redesdale knew what Nancy felt and, shortly before one of her visits, she wrote apprehensively to Jessica, '[I] have warned her she will be terribly bored as there's only me and nothing to do and nowhere to go, anyhow she's fairly warned.'[63] Diana later discussed with Debo how 'vile' Nancy sometimes was to Sydney. She recalled her elder sister unkindly complaining about the superb food her mother served.[64] Nancy moaned that Muv's helpings were too small, but Lady Redesdale retaliated by telling her eldest daughter to go back to France if she was starving.[65] Nancy's remarks harked back to her belief that her mother underfed her as a child, setting her up for the health problems she suffered from in later life.[66] Diana believed that her elder sister was just being unpleasant for the sake of it and to upset Sydney.[67]

Lady Redesdale's grandchildren and great-grandchildren remember idyllic holidays spent with her on Inch Kenneth. She drove them across Mull in her 1930 Morris at top speed, like a New York cab driver, honking at any vehicle which got in her way.[68] Once on her island, she swam with them in the icy waters most days. Having loved the sea since her childhood, Inch Kenneth was the next best thing to living on a boat.[69] If the seas were rough and it was pouring with rain she would just put on her oilskins and still go out in her boat, *The Puffin*, shouting to her queasy companions, 'Great fun, isn't it?'[70] She enjoyed being surrounded by young people and they loved being with her. Her great-granddaughter, Marina Guinness, has happy memories of staying with her on the island every summer. 'She was very deaf by then and she taught me to play scrabble, which I still love,' she remembers. A real bond developed between the elderly lady and the little girl. Marina adds, 'She was the first person to die that I loved.'[71]

When Jessica and her son came to Britain for a visit, Ben also enjoyed his time on the island.* He became friends with the boatman, Mr MacGillivray's son. As they went around the island together, he used to show Ben where the seagull's eggs could be found. Jessica got on well with Mr and Mrs MacGillivray, too, feeling that they provided 'an incongruous note of sanity in this fairly nutty place'.[72] When Jessica asked her son what he thought of his grandmother, he told her, 'I love Muv, she's exactly like you, always roaring and awfully vague.'[73] Decades later, Ben remembers Lady Redesdale as being 'a nice doddery old lady. I can picture her in Scottish tweed.' Her outward appearance was different from the way she came across to the little boy and, like his sister, he did not find her a warm granny figure, partly because he was influenced by Jessica's feelings towards her. He explains:

My impression of her was completely ruled by my mother's actual impressions of her. She used to impersonate Muv saying 'Ohhr dear, Ohrr dear.' She also told us stories about her. Muv was very deaf and one day when she was crossing from Oban to Mull on the ferry with her friend Lady So-and-So, Muv thought they were just making polite chit-chat. Actually, her friend had said that her best friend

---

*   They came in 1959.

had just died unexpectedly, but, Muv said 'Ohrr lovely, lovely.' She couldn't hear a thing.[74]

During the winter, Muv lived in London, where Diana, Debo, Nancy and Pam visited her regularly. Her circle and routine had hardly changed over the years. At nine o'clock every weekday morning she rushed out of the house immediately after breakfast for Harrods' opening.[75] As she became less mobile, she thought about getting a motorised wheelchair. Her daughters joked that it should be called the 'Racing Bath Chair' and have a side seat for her dachshund, Jose, and it should be programmed to just whizz down the Brompton Road to Harrods. Unfortunately, it never materialised, but the thought of it gave them all a good laugh.[76] In London, Lady Redesdale enjoyed hosting small lunches or tea parties for her friends. She regularly saw Violet Hammersley and Geoffrey, while Nanny Blor occasionally visited. Weenie came to stay with her for long periods and enjoyed it so much she bought a flat virtually next door in Rutland Gate. Their brother George had died of a coronary in 1954, but the sisters remained close to his widow, Madeleine. When she also bought a flat in Knightsbridge, Sydney said they formed 'quite a colony'.[77]

As the older generation gradually died out, Sydney became friends with the younger one. Lady Redesdale's niece, Julia's husband, David Budworth, who only knew his wife's aunt in her old age, thought she was an exceptional person. He considered her to be 'far more clever and beautiful than any of her daughters. Far more graceful too.'[78] The granddaughter of Tello and Thomas, Madeau Stewart was a particular favourite. The younger woman shared Sydney's birthday and her sense of humour. Using the German term from Goethe's novel, Diana claimed that there was a '*Wahlverwandtschaften*' between them, meaning an elective affinity or that they were kindred by choice.[79] Lady Redesdale often invited Madeau up to Inch Kenneth to stay. Both women were musical and, in the evenings, Madeau would play the flute while Sydney accompanied her on the piano. The flautist would sometimes sit on the rocks playing 'Danny Boy' and J.S. Bach to the appreciative seals.[80] Madeau worked for the BBC's Sound Archives and made programmes about music. When she decided to record one of her sessions with the seals for the radio, the press was interested. Lady Redesdale agreed to journalists coming to the island, but she refused to give an interview or be photographed. From bitter experience, she was wary of how she would be portrayed. She wrote to Madeau, 'I suppose it will all be arranged to show the Mad Mitfords at their maddest with a completely lunatic parent.'[81]

Madeau enjoyed Lady Redesdale's company and recalled that they had great fun together because they shared a delight in the absurd. One day when they went rowing around the island, the dog fell in the water, the boat nearly overturned and then they crashed into the bank. The two women saw the funny side and became helpless with laughter. On another occasion, when a storm suddenly blew up, Madeau nearly got swept out to sea. Lady Redesdale could not stop laughing and joked that her guest would probably have ended up in Mexico. Muv found this idea so funny that she lent Madeau several books about Montezuma, presumably, in preparation for subsequent storms.[82]

In her late seventies Lady Redesdale was diagnosed with Parkinson's disease. When her oldest friend Violet Hammersley heard, she could not resist saying to Sydney, 'What about the good body now?'[83] Muv was equally caustic about 'the Wid', writing to Jessica, 'She is well over eighty and been ill all her life, but always turns up for anything she wants to do.'[84] These barbs were just part of their repartee, and their friendship ran deep. Mrs Hammersley told Jessica that Sydney was 'a very dear friend through the last distance of years – never changing and tied by a hundred memories'.[85] A symptom of Lady Redesdale's illness was shaking hands, which made writing and playing the piano increasingly hard, but overall she remained fit and independent. In her late seventies she still swam in the sea every day during the summer and enjoyed walks around the island.[86] She took a keen interest in the farm animals and still chased the goats with her umbrella.[87] As the disease progressed, she became increasingly unsteady on her feet, so her daughters gave her a whistle to take with her to summon help if necessary. One day, Sydney fell in some deep mud and could not get herself up. Fortunately, after half an hour her boatman's sheep dog found her and fetched help. When she heard the story, Nancy reacted in her usual humorous way, telling her mother that mud baths were very beneficial, but she would not advise her in the future to 'Wallow and Whistle'.[88]

When Lady Redesdale's tremors worsened, her daughters made her see a doctor, who gave her some tablets to help.[89] Inevitably, old habits died hard, as Sydney's great-granddaughter Marina explains, 'Someone thought that she should go to the mainland and occasionally see a doctor. On the way back in the small rowing boat she would fling whatever pills she had been given overboard.'[90] She still preferred her own eccentric remedies for illnesses, leaving the 'good body' to heal itself. When Jessica told her mother she sometimes got cramp in her feet, Muv put a potato in her bed – to her sceptical daughter's surprise, it seemed to work.[91] Lady Redesdale had become so deaf that she could hardly hear a word in conversations. Jessica got her a modern hearing aid, but it remained on the shelf because Lady Redesdale refused to use it. She told her daughter that her health problems were 'just Nature's warnings that it is time to step off the stage'.[92]

When Sydney turned eighty in May 1960, she wrote to Jessica that, as an octogenarian, 'one begins to feel quite grown up'.[93] She told Nancy that at her age you did not mind about anything anymore.[94] However, Sydney admitted that it was odd to find herself and her contemporaries had become so old.[95] Her daughters found it difficult, too. Diana wrote that she could hardly bear to contemplate that one day her mother would no longer be alive. When she took her mother to the airport after a trip to Paris, Diana had a premonition that it would be Sydney's last visit to France, and she was blinded with tears.[96] Debo confessed to her older sister that she felt the same. Knowing the time they had left with their mother was coming to an end, she found it painful leaving Muv, and felt sad that she was getting old. The woman who had always been so self-contained now seemed reluctant to let her daughter go.[97]

While in London in October 1962, Sydney was involved in a car crash. She was the only person hurt, but she suffered a deep wound which bled heavily. Characteristically, after being put in an ambulance, she insisted on getting out again and taking a taxi because she did not want to be kept in hospital overnight and wanted to go home. Although her face was in a mess and she had a black eye, the doctor pleased her by just dressing the wound and then not looking at it again for ten days, leaving the 'Good Body' to heal itself.[98] She spent Christmas in London with Weenie rather than travelling up to Chatsworth. By April 1963, she was well enough to go with Nancy to the wedding of Princess Alexandra to Angus Ogilvy, followed by a ball at Windsor. Dressed in black velvet, lace and diamonds, Sydney was described by her daughter as the most elegant woman there.[99]

In one of her final letters to Jessica, Sydney acknowledged that she was becoming frail and that her lifestyle would have to change. She explained that she was increasingly vague and found it hard to remember anything. She had not invited many guests to the island because it was too much effort.[100] Her daughters did not want her to go to the island and they tried to persuade her to spend the summer with Pam in Gloucestershire instead, but Lady Redesdale was determined to go.[101] In early May, Madeau Stewart agreed to travel with her. As there was no restaurant car on the sleeper train, they brought sandwiches and a small bottle of claret, on Weenie's suggestion.[102] It was a tiring journey: Sydney could not sleep on the overnight train, then there was a rough Hebridean crossing to the island. When Muv arrived, she felt so ill that she went straight to bed to rest and stayed there until the following day. At dinner she choked badly, then during the night she woke her maid, who was sleeping in the adjoining room, wondering where she was. Knowing she was increasingly unwell, Lady Redesdale said that she would like to see her doctor, Flora MacDonald. After examining her, Dr MacDonald recognised that she was in the final stages of Parkinson's disease.[103] Madeau telephoned the sisters and told them the situation. Pam, Nancy and Diana hurried up to Inch Kenneth and Debo joined them later. Diana's grandchildren, Patrick and Marina Guinness, aged five and six, also stayed. Two nurses joined them on the island to provide round-the-clock care.

As Sydney's birthday was on 10 May, the family used the pretext of celebrating the occasion to explain their arrival.[104] They could not deceive their mother and, frank as ever, Sydney told them that of course she knew why they had come – she was dying.[105] The sisters endured a gruelling fortnight on the remote island, watching as their mother fought her final battle. Gales set in, so for a few days they were cut off from the mainland. Isolated together, it was like being in a novel, as Madeau wrote afterwards, 'nothing seemed quite real on that strange and remote island'.[106] Nancy thought of herself as like her hero, Captain Scott of the Antarctic, on his final voyage, surviving in an isolated hut.[107] The four sisters used humour to cope; they spent half the time in tears, the other half shrieking with laughter.[108] Lady Redesdale also kept her sense of humour almost to the end. Her great-grandchildren amused her. When Diana told Patrick that Granny Muv was very poorly, he thought it meant she was poor and replied that she must have been a wealthy young lady once because her home was so nice. When Sydney heard his comment, she laughed and said that she did not feel a very wealthy young lady today.[109] On another occasion, Muv told her daughters to alter anything in her will if they did not like it. When Nancy told her they would go to prison if they did, it made her laugh too.[110]

Her daughters took it in turns to sit with her so that they could talk to her or hold her hand if she woke up and was distressed during the long nights.[111] At one point she seemed to have a vision, seeing bright lights and people she had known. Her voice became stronger and she said, 'Perhaps, who knows, Tom and Unity?' As the days slowly passed, she suffered a minor stroke and became increasingly uncomfortable. She could not eat and was only able to swallow sips of water because her throat was constricting. At times, she experienced what she called her 'horrors' and could not lie still.[112] Both Sydney and her daughters wanted her to be released from her suffering. After eleven days she went into a coma, which lasted for nearly a week.

On 25 May 1963, Lady Redesdale died aged eighty-three in her beloved Scottish home, surrounded by all her daughters, except Jessica. There was calm after the storm and, on a still evening, Sydney's coffin was taken to the mainland in *The Puffin*, escorted by a flotilla of her neighbours' boats. Her ensign flew at half-mast and a lone piper played a lament.[113] It was a fitting ending for the daughter of Thomas Bowles, the master mariner. Like him, she had always steered her own course, no matter what the consequences. On 30 May, Lady Redesdale's funeral was held at Swinbrook. Taking place on a golden spring day as the wildflowers in the hedgerows were coming out, in the village where Sydney had spent so much of her life, it was a classic Mitford service. Her daughters could not hold back their tears when 'Holy, Holy, Holy' was sung. However, humour remained amidst the sadness and no family occasion was complete without an amusing anecdote. Sydney's brother and sister were at the service and afterwards, Weenie phoned Geoffrey to suggest that, as their other siblings were now dead, perhaps they should meet up. Geoffrey replied, 'But we have met,' and that was the end of the conversation.[114] When James Lees-Milne's obituary appeared in *The Times*, describing Sydney as having 'the soul of a mariner', Jessica thought it was all very well for him, 'but who wants to be brought up by a mariner? And at that, a fairly ancient mariner by the time I came along.'[115] Inevitably, beneath the humour, all her daughters felt a deep sense of loss. They would miss her for the rest of their lives. Diana wrote that her mother's death made her feel twenty years older.[116] Nancy, who had had the most difficult relationship with her, found it particularly hard. She wrote that losing Muv made her so sad because she felt that she would never experience anything genuinely nice in her life again.[117] They all agreed that she had been a 'very unusual person'.[118]

Sydney was buried in the quiet country churchyard next to her husband and close to her daughter Unity. Over the next decades, Lady Redesdale's daughters Nancy, Diana and Pam would join her there. The fractured family was reunited in death. On the wall in the entrance to the church, a simple blackboard commemorates the Swinbrook men who served and lost their lives in the Second World War. Halfway down is Tom's name with the date of his death inscribed beside it. The scene of the simple graves in the timeless graveyard calls to mind Thomas Gray's 'Elegy Written in a Country Churchyard', but none of the Mitfords blushed unseen – their lives were very public. It is fitting that in death, four out of her six daughters are buried close to Lady Redesdale, rather than with the men they had so revered. Rebel against her as they might, they were always very much Sydney's children; their inheritance from their mother had shaped their lives for good or ill. The men had been temporary; her influence was permanent.

Notes

Introduction

1. After Sydney's death, her niece, Madeau Stewart, wrote to Lady Redesdale's surviving daughters describing her as this, and they agreed. Pamela Jackson to Madeau Stewart, 8 June 1963. Madeau Stewart Papers, Redesdale Correspondence, Oxford History Centre, P143/12/C2/005.
2. Interview with Charlotte Mosley, 9 August 2024.
3. Mary S. Lovell, *The Mitford Girls: The Biography of an Extraordinary Family* (London: Little Brown and Co, 2001), p. 2.
4. Interview with Charlotte Mosley, 9 August 2024.
5. Lovell, *The Mitford Girls*, pp. 200, 258.
6. Interview with Constancia Romilly, 1 August 2024.
7. Richard Griffiths, *Fellow Travellers of the Right: British Enthusiasts for Nazi Germany 1933–1939* (London: Faber and Faber, 2010), p. 175.
8. Sydney Redesdale to Neville Chamberlain, 11 November 1938. Jessica Mitford Papers, Ohio State University Special and Rare Manuscripts, 0089 Box 204, Folder 10.
9. James Lees-Milne, 'Obituary of Sydney, Lady Redesdale', *The Times*, 28 May 1963.

Chapter 1: An Adventurous Childhood

1. *Ibid.*
2. Jonathan Guinness made this point to Mary S. Lovell. Lovell, *The Mitford Girls*, p. 20.
3. Geoffrey Bowles, *Writings of a Rebel* (London: The Sterling Press, 1944), p. 1.
4. For a full discussion of Thomas's history, see Julia M. Budworth, *Never Forget: George F.S. Bowles: A Biography* (privately published, 2001), pp. 51–9.

5. Quoted in Jonathan Guinness with Catherine Guinness, *The House of Mitford* (London: Hutchinson, 1984), p. 123.

6. Thomas Gibson Bowles quoted in Budworth, *Never Forget*, p. 255.

7. According to Julia Budworth, no one knew Susan Bowles's story until research in the 1980s, Budworth, *Never Forget*, p. 97.

8. Leonard E. Naylor, *The Irrepressible Victorian: The Story of Thomas Gibson Bowles* (London: MacDonald, 1965), p. 11.

9. John B. Osborne, 'Governed by Mediocrity: Image and Text in *Vanity Fair*'s Political Caricatures, 1869–1889', *Victorian Periodicals Review*, Vol. 40, No. 4 (Winter 2007), p. 308.

10. *Ibid.*, p. 310.

11. Guinness, *The House of Mitford*, p. 138.

12. *Ibid.*, p. 130.

13. Osborne, 'Governed by Mediocrity', p. 321.

14. *Ibid.*, p. 320.

15. Thomas Gibson Bowles, *Flotsam and Jetsam: A Yachtsman's Experience at Sea and Ashore* (New York: Funk and Wagnalls Publisher, 1883), p. 197.

16. For a full discussion of these myths, see Budworth, *Never Forget*.

17. *Ibid.*, p. 81.

18. *Ibid.*

19. Guinness, *The House of Mitford*, p. 154.

20. Budworth, *Never Forget*, p. 94.

21. Guinness, *The House of Mitford*, p. 156.

22. Budworth, *Never Forget*, p. 94.

23. Naylor, *The Irrepressible Victorian*, p. 122.

24. Budworth, *Never Forget*, p. 375.

25. Guinness, *The House of Mitford*, p. 187.

26. Thomas Gibson Bowles, *The Log of the Nereid* (London: Simpkin, Marshall and Co., 1889), 'Dedication'.

27. Sydney Redesdale, 'The Dolphin'. Jessica Mitford correspondence, Special and Rare Manuscripts, Box 205, Folder 3, Ohio State University.

28. Deborah Devonshire, *Wait for Me!* (London: John Murray, 2011), p. 29.

29. *Ibid.*

30. For a full discussion of this incident, see Naylor, *The Irrepressible Victorian*, pp. 60–6.

31. Martin Pugh, *'Hurrah for the Blackshirts!': Fascists and Fascism in Britain Between the Wars* (London: Pimlico, 2006), p. 214.

32. For a full discussion of this ambivalence in late nineteenth-century English culture, see Neil R. Davison, 'The Jew as Homme/Femme-Fatale: Jewish (Art)ifice, "Trilby" and Dreyfus', *Jewish Social Studies, New Series*, Vol. 8, No. 2/3 (Winter/Spring 2002), pp. 73–111.

33. Bowles, *Flotsam and Jetsam*, pp. 31–2.

34. Thomas Gibson Bowles, quoted in John Franks, 'Jews in "Vanity Fair"', *Jewish Historical Studies*, Vol. 35, 1996–98, pp. 201–3.

35. Pugh, *'Hurrah for the Blackshirts!'*, pp. 215, 13.

36. Guinness, *The House of Mitford*, p. 160.
37. James Lees-Milne, 15 December 1972, *A Mingled Measure: Diaries 1953–1972* (London: John Murray, 1994), p. 307.
38. Devonshire, *Wait for Me!*, p. 29.
39. Guinness, *The House of Mitford*, p. 162.
40. *Ibid.*, p. 163.
41. Budworth, *Never Forget*, p. 135.
42. *Ibid.*, p. 155.
43. *Ibid.*, p. 117.
44. For a full discussion of Thomas, see Budworth, *Never Forget*, pp. 30–2, 155–6.
45. Guinness, *The House of Mitford*, p. 190.
46. *Ibid.*, p. 159.
47. Budworth, *Never Forget*, p. 154.
48. Guinness, *The House of Mitford*, p. 177.
49. *Ibid.*, p. 178.
50. Peter Y. Sussman (ed.), *Decca: The Letters of Jessica Mitford*, (London: Weidenfeld and Nicolson, 2006), p. 235, note 80.
51. Naylor, *The Irrepressible Victorian*, p. 156.
52. Guinness, *The House of Mitford*, p. 178.
53. Joseph Jaconelli, 'The "Bowles Act" – Cornerstone of the Fiscal Constitution', *The Cambridge Law Journal*, Vol. 69, No. 3, November 2010, p. 582.
54. Bowles, *The Log of the Nereid*, p. 19.
55. Naylor, *The Irrepressible Victorian*, p. 188.
56. Thomas Gibson Bowles, quoted in Budworth, *Never Forget*, p. 257.

Chapter 2: Love and Marriage

1. Guinness, *The House of Mitford*, pp. 183–4.
2. Lovell, *The Mitford Girls*, p. 10.
3. Guinness, *The House of Mitford*, pp. 184–5.
4. Budworth, *Never Forget*, p. 154.
5. Guinness, *The House of Mitford*, p. 222.
6. Jessica Mitford to Nancy Mitford, 13 October 1971. Charlotte Mosley (ed.), *The Mitfords: Letters Between Six Sisters* (London: Fourth Estate, 2012), p. 557.
7. Budworth, *Never Forget*, p. 153.
8. *Ibid.*, p. 155.
9. Guinness, *The House of Mitford*, p. 185.
10. *Ibid.*, p. 218.
11. Lovell, *The Mitford Girls*, p. 12.
12. Bowles, *The Log of the Nereid*, p. 143.
13. Devonshire, *Wait for Me!*, p. 31.
14. Guinness, *The House of Mitford*, p. 173.
15. *Ibid.*, p. 223.
16. Devonshire, *Wait for Me!*, p. 32.

17. Guinness, *The House of Mitford*, p. 223.
18. Budworth, *Never Forget*, p. 152.
19. Guinness, *The House of Mitford*, p. 226.
20. Budworth, *Never Forget*, p. 155.
21. Edgar Syers, *The Badminton Magazine of Sports and Pastimes*, January 1899.
22. T.D. Richardson, *Modern Figure Skating*, quoted in Skate Guard Blog, 24 June 2017.
23. Guinness, *The House of Mitford*, p. 225.
24. Lovell, *The Mitford Girls*, p. 13.
25. Anne de Courcy, *Diana Mosley* (London: Vintage, 2004), p. 26.
26. Guinness, *The House of Mitford*, p. 228.
27. *Ibid.*, p. 225.
28. *Ibid.*, p. 227.
29. *Ibid.*, p. 223.
30. Lovell, *The Mitford Girls*, p. 13.
31. Sophia Murphy, *The Mitford Family Album* (London: Sidgwick and Jackson, 1985).
32. Lovell, *The Mitford Girls*, p. 14.
33. Diana Mosley, *A Life of Contrasts* (London: Gibson Square, 2018), p. 31.
34. Budworth, *Never Forget*, p. 282.
35. Guinness, *The House of Mitford*, p. 217.
36. Lovell, *The Mitford Girls*, p. 11.
37. Guinness, *The House of Mitford*, p. 14.
38. *Ibid.*, p. 109.
39. Bertie Redesdale, quoted in David Pryce-Jones, *Unity Mitford: A Quest* (London: Weidenfeld and Nicolson, 1976), p. 13.
40. Guinness, *The House of Mitford*, p. 101.
41. Lovell, *The Mitford Girls*, p. 15.
42. *Ibid.*, p. 15.
43. 'A Simple Wedding', *The Daily Mirror*, 8 February 1904.
44. Jessica Mitford interview, *Chicago Tribune*, 23 October 1977, quoted in Lovell, *The Mitford Girls*, p. 15.
45. Interview with Charlotte Mosley, 9 August 2024.
46. Guinness, *The House of Mitford*, p. 229.
47. Budworth, *Never Forget*, p. 182.
48. *Ibid.*, p. 268.
49. Lovell, *The Mitford Girls*, p. 17.
50. Julia Budworth conversation with Mary S. Lovell. Lovell, *The Mitford Girls*, p. 17.
51. Devonshire, *Wait for Me!*, p. 21.
52. Budworth, *Never Forget*, p. 257.
53. *Ibid.*, p. 184.
54. Selina Hastings, *Nancy Mitford* (London: Vintage, 2002), p. 6.
55. Lovell, *The Mitford Girls*, p. 18.

Chapter 3: Motherhood

1. Devonshire, *Wait for Me!*, p. 37.
2. Guinness, *The House of Mitford*, p. 232.
3. Hastings, *Nancy Mitford*, p. 7.
4. Nancy Mitford, 'Blor', *The Water Beetle* (New York: Atheneum, 1986), p. 5.
5. Lovell, *The Mitford Girls*, p. 17.
6. Nancy Mitford, *The Pursuit of Love and Other Novels* (London: Penguin Random House, 2000), p. 18.
7. Lovell, *The Mitford Girls*, p. 110.
8. Nancy to Jessica, 1971, quoted in Jessica Mitford, *A Fine Old Conflict* (London: Michael Joseph, 1977), p. 128.
9. Lovell, *The Mitford Girls*, p. 26.
10. Nancy Mitford, 'Blor', *The Water Beetle*, p. 6.
11. Lovell, *The Mitford Girls*, p. 276.
12. Budworth, *Never Forget*, p. 183.
13. Nancy Mitford, 'Blor', *The Water Beetle*, p. 7.
14. Jessica Mitford, *Hons and Rebels* (London: Weidenfeld and Nicolson, 2007), p. 43.
15. Devonshire, *Wait for Me!*, p. 26.
16. Lovell, *The Mitford Girls*, p. 20.
17. See Rachel Trethewey, *The Churchill Girls* (Cheltenham: The History Press, 2021).
18. Interview with Charlotte Mosley, 9 August 2024.
19. Nancy to Jessica, 1971, quoted in Jessica Mitford, *A Fine Old Conflict*, p. 128.
20. Nancy Mitford, *The Pursuit of Love*, p. 9.
21. Nancy Mitford, 'Blor', *The Water Beetle*, p. 7.
22. Budworth, *Never Forget*, p. 278.
23. *Ibid.*, pp. 182–3.
24. Devonshire, *Wait for Me!*, p. 25.
25. Nancy Mitford, 'Blor', *The Water Beetle*, p. 13.
26. Hastings, *Nancy Mitford*, p. 32.
27. Guinness, *The House of Mitford*, p. 158.
28. Devonshire, *Wait for Me!*, p. 34.
29. *Ibid.*, p. 37.
30. Sydney Redesdale, 'Purity of Milk', *Daily Telegraph*, 2 March 1938.
31. Nancy Mitford, *The Pursuit of Love*, p. 222.
32. Lovell, *The Mitford Girls*, p. 31.
33. Jessica Mitford, *Hons and Rebels*, p. 46.
34. *Ibid.*, p. 47.

Chapter 4: The Family and Other Animals

1. 'Houses Wanted', *The Times*, 26 November 1931.
2. Lovell, *The Mitford Girls*, p. 27.
3. See Budworth, *Never Forget*, p. 276.

4. Nancy Mitford, *The Pursuit of Love*, p. 194.
5. *Ibid.*, p. 206.
6. Budworth, *Never Forget*, p. 514.
7. Lovell, *The Mitford Girls*, p. 31.
8. 'Home-Made Bread', *Banbury Advertiser*, 30 October 1924.
9. Pryce-Jones, *Unity Mitford*, p. 29.
10. Nancy Mitford, *The Pursuit of Love*, p. 65.
11. Budworth, *Never Forget*, p. 561.
12. Nancy Mitford to Jessica Mitford, 13 October 1971, Ohio State University Archive, quoted in Lovell, *The Mitford Girls*, p. 33.
13. Blanche Hozier, quoted in Lovell, *The Mitford Girls*, p. 42.
14. Hastings, *Nancy Mitford*, p. 31.
15. Devonshire, *Wait for Me!*, p. 134.
16. Deborah, Duchess of Devonshire to Diana Mosley, 27 August 2000. Mosley (ed.), *The Mitfords: Letters*, p. 801.
17. Devonshire, *Wait for Me!*, p. 14.
18. *Ibid.*, p. 25.
19. Lovell, *The Mitford Girls*, p. 43.
20. Devonshire, *Wait for Me!*, p. 47.
21. Pryce-Jones, *Unity Mitford*, p. 21.
22. Lovell, *The Mitford Girls*, p. 124.
23. Guinness, *The House of Mitford*, pp. 7–8.
24. Nancy Mitford, 'Blor', *The Water Beetle*, p. 14.
25. Hastings, *Nancy Mitford*, p. 31.
26. Interview with Charlotte Mosley, 9 August 2024.
27. Nancy Mitford, *The Pursuit of Love*, p. 231.
28. *Ibid.*, p. 341.
29. Mosley (ed.), *The Mitfords: Letters*, p. xx.
30. Lovell, *The Mitford Girls*, p. 21.
31. Harold Acton, *Nancy Mitford: The Biography* (London: Gibson Books, 2010), p. 119.
32. Budworth, *Never Forget*, p. 282.
33. Lovell, *The Mitford Girls*, p. 32.
34. Devonshire, *Wait for Me!*, p. 33.
35. Budworth, *Never Forget*, p. 281.
36. Nancy Mitford, 'Blor', *The Water Beetle*, p. 4.
37. Lovell, *The Mitford Girls*, p. 32.
38. Nancy Mitford, 'Blor', *The Water Beetle*, p. 5.

Chapter 5: Lady of the Manor

1. Lovell, *The Mitford Girls*, p. 34.
2. Guinness, *The House of Mitford*, p. 118.
3. Budworth, *Never Forget*, p. 318.
4. Lovell, *The Mitford Girls*, p. 37.

5. *Ibid.*, pp. 40–1.
6. 'Sale of Batsford', *Country Life*, 26 April 1919.
7. Sydney Redesdale to James Lees-Milne, 18 June 1948. James Lees-Milne Papers, Beinecke Library, Sydney, Lady Redesdale Series, Gen. Mss. 42, Box 13, f. 628.
8. Sydney Redesdale to James Lees-Milne, 30 March 1958. James Lees-Milne Papers, Beinecke Library, Sydney, Lady Redesdale Series, Gen. Mss. 42, Box 13, f. 628.
9. Lovell, *The Mitford Girls*, p. 45.
10. Devonshire, *Wait for Me!*, p. 2.
11. Jessica Mitford, *Hons and Rebels*, pp. 12–13.
12. *Ibid.*, p. 13.
13. Budworth, *Never Forget*, p. 561.
14. *Ibid.*, p. 358.
15. *Ibid.*, p. 329.
16. Lovell, *The Mitford Girls*, p. 61.
17. Pryce-Jones, *Unity Mitford*, p. 32.
18. Devonshire, *Wait for Me!*, p. 48.
19. *Ibid.*, p. 2.
20. 'Swinbrook', *Oxfordshire Weekly News*, 7 January 1920.
21. Devonshire, *Wait for Me!*, p. 7.
22. 'Swinbrook', *Oxfordshire Weekly News*, 7 January 1920.
23. Interview with Charlotte Mosley, 9 August 2024.
24. Jessica Mitford, *Hons and Rebels*, p. 27.
25. Devonshire, *Wait for Me!*, p. 232.
26. Lovell, *The Mitford Girls*, p. 44.
27. Mary S. Lovell agrees. See *The Mitford Girls*, p. 59.
28. *Ibid.*, p. 62.
29. Devonshire, *Wait for Me!*, p. 27.
30. *Ibid.*, p. 54.
31. Lovell, *The Mitford Girls*, p. 42.
32. Jessica Mitford, *Hons and Rebels*, pp. 22–3.
33. 'The Banbury Division. Women's Conservative Association. Annual Meeting at the Lorna Café. Address by Lady Redesdale', *Banbury Guardian*, 15 April 1926.
34. Pugh, *'Hurrah for the Blackshirts!'*, p. 4.
35. 'Home Secretary and the Coal Crisis: Conservative Fete at Eynsham Hall', *Oxford Chronicle and Reading Gazette*, 31 July 1925.
36. 'Conservative Fete at Bradwell Grove: The Minister of Pensions Eulogy of the Member of the Banbury Division', *Banbury Guardian*, 29 July 1926.
37. 'Brigadier Sir Henry Page Croft on the Political Situation', *Banbury Guardian*, 3 July 1924.
38. Nancy Mitford, *Christmas Pudding and Pigeon Pie* (London: Vintage Books, 2013), p. 64.
39. *Ibid.*, p. 109.
40. Sussman (ed.), *Decca*, p. 3.
41. Jessica Mitford, *Hons and Rebels*, p. 24.
42. *Ibid.*, p. 23.

43. Budworth, *Never Forget*, pp. 408–9.
44. Jessica Mitford, *Hons and Rebels*, p. 28.
45. *Ibid.*, p. 24.
46. 'At Random', *The Observer*, 24 October 1926.
47. Guinness, *The House of Mitford*, p. 265.
48. Nancy Mitford, *Wigs on the Green* (London: Penguin Books, 2015), p. 17.
49. Guinness, *The House of Mitford*, p. 186.
50. Nancy Mitford, *Wigs on the Green*, p. 17.
51. Guinness, *The House of Mitford*, p. 132.
52. Diana Mosley to Deborah, Duchess of Devonshire, 18 August 2000. Mosley (ed.), *The Mitfords: Letters*, p. 800.

Chapter 6: Home Education

1. James Lees-Milne, 8 August 1943, *Ancestral Voices: Prophesying Peace* (London: John Murray, 1977), pp. 201–2.
2. Interview with Charlotte Mosley, 9 August 2024.
3. Nancy Mitford, *The Pursuit of Love*, p. 16.
4. This was Uncle Matthew's view in Nancy Mitford, *The Pursuit of Love*, p. 45.
5. Sydney Redesdale to Jessica Mitford, 17 June 1937. Jessica Mitford Papers, Ohio State University, Special and Rare Manuscripts, 0089, Box 204, Folder 10.
6. Guinness, *The House of Mitford*, p. 220.
7. Budworth, *Never Forget*, p. 429.
8. Diana Mosley, *The Pursuit of Laughter* (London: Gibson Square, 2018), p. 27.
9. Jessica Mitford, *Hons and Rebels*, p. 35.
10. Lovell, *The Mitford Girls*, p. 53.
11. *Ibid.*, p. 117.
12. Devonshire, *Wait for Me!*, p. 75.
13. Nancy Mitford, 'Blor', *The Water Beetle*, p. 6.
14. Nancy Mitford, *The Pursuit of Love*, p. 27.
15. Guinness, *The House of Mitford*, p. 263.
16. Devonshire, *Wait for Me!*, p. 4.
17. James Lees-Milne, 'Sydney, Lady Redesdale', *The Times*, 28 May 1963.
18. Lovell, *The Mitford Girls*, p. 41.
19. Jessica Mitford, *Hons and Rebels*, p. 18.
20. *Ibid.*
21. Pryce-Jones, *Unity Mitford*, p. 34.
22. Guinness, *The House of Mitford*, p. 263.
23. 'Education at Home. Points from Letters', *The Times*, 26 September 1933.
24. Lovell, *The Mitford Girls*, p. 56.
25. Mosley, *The Pursuit of Laughter*, p. 150.
26. Lovell, *The Mitford Girls*, p. 54.
27. Jessica Mitford, *A Fine Old Conflict*, p. 18.
28. Lovell, *The Mitford Girls*, p. 105.

29. Jessica Mitford, *A Fine Old Conflict*, p. 18.
30. Nancy Mitford, *The Pursuit of Love*, p. 30.
31. Diana Mosley to Deborah Devonshire, 21 October 1971. Mosley (ed.), *The Mitfords: Letters*, p. 558.
32. Lovell, *The Mitford Girls*, p. 114.
33. Murphy, *The Mitford Family Album*.
34. Nancy Mitford, *The Pursuit of Love*, p. 268.
35. Nancy Mitford, quoted in Acton, *Nancy Mitford*, p. 41.
36. Charlotte Mosley (ed.), *Love from Nancy: The Letters of Nancy Mitford* (London: Hodder and Stoughton, 1993), p. 13.
37. Nancy Mitford, *The Pursuit of Love*, p. 30.
38. *Ibid.*, p. 15.
39. Jessica Mitford, *Hons and Rebels*, p. 45.
40. Devonshire, *Wait for Me!*, p. 28.
41. Lovell, *The Mitford Girls*, p. 43.
42. Jessica Mitford, *Hons and Rebels*, p. 13.
43. *Ibid.*, p. 14.
44. Budworth, *Never Forget*, p. 429.
45. Devonshire, *Wait for Me!*, p. 53.
46. Programme, 6 August 1932. Jessica Mitford Collection, Ohio State University, Special and Rare Manuscripts, 0089, Box 204, Folder 10.
47. Jessica Mitford, *Hons and Rebels*, pp. 56–7.
48. Devonshire, *Wait for Me!*, p. 5.
49. Jessica Mitford, *Hons and Rebels*, pp. 57–9.
50. Guinness, *The House of Mitford*, p. 577.
51. Jessica Mitford, *Hons and Rebels*, p. 256.

Chapter 7: Escapades

1. Jessica Mitford, *A Fine Old Conflict*, p. 22.
2. *Ibid.*, p. 23.
3. *Ibid.*, p. 20.
4. D.J. Taylor, *Bright Young People: The Rise and Fall of a Generation 1918–1940* (London: Vintage Books, 2008), p. 81.
5. Nancy Mitford, *Wigs on the Green*, p. 38.
6. Published in 1931.
7. Nancy Mitford, *Highland Fling* (London: Capuchin Classics, 2010), p. 98.
8. James Lees-Milne, *Another Self* (Norwich: Michael Russell (Publishing), 2003), p. 62.
9. Lovell, *The Mitford Girls*, p. 70.
10. *Ibid.*, p. 71.
11. Lees-Milne, *Another Self*, pp. 63–4.
12. *Ibid.*, p. 62.
13. Jessica Mitford, *Hons and Rebels*, p. 39.

14. Devonshire, *Wait for Me!*, p. 8.
15. Michael Mason to Sydney Redesdale, 23 August 1951. Jessica Mitford Correspondence, Ohio State University, Special and Rare Manuscripts, 0089, Box 205, Folder 1.
16. Lees-Milne, *Another Self*, p. 61.
17. James Lees-Milne, 'Obituary of Sydney, Lady Redesdale', *The Times*, 28 May 1963.
18. Lees-Milne, *Another Self*, p. 61.
19. Nancy Mitford, *Highland Fling*, p. 43.
20. Pryce-Jones, *Unity Mitford*, p. 18.
21. Budworth, *Never Forget*, p. 360.
22. Mosley, *A Life of Contrasts*, p. 42.
23. *Ibid.*, p. 48.
24. The Duchess of Devonshire, *The House: A Portrait of Chatsworth* (London: Macmillan, 1982), p. 172.
25. Murphy, *The Mitford Family Album*.
26. Jessica Mitford, quoted in Pryce-Jones, *Unity Mitford*, p. 30.
27. Nancy to Tom, 17 July 1927. Mosley (ed.), *Love from Nancy*, p. 23.
28. Guinness, *The House of Mitford*, p. 272.
29. Nancy Mitford, *The Pursuit of Love*, p. 245.
30. *Ibid.*, p. 230.
31. Nancy Mitford to Evelyn Waugh, 13 January 1950. Mosley, *The Letters of Nancy Mitford and Evelyn Waugh* (London: Penguin, 2010), p. 173.
32. Guinness, *The House of Mitford*, pp. 290–1.
33. Taylor, *Bright Young People*, p. 37.
34. Devonshire, *Wait for Me!*, p. 24.
35. Diana Mosley to Deborah Devonshire, 20 April 1994. Mosley (ed.), *The Mitfords: Letters*, p. 746.
36. Mosley, *A Life of Contrasts*, p. 44.
37. 'The Marquise Not Slandered', *The Manchester Guardian*, 29 January 1930.
38. Mosley, *A Life of Contrasts*, p. 44.
39. Devonshire, *Wait for Me!*, p. 15.
40. Budworth, *Never Forget*, p. 439.
41. Lady Redesdale memoir, quoted in Murphy, *The Mitford Family Album*.
42. Devonshire, *Wait for Me!*, p. 27.
43. Nancy Mitford, *The Pursuit of Love*, p. 34.
44. Mosley, *A Life of Contrasts*, p. 58.
45. Sussman (ed.), *Decca*, p. xviii.
46. Devonshire, *Wait for Me!*, p. 64.
47. *Ibid.*, p. 63.
48. Nancy Mitford, *The Pursuit of Love*, p. 49.
49. Hastings, *Nancy Mitford*, p. 46.
50. Jessica Mitford, *Hons and Rebels*, p. 51.
51. *Ibid.*, p. 357.
52. Nancy to Tom, 27 November 1926. Mosley (ed.), *Love from Nancy*, p. 19.

53. Jessica Mitford, *A Fine Old Conflict*, p. 22.
54. Nancy to Tom, 17 July 1927. Mosley (ed.), *Love from Nancy*, p. 23.
55. Jessica Mitford, *Hons and Rebels*, p. 40.
56. Mosley (ed.), *The Mitfords: Letters*, p. 34, note 8.
57. Jessica Mitford, *Hons and Rebels*, p. 35.
58. Nancy to Diana, March 1931. Mosley (ed.), *The Mitfords: Letters*, p. 22.
59. Lovell, *The Mitford Girls*, p. 148.
60. Sydney Redesdale to Jessica Mitford, 23 February 1934. Jessica Mitford Collection, Ohio State University, Special and Rare Manuscripts, 0089, Box 204, Folder 10.
61. Guinness, *The House of Mitford*, pp. 300–1.
62. Jessica Mitford, *A Fine Old Conflict*, p. 23.
63. Nancy Mitford to Jessica Mitford, 18 October 1971. Mosley (ed.), *Love from Nancy*, p. 510.
64. Nancy Mitford, *Highland Fling*, pp. 161, 165.
65. Jessica Mitford, *Hons and Rebels*, p. 99.
66. Nancy Mitford, *The Pursuit of Love*, p. 223.
67. *Ibid.*, p. 233.
68. Budworth, *Never Forget*, p. 282.
69. Nancy Mitford, *The Pursuit of Love*, pp. 18–19.
70. *Ibid.*, pp. 238–9.
71. Devonshire, *Wait for Me!*, pp. 10, 25.
72. Interview with Charlotte Mosley, 9 August 2024.
73. Guinness, *The House of Mitford*, p. 279.
74. Devonshire, *Wait for Me!*, p. 60.
75. De Courcy, *Diana Mosley*, p. 39.
76. Jessica Mitford, *Hons and Rebels*, p. 52.
77. Mosley, *A Life of Contrasts*, p. 67.
78. Dora Carrington to Lytton Strachey, quoted in Lovell, *The Mitford Girls*, p. 126.
79. Mosley, *A Life of Contrasts*, p. 72.
80. Nancy Mitford, *The Pursuit of Love*, p. 77.

Chapter 8: Political Divides

1. Jessica Mitford, *A Fine Old Conflict*, p. 25.
2. Guinness, *The House of Mitford*, p. 10.
3. *Ibid.*
4. For a full discussion of the Mitford girls' need for a cause which linked a man and a political ideal, see Guinness, *The House of Mitford*, pp. 325–7.
5. Budworth, *Never Forget*, p. 526.
6. Guinness, *The House of Mitford*, p. 312.
7. *Ibid.*
8. *Ibid.*, p. 331.
9. Lovell, *The Mitford Girls*, p. 136.
10. De Courcy, *Diana Mosley*, p. 102.

11. Nancy Mitford to Hamish Erskine, 24 December 1932. Mosley (ed.), *Love from Nancy*, p. 53.
12. Devonshire, *Wait for Me!*, p. 71.
13. Nancy Mitford, *Wigs on the Green*, p. 38.
14. Nancy Mitford, *The Pursuit of Love*, p. 87.
15. Mosley, *A Life of Contrasts*, p. 277.
16. Guinness, *The House of Mitford*, p. 287.
17. Pryce-Jones, *Unity Mitford*, p. 36.
18. *Ibid.*, p. 43.
19. Lovell, *The Mitford Girls*, p. 125.
20. Pryce-Jones, *Unity Mitford*, p. 56.
21. Devonshire, *Wait for Me!*, p. 73.
22. Mosley (ed.), *The Mitfords: Letters*, p. 11.
23. Guinness, *The House of Mitford*, p. 333.
24. Lady Glenconner interview, quoted in Pryce-Jones, *Unity Mitford*, p. 50.
25. *Ibid.*, p. 75.
26. Interview with Constancia Romilly, 1 August 2024.
27. Jessica Mitford, *Hons and Rebels*, p. 71.
28. Lovell, *The Mitford Girls*, p. 162.
29. Lauren Young, *Hitler's Girl: The British Aristocracy and the Third Reich on the Eve of World War Two* (London: HarperCollins, 2022), p. 69.
30. Guinness, *The House of Mitford*, p. 361.
31. Sydney Redesdale to Jessica Mitford, 24 March 1937. Jessica Mitford Papers, Ohio State University, Special and Rare Manuscripts, 0089, Box 203.
32. Jessica Mitford, *Hons and Rebels*, p. 73.
33. *Ibid.*, p. 65.
34. Pryce-Jones, *Unity Mitford*, p. 31.
35. Guinness, *The House of Mitford*, p. 364.
36. Sydney Redesdale, quoted in Guinness, *The House of Mitford*, p. 365.
37. Unity Mitford to Nancy Mitford, July 1934. Mosley (ed.), *The Mitfords: Letters*, p. 49.
38. Guinness, *The House of Mitford*, p. 365.
39. Pryce-Jones, *Unity Mitford*, p. 162.
40. Guinness, *The House of Mitford*, p. 367.
41. *Ibid.*, p. 369.
42. Unity Mitford to Sydney Redesdale, 11 February 1935, quoted in Guinness, *The House of Mitford*, p. 369.
43. Unity Mitford to Diana Guinness, 25 April 1935. Mosley (ed.), *The Mitfords: Letters*, pp. 54–6.
44. Unity Mitford to Diana Guinness, 25 April 1935. Guinness, *The House of Mitford*, p. 375.
45. Guinness, *The House of Mitford*, p. 440.
46. Julie V. Gottlieb, *Feminine Fascism: Women in Britain's Fascist Movement* (London, New York: I.B. Tauris, 2003), p. 125.
47. Griffiths, *Fellow Travellers*, p. 169.

48. Young, *Hitler's Girl*, p. 96.
49. *Ibid.*, p. 28.
50. Mosley (ed.), *The Mitfords: Letters*, p. 61, note 3.
51. Young, *Hitler's Girl*, p. 92.
52. Pryce-Jones, *Unity Mitford*, p. 117.
53. Unity Mitford, quoted in Guinness, *The House of Mitford*, p. 377.
54. Lovell, *The Mitford Girls*, p. 192.
55. Nancy Mitford to Unity Mitford, 29 June 1935. Mosley (ed.), *The Mitfords: Letters*, p. 61.
56. De Courcy, *Diana Mosley*, p. 122.
57. Jessica Mitford, *Hons and Rebels*, p. 93.
58. Lovell, *The Mitford Girls*, pp. 177–8.
59. *Ibid.*, pp. 177, 196.
60. Griffiths, *Fellow Travellers*, pp. 77–8.
61. Pugh, '*Hurrah for the Blackshirts!*', p. 14.
62. Email from Andrew Roberts, 29 November 2024.
63. Griffiths, *Fellow Travellers*, pp. 11, 59, 65.
64. Email from Andrew Roberts, 29 November 2024.
65. Andrew Roberts, *Churchill: Walking With Destiny* (London: Allen Lane, 2018), pp. 95, 368.
66. Quoted in *ibid.*, pp. 363–4.
67. Jessica Mitford, *Hons and Rebels*, p. 104.
68. Pugh, '*Hurrah for the Blackshirts!*', p. 218.
69. Quoted in de Courcy, *Diana Mosley*, p. 153.
70. Jan Dalley, *Diana Mosley: A Life* (London: Faber and Faber, 1999), p. 253.
71. Lovell, *The Mitford Girls*, pp. 177–8.
72. Jessica Mitford, *Hons and Rebels*, p. 250.
73. Nancy Mitford to Mark Ogilvie-Grant, 9 November 1935. Mosley (ed.), *Love from Nancy*, p. 71.
74. Jessica Mitford, *Hons and Rebels*, p. 94.
75. *Ibid.*, p. 66.
76. Nancy Mitford, *Wigs on the Green*, p. 5.
77. *Ibid.*, p. 125.
78. *Ibid.*, p. 127.

Chapter 9: Parting of the Ways

1. Jessica Mitford, *Hons and Rebels*, p. 77.
2. *Ibid.*, p. 66.
3. *Ibid.*, p. 67.
4. Lord Redesdale's letter, *The Times*, 14 March 1936.
5. 'Restoration of Colonial Territories to Germany', *The Scotsman*, 26 March 1936.
6. Griffiths, *Fellow Travellers*, p. 207.
7. 'Court Circular', *The Times*, 15 July 1936.

8. Charles Spicer, *Coffee with Hitler: The British Amateurs Who Tried to Civilise the Nazis* (London: Oneworld, 2022), p. 1.

9. *Ibid.*, p. 325.

10. Lawrence James, *Aristocrats: Power, Grace and Decadence* (London: Little Brown, 2009), p. 371.

11. Quoted in Young, *Hitler's Girl*, p. 99.

12. 'Germany's Need of Colonies: Vital to Standard of Life: Herr Von Ribbentrop on Bolshevism', *The Times*, 16 December 1936.

13. Harold Nicolson, quoted in Pugh, *'Hurrah for the Blackshirts!'*, p. 271.

14. Jessica Mitford to Nancy Mitford, 13 October 1971, quoted in Lovell, *The Mitford Girls*, p. 60.

15. Jessica Mitford, *Hons and Rebels*, p. 41.

16. *Ibid.*, p. 96.

17. *Ibid.*, pp. 91–2.

18. *Ibid.*, p. 99.

19. *Ibid.*, p. 101.

20. Guinness, *The House of Mitford*, p. 380.

21. Jessica Mitford, *Hons and Rebels*, p. 102.

22. Lord Queenborough and Lady Houston were her adversaries. Griffiths, *Fellow Travellers*, p. 235.

23. Duchess of Atholl to Unity Mitford, quoted in Guinness, *The House of Mitford*, p. 379.

24. 'Refugee History', *BCA UK – The Association for the UK Basque Children* website.

25. Sydney Redesdale to Jessica Mitford, 17 June 1937. Jessica Mitford Collection, Ohio State University, Special and Rare Manuscripts, 0089, Box 204, Folder 10.

26. Sydney Redesdale, 'The Basque Children', *Daily Telegraph*, 21 October 1937.

27. Devonshire, *Wait for Me!*, p. 84.

28. Jessica Mitford, *Hons and Rebels*, p. 110.

29. Jessica Mitford to Deborah, Duchess of Devonshire, 14 May 1993, quoted in Lovell, *The Mitford Girls*, p. 171.

30. Lovell, *The Mitford Girls*, p. 121.

31. Guinness, *The House of Mitford*, pp. 399–400.

32. Devonshire, *Wait for Me!*, p. 84.

33. Jessica Mitford to Sydney Redesdale, late February 1937. Sussman (ed.), *Decca*, p. 23.

34. Jessica Mitford, *Hons and Rebels*, p. 148.

35. Griffiths, *Fellow Travellers*, p. 263.

36. Sydney Redesdale to Jessica Mitford, 23 February 1937. Jessica Mitford Collection, Ohio State University, Special and Rare Manuscripts, 0089, Box 204, Folder 10.

37. Nancy Mitford, *The Pursuit of Love*, p. 109.

38. Sydney Redesdale to Jessica Mitford, 3 March 1937. Jessica Mitford Papers, Ohio State University, Special and Rare Manuscripts, 0089, Box 204, Folder 10.

39. Budworth, *Never Forget*, p. 480.

40. Lovell, *The Mitford Girls*, p. 231.

41. Unity Mitford to Jessica Mitford, 11 April 1937. Mosley (ed.), *The Mitfords: Letters*, pp. 90–1.

42. Nanny Laura Dix to Jessica Mitford, 3 March 1937. Jessica Mitford Papers, Ohio State University, Special and Rare Manuscripts, 0089, Box 203, Folder 6.
43. Nanny Laura Dix to Jessica, 13 March 1937. Jessica Mitford Papers, Ohio State University, Special and Rare Manuscripts, 0089, Box 203, Folder 6.
44. Guinness, *The House of Mitford*, p. 405.
45. Lovell, *The Mitford Girls*, p. 229.
46. Jessica Mitford, *Hons and Rebels*, p. 145.
47. *Ibid.*, p. 146.
48. Nanny Laura Dix to Jessica, 25 March 1937. Jessica Mitford Papers, Ohio State University, Special and Rare Manuscripts, 0089, Box 203, Folder 6.
49. For a full discussion of Phyllis Bowles's love life, see Budworth, *Never Forget*, pp. 418–21.
50. For a full discussion of Sarah's relationship, see Trethewey, *The Churchill Girls*.
51. Jessica Mitford to Deborah Mitford, 3 August 1937. Mosley (ed.), *The Mitfords: Letters*, p. 109.
52. Jessica Mitford, *Hons and Rebels*, p. 167.
53. De Courcy, *Diana Mosley*, pp. 186–7.
54. Lovell, *The Mitford Girls*, p. 236.
55. Sydney Redesdale to Jessica Mitford, 24 March 1937. Jessica Mitford Papers, Ohio State University, Special and Rare Manuscripts, 0089, Box 204, Folder 10.
56. Sydney Redesdale to Esmond Romilly, 14 April 1937. Jessica Mitford Papers, Ohio State University, Special and Rare Manuscripts, 0089, Box 204, Folder 10.
57. Sydney Redesdale to Jessica Mitford, 5 May 1937. Jessica Mitford Papers, Ohio State University, Special and Rare Manuscripts, 0089, Box 204, Folder 10.
58. Lovell, *The Mitford Girls*, p. 237.
59. Nanny Laura Dix to Jessica, 30 April 1937. Jessica Mitford Papers, Ohio State University, Special and Rare Manuscripts, 0089, Box 203, Folder 6.
60. Deborah Mitford to Jessica Mitford, 12 May 1937. 94.
61. Sydney Redesdale to Jessica Mitford, 10 May 1937. Jessica Mitford Papers, Ohio State University. Special and Rare Manuscripts, 0089, Box 204, Folder 10.
62. Devonshire, *Wait for Me!*, p. 87.
63. *Ibid.*
64. Jessica Mitford, *Hons and Rebels*, p. 155.
65. Sydney Redesdale to Jessica Mitford, 20 May 1937. Jessica Mitford Papers, Ohio State University, Special and Rare Manuscripts, 0089, Box 204, Folder 10.
66. 'Strong and exuberant', Sydney Redesdale to Jessica Mitford, 20 May 1937. Jessica Mitford Papers, Ohio State University, Special and Rare Manuscripts, 0089, Box 204, Folder 10.
67. Sydney Redesdale to Jessica Mitford, 17 June 1937. Jessica Mitford Papers, Ohio State University, Special and Rare Manuscripts, 0089, Box 204, Folder 10.
68. Jessica Mitford, *Hons and Rebels*, p. 132.
69. Lovell, *The Mitford Girls*, p. 254.
70. Unity Mitford to Jessica Mitford, 10 August 1937. Mosley (ed.), *The Mitfords: Letters*, p. 113.
71. Jessica Mitford, *Hons and Rebels*, p. 245.

Chapter 10: On the Move

1. Sydney Redesdale to Jessica Mitford, 26 May 1937. Jessica Mitford Papers, Ohio State University, Special and Rare Manuscripts, 0089, Box 204, Folder 10.
2. Sydney Redesdale to Jessica Mitford, 16 June 1937. Jessica Mitford Papers, Ohio State University, Special and Rare Manuscripts, 0089, Box 204, Folder 10.
3. Lovell, *The Mitford Girls*, p. 244.
4. Devonshire, *Wait for Me!*, p. 89.
5. Lovell, *The Mitford Girls*, p. 244.
6. Sydney Redesdale to Jessica Mitford, 12 June 1937. Jessica Mitford Papers, Ohio State University, Special and Rare Manuscripts, 0089, Box 204, Folder 10.
7. Lovell, *The Mitford Girls*, p. 293.
8. Deborah Mitford to Jessica Mitford, 30 June 1937. Mosley (ed.), *The Mitfords: Letters*, p. 106.
9. Spicer, *Coffee with Hitler*, p. 121.
10. Jessica Mitford, *A Fine Old Conflict*, p. 23.
11. Redesdale, 'Purity of Milk', *The Telegraph*.
12. Interview with Constancia Romilly, 1 August 2024.
13. Interview with Charlotte Mosley, 9 August 2024.
14. Gottlieb, *Feminine Fascism*, pp. 70–4.
15. Guinness, *The House of Mitford*, p. 439.
16. *Ibid.*, p. 19.
17. *Ibid.*, p. 356.
18. *Ibid.*, p. 296.
19. 'Sale of Swinbrook', *Banbury Guardian*, 21 May 1936.
20. Jessica Mitford, *Hons and Rebels*, p. 61.
21. Young, *Hitler's Girl*, p. 62.
22. Pugh, *'Hurrah for the Blackshirts!'*, p. 82.
23. Sydney Redesdale to Jessica Mitford, 8 August 1937. Jessica Mitford Papers, Ohio State University, Special and Rare Manuscripts, 0089, Box 204, Folder 10.
24. Deborah Mitford to Jessica Mitford, 20 June 1937. Mosley (ed.), *The Mitfords: Letters*, p. 102.
25. Sydney Redesdale to Jessica Mitford, 3 July 1937. Jessica Mitford Papers, Ohio State University, Special and Rare Manuscripts, 0089, Box 204, Folder 10.
26. Deborah Mitford to Jessica Mitford, 18 June 1937. Mosley (ed.), *The Mitfords: Letters*, pp. 101–2.
27. 'The Debut of a Beauty', *The Observer*, 27 March 1938.
28. Devonshire, *Wait for Me!*, p. 97.
29. 'The Debut of a Beauty', *The Observer*, 27 March 1938.
30. Devonshire, *Wait for Me!*, p. 95.
31. *Ibid.*, p. 98.
32. Sydney Redesdale to Jessica Mitford, 12 July 1937. Jessica Mitford Papers, Ohio State University, Special and Rare Manuscripts, 0089, Box 204, Folder 10.
33. Mary S. Lovell interview with Diana Mosley, 15 January 2000, quoted in Lovell, *The Mitford Girls*, p. 258.

34. Sydney Redesdale to Jessica Mitford, 22 June 1937. Jessica Mitford Papers, Ohio State University, Special and Rare Manuscripts, 0089, Box 204, Folder 10.
35. Jessica Mitford, *Hons and Rebels*, p. 167.
36. Lovell, *The Mitford Girls*, p. 259; Devonshire, *Wait for Me!*, p. 110.

Chapter 11: Causing Controversy

1. 'Debate Fiasco in the Lords', *Sunderland Daily Echo*, 30 March 1938.
2. 'The National Effort', *The Times*, 30 March 1938.
3. 'Ambassadors Listen to Lords Debate', *Bradford Observer*, 30 March 1938.
4. Griffiths, *Fellow Travellers*, p. 296.
5. Spicer, *Coffee with Hitler*, p. 178.
6. Griffiths, *Fellow Travellers*, p. 292.
7. *Ibid.*, p. 277.
8. *Ibid.*, p. 313.
9. Hastings, *Nancy Mitford*, p. 119.
10. Guinness, *The House of Mitford*, p. 416.
11. Unity Mitford to Diana Mosley, 14 August 1938. Mosley (ed.), *The Mitfords: Letters*, p. 134.
12. Mary S. Lovell interview with Diana Mosley, 15 January 2000, quoted in Lovell, *The Mitford Girls*, p. 269.
13. Mosley, *A Life of Contrasts*, p. 150.
14. Virginia Cowles, *Looking for Trouble* (London: Faber, 2021), pp. 171–2.
15. 'Sudeten Leader Visits Hitler', *The Scotsman*, 2 September 1938.
16. Cowles, *Looking for Trouble*, pp. 171–2, 178.
17. Sydney Redesdale to Jessica Mitford, 5 July 1941. Jessica Mitford Correspondence, Ohio State University, Special and Rare Manuscripts, 0089, Box 203, Folder 6.
18. Cowles, *Looking for Trouble*, pp. 163, 171–2.
19. *Ibid.*, p. 171.
20. *Ibid.*, p. 174.
21. Guinness, *The House of Mitford*, p. 418.
22. Jessica Mitford, *Hons and Rebels*, p. 74.
23. Email from Professor Simon Heffer, 2 December 2024.
24. Email from Professor Richard Toye, 6 December 2024.
25. James, *Aristocrats*, p. 372.
26. Lord Redesdale, *The Sunday Pictorial*, April 1938, quoted in Pryce-Jones, *Unity Mitford*, p. 183.
27. Pryce-Jones, *Unity Mitford*, p. 5.
28. Guinness, *The House of Mitford*, p. 370.
29. Mary S. Lovell interview with Diana Mosley, 15 January 2000, quoted in Lovell, *The Mitford Girls*, p. 250.
30. Guinness, *The House of Mitford*, p. 370.
31. Cowles, *Looking for Trouble*, pp. 177–8.
32. Mosley, *A Life of Contrasts*, p. 157.
33. 'Munich Agreement', *Holocaust Encyclopedia* website.

34. Spicer, *Coffee with Hitler*, p. 213.
35. Young, *Hitler's Girl*, p. 43.
36. The Link Letter to *The Times*, 1938.
37. Mosley, *A Life of Contrasts*, p. 161.
38. Sydney Redesdale to Unity, quoted in Guinness, *The House of Mitford*, p. 418.
39. Email from Professor Richard Toye, 6 December 2024.
40. Sydney Redesdale to Neville Chamberlain, 11 November 1938. Jessica Mitford Papers, Ohio State University, Special and Rare Manuscripts, 0089, Box 204, Folder 10.
41. Julie V. Gottlieb, *'Guilty Women': Foreign Policy, and Appeasement in Inter-War Britain* (Basingstoke: Palgrave Macmillan, 2015), p. 197.
42. *Ibid.*, p. 205.
43. *Ibid.*, p. 198.
44. Richard J. Evans, *Hitler's People: The Faces of the Third Reich* (London: Allen Lane, 2024), p. 143.
45. 'Kristallnacht', *Holocaust Encyclopedia* online.
46. Chips Channon, 21 November 1938, quoted in Griffiths, *Fellow Travellers*, p. 338.
47. Spicer, *Coffee with Hitler*, p. 218.
48. Pugh, *'Hurrah for the Blackshirts!'*, p. 278.
49. Pryce-Jones, *Unity Mitford*, p. 206.
50. 'Redesdale Supports Nazis: High Time Colonies Were Returned', *Shields Daily News*, 1 February 1939.
51. *Ibid.*
52. Unity Mitford, *Daily Mirror*, quoted in Guinness, *The House of Mitford*, p. 419.
53. Griffiths, *Fellow Travellers*, p. 344.
54. Guinness, *The House of Mitford*, p. 419.
55. Spicer, *Coffee with Hitler*, p. 245.
56. *Ibid.*, p. 239.
57. Guinness, *The House of Mitford*, p. 439.
58. Lovell, *The Mitford Girls*, p. 276.
59. Jessica Mitford, *Hons and Rebels*, pp. 177–8.
60. Guinness, *The House of Mitford*, p. 310.
61. Nancy Mitford to Sydney Redesdale, 25 May 1939. Mosley (ed.), *Love from Nancy*, p. 80.
62. Mosley (ed.), *The Mitfords: Letters*, p. 43, note 1.
63. Diana Mosley, *Loved Ones: Pen Portraits by Diana Mosley* (London: Sidgwick and Jackson, 1985), p. 49.
64. Budworth, *Never Forget*, p. 487.
65. Lady Redesdale, 'Where Nazism Differs', *Daily Record*, 10 June 1939.
66. Evans, *Hitler's People*, p. 311.
67. Griffiths, *Fellow Travellers*, p. 249.
68. De Courcy, *Diana Mosley*, p. 200.
69. *Ibid.*, p. 206.
70. Richard Griffiths, *Patriotism Perverted: Captain Ramsay, the Right Club, and British Anti-Semitism 1939–1940* (London: Faber and Faber, 2010), p. 128.

71. *Ibid.*, p. 77.
72. Archibald Ramsay, quoted in *ibid.*, p. 122.
73. Griffiths, *Patriotism Perverted*, p. 123.
74. *Ibid.*, pp. 4, 125.
75. *Ibid.*
76. 'Nazi Gold Paid to Agent of "Link"', *Daily Mirror*, 4 August 1939.
77. Simon Haxey was a pseudonym.
78. 'A Warning to Hitler's Friends in Britain', *Sunday Mirror*, 13 August 1939.
79. 'Inch Kenneth Bought by Lady Redesdale', *Oban Times and Argyllshire Advertiser*, 10 December 1938.
80. Sydney Redesdale to Jessica Mitford, 2 October 1960. Jessica Mitford Correspondence, Ohio State University, Special and Rare Manuscripts, 0089, Box 205, Folder 1.
81. Budworth, *Never Forget*, p. 490.
82. *Ibid.*, p. 491.

Chapter 12: Unity's War

1. Lovell, *The Mitford Girls*, pp. 289, 291.
2. Guinness, *The House of Mitford*, p. 431.
3. *Ibid.*, p. 428.
4. Lovell, *The Mitford Girls*, p. 296.
5. Budworth, *Never Forget*, p. 493.
6. Sydney Redesdale to Jessica Mitford, 29 September 1939. Jessica Mitford Correspondence, Ohio State University, Special and Rare Manuscripts, 0089, Box 203, Folder 6.
7. Guinness, *The House of Mitford*, p. 579.
8. *Ibid.*, p. 580.
9. Mosley (ed.), *Love from Nancy*, p. 59.
10. Hastings, *Nancy Mitford*, p. 121.
11. Nancy Mitford to Violet Hammersley, 15 September 1939. Mosley (ed.), *Love from Nancy*, p. 83.
12. Nancy Mitford to Jessica Mitford, 21 September 1939. Mosley (ed.), *The Mitfords: Letters*, p. 151.
13. Nancy Mitford to Violet Hammersley, 15 September 1939. Mosley (ed.), *Love from Nancy*, p. 89.
14. Nancy Mitford to Deborah Mitford, 20 September 1939. Mosley (ed.), *The Mitfords: Letters*, p. 150.
15. Nancy Mitford to Violet Hammersley, 14 October 1939. Mosley (ed.), *Love from Nancy*, p. 86.
16. Nancy Mitford, *Christmas Pudding and Pigeon Pie*, p. 220.
17. Justine Picardie, *Coco Chanel: The Legend and the Life* (London: HarperCollins, 2023), p. 258.
18. Jessica Mitford, *Hons and Rebels*, p. 253.
19. Nancy Mitford, *The Pursuit of Love*, p. 64.

20. 'Unity Still in Germany', *Daily Mirror*, 5 September 1939.
21. Nancy Mitford to Jessica Mitford, 21 September 1939. Mosley (ed.), *The Mitfords: Letters*, p. 151.
22. Sydney Redesdale to Jessica Mitford, 29 September 1939. Jessica Mitford Correspondence, Ohio State University, Special and Rare Manuscripts, 0089, Box 203, Folder 6.
23. Sydney Redesdale to Jessica Mitford, 5 October 1939. Jessica Mitford Correspondence, Ohio State University, Special and Rare Manuscripts, 0089, Box 203, Folder 6.
24. Mosley, *A Life of Contrasts*, p. 165.
25. Sydney Redesdale to Jessica Mitford, 16 October 1939. Jessica Mitford Correspondence, Ohio State University, Special and Rare Manuscripts, 0089, Box 203, Folder 6.
26. Sydney Redesdale to Jessica Mitford, 8 December 1939. Jessica Mitford Correspondence, Ohio State University, Special and Rare Manuscripts, 0089, Box 203, Folder 6.
27. Sydney Redesdale to Jessica Mitford, 29 October 1939. Jessica Mitford Correspondence, Ohio State University, Special and Rare Manuscripts, 0089, Box 203, Folder 6.
28. Lovell, *The Mitford Girls*, p. 303.
29. Sydney Redesdale to Jessica Mitford, 29 October 1939. Jessica Mitford Correspondence, Ohio State University, Special and Rare Manuscripts, 0089, Box 203, Folder 6.
30. Mosley, *A Life of Contrasts*, p. 165.
31. Sydney Redesdale to Jessica Mitford, 8 November 1939. Jessica Mitford Correspondence, Ohio State University, Special and Rare Manuscripts, 0089, Box 203, Folder 6.
32. Sydney Redesdale to Jessica Mitford, 8 December 1939. Jessica Mitford Correspondence, Ohio State University, Special and Rare Manuscripts, 0089, Box 203, Folder 6.
33. Guinness, *The House of Mitford*, p. 432.
34. *Ibid.*, p. 580.
35. Sydney Redesdale to Jessica Mitford, 9 January 1939. Jessica Mitford Correspondence, Ohio State University, Special and Rare Manuscripts, 0089, Box 203, Folder 6.
36. Guinness, *The House of Mitford*, p. 434.
37. Mosley, *A Life of Contrasts*, p. 167.
38. Guinness, *The House of Mitford*, p. 435.
39. *Ibid.*, p. 435.
40. Young, *Hitler's Girl*, pp. 177–8.
41. Guinness, *The House of Mitford*, p. 436.
42. 'Cassandra', *Daily Mirror*, 4 January 1940.
43. Mosley, *A Life of Contrasts*, p. 167.
44. 'Abuse of Freedom', *The Times*, 13 January 1940.
45. Lord Denham, 23 January 1940, Hansard online.
46. 'Cassandra', *Daily Mirror*, 26 January 1940.

47. 'Unity Enters Home for Operation', *Daily Mirror*, 23 January 1940.
48. Quoted in Young, *Hitler's Girl*, p. 180.
49. Lovell, *The Mitford Girls*, p. 311.
50. Sydney Redesdale to Jessica Mitford, 1 April 1940. Jessica Mitford Correspondence, Ohio State University, Special and Rare Manuscripts, 0089, Box 203, Folder 6.
51. Guinness, *The House of Mitford*, p. 437.
52. Sydney Redesdale to Jessica Mitford, 28 January 1940. Jessica Mitford Correspondence, Ohio State University, Special and Rare Manuscripts, 0089, Box 203, Folder 6.
53. Sydney Redesdale to Jessica Mitford, 28 January 1940. Jessica Mitford Correspondence, Ohio State University, Special and Rare Manuscripts, 0089, Box 203, Folder 6.
54. *Hitler's British Girl*, Channel 4, 2007. Available on YouTube.
55. Devonshire, *Wait for Me!*, p. 108.
56. Sydney Redesdale to Jessica Mitford, 22 February and 11 March 1940. Jessica Mitford Correspondence, Ohio State University, Special and Rare Manuscripts, 0089, Box 203, Folder 6.
57. Devonshire, *Wait for Me!*, p. 116.
58. Budworth, *Never Forget*, p. 525.
59. 'Lord Redesdale', *The Times*, 9 March 1940.
60. Hastings, *Nancy Mitford*, p. 120.
61. Lovell, *The Mitford Girls*, p. 310.
62. Mosley, *A Life of Contrasts*, p. 192.
63. Sydney Redesdale to Jessica Mitford, 7 October 1940. Jessica Mitford Correspondence, Ohio State University, Special and Rare Manuscripts, 0089, Box 203, Folder 6.
64. Guinness, *The House of Mitford*, p. 311.
65. Nancy Mitford to Violet Hammersley, 10 February 1940. Mosley (ed.), *Love from Nancy*, p. 95.
66. Mosley, *A Life of Contrasts*, p. 164.
67. De Courcy, *Diana Mosley*, p. 203.
68. For a full discussion, see Griffiths, *Patriotism Perverted*, pp. 200–1.
69. Guinness, *The House of Mitford*, p. 311.
70. Devonshire, *Wait for Me!*, p. 116.
71. Guinness, *The House of Mitford*, p. 438.
72. Sydney Redesdale to Jessica Mitford, 14 September 1940. Jessica Mitford Correspondence, Ohio State University, Special and Rare Manuscripts, 0089, Box 203, Folder 6.
73. Sydney Redesdale to Jessica Mitford, 1 January 1943. Jessica Mitford Correspondence, Ohio State University, Special and Rare Manuscripts, 0089, Box 203, Folder 6.
74. Email from Jonathan Guinness, January 2025.
75. Devonshire, *Wait for Me!*, p. 25.
76. Budworth, *Never Forget*, pp. 526, 561.
77. *Ibid.*, p. 503.

78. Guinness, *The House of Mitford*, p. 440.
79. 'Mitfords' Island Home', *Daily News*, 12 July 1940.
80. 'Lord Redesdale and His Family: References in the House of Commons', *Oban Times and Argyllshire Advertiser*, 27 July 1940.
81. Budworth, *Never Forget*, p. 525.
82. 'Lord Redesdale says "Bitterly Opposed to Fascism"', *Dundee Courier*, 20 July 1940.
83. Lovell, *The Mitford Girls*, p. 311.
84. De Courcy, *Diana Mosley*, p. 239.
85. Sydney Redesdale to Jessica Mitford, 23 February 1942. Jessica Mitford Correspondence, Ohio State University, Special and Rare Manuscripts, 0089, Box 203, Folder 6.
86. Sydney Redesdale to Jessica Mitford, 1 December 1940. Jessica Mitford Correspondence, Ohio State University, Special and Rare Manuscripts, 0089, Box 203, Folder 6.
87. Sydney Redesdale to Jessica Mitford, 29 August 1940. Jessica Mitford Correspondence, Ohio State University, Special and Rare Manuscripts, 0089, Box 203, Folder 6.
88. Mosley (ed.), *Love from Nancy*, p. 105, note 3.
89. Budworth, *Never Forget*, p. 526.
90. Guinness, *The House of Mitford*, p. 442.
91. Sydney Redesdale to Jessica Mitford, 26 September 1940. Jessica Mitford Correspondence, Ohio State University, Special and Rare Manuscripts, 0089, Box 203, Folder 6.
92. Sydney Redesdale to Jessica Mitford, 6 January 1941. Jessica Mitford Correspondence, Ohio State University, Special and Rare Manuscripts, 0089, Box 203, Folder 6.
93. Sydney Redesdale to Jessica Mitford, 18 January 1942. Jessica Mitford Correspondence, Ohio State University, Special and Rare Manuscripts, 0089, Box 203, Folder 6.
94. Deborah Mitford to Jessica Mitford, 6 May 1940. Mosley (ed.), *The Mitfords: Letters*, p. 157.
95. Lovell, *The Mitford Girls*, p. 334.
96. Deborah Mitford to Jessica Mitford, 7 October 1940, Jessica Mitford Papers, Ohio State Papers, quoted in Lovell, *The Mitford Girls*, p. 334.
97. Devonshire, *Wait for Me!*, p. 108.
98. Guinness, *The House of Mitford*, p. 438.
99. Deborah Mitford to Jessica Mitford, 24 June 1941. Mosley (ed.), *The Mitfords: Letters*, p. 178.
100. Budworth, *Never Forget*, pp. 514, 517.

Chapter 13: War On Many Fronts

1. Lovell, *The Mitford Girls*, p. 321.
2. Gottlieb, *Feminine Fascism*, p. 227.

3. Lovell, *The Mitford Girls*, p. 323.
4. Nancy Mitford to Deborah Mitford, 20 September 1939. Mosley (ed.), *The Mitfords: Letters*, p. 150.
5. Spicer, *Coffee with Hitler*, p. 274.
6. Mosley, *A Life of Contrasts*, pp. 171–2.
7. *Ibid.*, p. 173.
8. Lovell, *The Mitford Girls*, p. 325.
9. Mosley, *A Life of Contrasts*, p. 181.
10. Mosley (ed.), *The Mitfords: Letters*, p. 146.
11. Lovell, *The Mitford Girls*, p. 327.
12. Email from Jonathan Guinness, January 2025.
13. Sydney Redesdale to Jessica Mitford, 20 July 1942. Jessica Mitford Correspondence, Ohio State University, Special and Rare Manuscripts, 0089, Box 203, Folder 6.
14. Mosley, *A Life of Contrasts*, p. 189.
15. Devonshire, *Wait for Me!*, p. 112.
16. Guinness, *The House of Mitford*, p. 494.
17. Mosley, *A Life of Contrasts*, p. 186.
18. Interview with Charlotte Mosley, 9 August 2024.
19. Lovell, *The Mitford Girls*, p. 330.
20. Mosley (ed.), *The Mitfords: Letters*, p. 144.
21. 'Lord Redesdale's Guests', *Birmingham Mail*, 24 September 1940.
22. 'Lord Redesdale's Town Residence', *Oban Times and Argyllshire Advertiser*, 28 September 1940.
23. Nancy Mitford to Jessica Mitford, 26 December 1940. Mosley (ed.), *Love from Nancy*, p. 108.
24. Guinness, *The House of Mitford*, p. 463.
25. Sydney Redesdale to Jessica Mitford, 7 October 1940. Jessica Mitford Correspondence, Ohio State University, Special and Rare Manuscripts, 0089, Box 203, Folder 6.
26. Sydney Redesdale to Jessica Mitford, 26 September 1940. Jessica Mitford Correspondence, Ohio State University, Special and Rare Manuscripts, 0089, Box 203, Folder 6.
27. Sydney Redesdale to Jessica Mitford, 26 September 1940. Jessica Mitford Correspondence, Ohio State University, Special and Rare Manuscripts, 0089, Box 203, Folder 6.
28. Sydney Redesdale to Jessica Mitford, 11 February 1941. Jessica Mitford Correspondence, Ohio State University, Special and Rare Manuscripts, 0089, Box 203, Folder 6.
29. Sydney Redesdale to Jessica Mitford, 20 May 1942. Jessica Mitford Correspondence, Ohio State University, Special and Rare Manuscripts, 0089, Box 203, Folder 6.
30. Budworth, *Never Forget*, p. 513.
31. Devonshire, *Wait for Me!*, p. 120.
32. Devonshire, *The House*, p. 73.
33. Pryce-Jones, *Unity Mitford*, p. 253.
34. Lovell, *The Mitford Girls*, p. 352.

35. *Ibid.*, p. 352.
36. Nancy Mitford to Deborah Mitford, 22 November 1941. Mosley (ed.), *Love from Nancy*, p. 114.
37. Mosley (ed.), *The Mitfords: Letters*, p. 357, note 1.
38. Unity Mitford to Jessica Mitford, 10 May 1941. *Ibid.*, p. 175.
39. Sydney Redesdale to Jessica Mitford, 11 February 1941. Jessica Mitford Correspondence, Ohio State University, Special and Rare Manuscripts, 0089, Box 203, Folder 6.
40. Sydney Redesdale to Jessica Mitford, 28 April 1941. Jessica Mitford Correspondence, Ohio State University, Special and Rare Manuscripts, 0089, Box 203, Folder 6.
41. Jessica Mitford, *Hons and Rebels*, p. 258.
42. Sussman (ed.), *Decca*, p. 48.
43. Virginia Durr to Sydney Redesdale, no date. Jessica Mitford Correspondence, Ohio State University, Special and Rare Manuscripts, 0089, Box 203, Folder 6.
44. Sydney Redesdale to Virginia Durr, 25 March 1942. Jessica Mitford Correspondence, Ohio State University, Special and Rare Manuscripts, 0089, Box 203, Folder 6.
45. Virginia Durr to Sydney Redesdale, 6 May 1942. Jessica Mitford Correspondence, Ohio State University, Special and Rare Manuscripts, 0089, Box 203, Folder 6.
46. Virginia Durr to Sydney Redesdale, May 1943. Jessica Mitford Correspondence, Ohio State University, Special and Rare Manuscripts, 0089, Box 203, Folder 6.
47. Virginia Durr to Sydney Redesdale, no date. Jessica Mitford Correspondence, Ohio State University, Special and Rare Manuscripts, 0089, Box 203, Folder 6.
48. Sydney Redesdale to Jessica Mitford, no date. Jessica Mitford Correspondence, Ohio State University, Special and Rare Manuscripts, 0089, Box 203, Folder 6.
49. Jessica Mitford to Sydney Redesdale, 24 November 1942. Sussman (ed.), *Decca*, p. 95.
50. Mosley (ed.), *The Mitfords: Letters*, p. 148.
51. Jessica Mitford to Sydney Redesdale, 21 July 1943. Jessica Mitford Correspondence, Ohio State University, Special and Rare Manuscripts, 0089, Box 203, Folder 6.
52. Sussman (ed.), *Decca*, p. 51.
53. Lady Redesdale's campaign is documented in the Sydney, Lady Redesdale Correspondence, The Oswald Mosley Papers, Cadbury Research Library: Special Collections, OMD/6/3/1.
54. Gottlieb, *Feminine Fascism*, p. 247.
55. *Ibid.*, p. 232.
56. Sydney Redesdale to Lord Cranborne, 13 December 1940. Sydney, Lady Redesdale Correspondence, The Oswald Mosley Papers, Cadbury Research Library: Special Collections, OMD/6/3/1.
57. Lord Cranborne to Sydney Redesdale, 30 December 1940. Sydney, Lady Redesdale Correspondence, The Oswald Mosley Papers, Cadbury Research Library: Special Collections, OMD/6/3/1.
58. Lord Simon to Sydney Redesdale, 19 May 1942. Sydney, Lady Redesdale Correspondence, The Oswald Mosley Papers, Cadbury Research Library: Special Collections, OMD/6/3/1.

59. 'Lord Simon of the Fifth Freedom', *The Times*, 28 April 1942.
60. Mosley, *A Life of Contrasts*, p. 192.
61. Sydney Redesdale to Winston Churchill, 1 April 1943. Lady Redesdale Correspondence, The Oswald Mosley Papers, Cadbury Research Library: Special Collections, OMD/6/3/1.
62. Memorandum from Winston Churchill to the Home Secretary, 25 November 1943. The Churchill Archives, Churchill College, Cambridge, CHAR 10/130.
63. Mosley, *A Life of Contrasts*, p. 195.
64. Jessica Mitford to Sydney Redesdale, 23 November 1943. Jessica Mitford Correspondence, Ohio State University, Special and Rare Manuscripts, 0089, Box 203, Folder 6.
65. Jessica Mitford to Sydney Redesdale, 21 July 1943. Jessica Mitford Correspondence, Ohio State University, Special and Rare Manuscripts, 0089, Box 203, Folder 6.
66. Jessica Mitford to Sydney Redesdale, 27 March 1944. Jessica Mitford Correspondence, Ohio State University, Special and Rare Manuscripts, 0089, Box 203, Folder 6.
67. David Redesdale to Jessica Mitford, 21 May 1944. Jessica Mitford Correspondence, Ohio State University, Special and Rare Manuscripts, 0089, Box 203, Folder 6.
68. Young, *Hitler's Girl*, p. 186.
69. Mosley (ed.), *The Mitfords: Letters*, p. 200.
70. Sydney Redesdale to Jessica Mitford, 15 May 1944. Jessica Mitford Correspondence, Ohio State University, Special and Rare Manuscripts, 0089, Box 203, Folder 6.
71. Sydney Redesdale to Jessica Mitford, 25 July 1944. Jessica Mitford Correspondence, Ohio State University, Special and Rare Manuscripts, 0089, Box 203, Folder 6.
72. Devonshire, *Wait for Me!*, p. 135.
73. *Ibid.*, p. 134.
74. Deborah Mitford to Diana Mitford, 19 August 1944. Mosley (ed.), *The Mitfords: Letters*, p. 202.
75. *Ibid.*
76. Devonshire, *Wait for Me!*, p. 134.
77. Deborah Mitford to Diana Mitford, 19 August 1944. Mosley (ed.), *The Mitfords: Letters*, p. 202.
78. Budworth, *Never Forget*, p. 525.
79. Sydney Redesdale to Jessica Mitford, 11 September 1944. Jessica Mitford Correspondence, Ohio State University, Special and Rare Manuscripts, 0089, Box 203, Folder 6.
80. Sydney Redesdale to Jessica Mitford, 3 February 1945. Jessica Mitford Correspondence, Ohio State University, Special and Rare Manuscripts, 0089, Box 203, Folder 6.
81. Budworth, *Never Forget*, p. 545.
82. Lovell, *The Mitford Girls*, p. 391.
83. Lees-Milne, 23 December 1944, *Ancestral Voices*, p. 394.
84. *Ibid.*, 27 December 1944, pp. 394–5.
85. Devonshire, *Wait for Me!*, p. 133.
86. Sydney Redesdale to Jessica Mitford, 22 April 1945. Jessica Mitford Correspondence, Ohio State University, Special and Rare Manuscripts, 0089, Box 203, Folder 6.

87. James Lees- Milne, 10 April 1945, *Ancestral Voices*, p. 425.
88. Sydney Redesdale to Jessica Mitford, 22 April 1945. Jessica Mitford Correspondence, Ohio State University, Special and Rare Manuscripts, 0089, Box 203, Folder 6.
89. Interview with Charlotte Mosley, 9 August 2024.
90. Sydney Redesdale to James Lees-Milne, 21 April 1945. James Lees-Milne Papers, Beinecke Library, Yale University, Gen. Mss. 46, Box 13, f. 628.
91. Sydney Redesdale to James Lees-Milne, 4 May 1945. James Lees-Milne Papers, Beinecke Library, Yale University, Gen. Mss. 46, Box 13, f. 628.
92. Sydney Redesdale to Jessica Mitford, 14 June 1945. Jessica Mitford Correspondence, Ohio State University, Special and Rare Manuscripts, 0089, Box 203, Folder 6.
93. Budworth, *Never Forget*, p. 530.
94. Sydney Redesdale to Jessica Mitford, 15 May 1945. Jessica Mitford Correspondence, Ohio State University, Special and Rare Manuscripts, 0089, Box 203, Folder 6.
95. Nancy Mitford to Jessica Mitford, 4 July 1941. Mosley (ed.), *The Mitfords: Letters*, p. 180.
96. Sydney Redesdale to Jessica Mitford, 14 June 1945. Jessica Mitford Correspondence, Ohio State University, Special and Rare Manuscripts, 0089, Box 203, Folder 6.

Chapter 14: Keeping the Family Together

1. Deborah Devonshire to Diana Mosley, 4 October 1945. Mosley (ed.), *The Mitfords: Letters*, p. 218.
2. Pryce-Jones, *Unity Mitford*, p. 258.
3. Budworth, *Never Forget*, p. 562.
4. Lovell, *The Mitford Girls*, p. 400.
5. James Lees-Milne, 10 August 1945, *Ancestral Voices*, p. 461.
6. Budworth, *Never Forget*, p. 518.
7. Devonshire, *Wait for Me!*, p. 116.
8. Acton, *Nancy Mitford*, p. 118.
9. Nancy Mitford to Diana Mosley, 7 July 1948. Mosley (ed.), *The Mitfords: Letters*, p. 248.
10. Lord Redesdale to Sydney Redesdale, 25 February 1954. Jessica Mitford Correspondence, Ohio State University, Special and Rare Manuscripts, 0089, Box 205, Folder 1.
11. Lees-Milne, 23 December 1944, *Ancestral Voices*, p. 394.
12. Mosley, *A Life of Contrasts*, p. 208.
13. Jessica Mitford Correspondence, Ohio State University, Special and Rare Manuscripts, 0089, Box 204, Folder 11.
14. Sydney Redesdale to Jessica Mitford, 22 April 1945. Jessica Mitford Correspondence, Ohio State University, Special and Rare Manuscripts, 0089, Box 203, Folder 6.
15. Mosley, *A Life of Contrasts*, p. 213.
16. *Ibid.*, p. 210.
17. Email from Jonathan Guinness, January 2025.

18. Lovell, *The Mitford Girls*, pp. 402–3.
19. Jessica Mitford to Sydney Redesdale, 21 May 1946. Jessica Mitford Correspondence, Ohio State University, Special and Rare Manuscripts, 0089, Box 204, Folder 11.
20. Sydney Redesdale, letter to the editor of the *Scottish Sunday Express*, June 1953, quoted in Mosley, *A Life of Contrasts*, p. 234.
21. Guinness, *The House of Mitford*, p. 445.
22. Budworth, *Never Forget*, p. 546.
23. Interview with Constancia Romilly. 1 August 2024.
24. Mosley (ed.), *The Mitfords: Letters*, p. 37.
25. De Courcy, *Diana Mosley*, p. xii.
26. Mosley (ed.), *The Mitfords: Letters*, p. 37.
27. 'The Lost Interview by Duncan Fallowell. Paris. Spring 2002 and 2003', Diana Mosley, *The Pursuit of Laughter*, p. 354.
28. Mosley (ed.), *The Mitfords: Letters*, p. 38.
29. *Ibid.*, p. 213.
30. Email from Professor Richard Toye, 6 December 2024.
31. Email from Andrew Lownie, 2 December 2024.
32. Jessica Mitford, *A Fine Old Conflict*, p. 185.
33. Budworth, *Never Forget*, p. 493.
34. Guinness, *The House of Mitford*, p. 186.
35. *Ibid.*, p. 440.
36. Pryce-Jones, *Unity Mitford*, p. 257.
37. *Ibid.*, p. 1.
38. Geoffrey Bowles, *The Weekly Review*, 28 November 1946, quoted in Pryce-Jones, *Unity Mitford*, p. 15.
39. Simon Heffer to author, 2 December 2024.
40. Budworth, *Never Forget*, p. 542.
41. Pryce-Jones, *Unity Mitford*, p. 253.
42. Budworth, *Never Forget*, p. 544.
43. *Ibid.*
44. Pryce-Jones, *Unity Mitford*, p. 6.
45. *Ibid.*, p. 253.
46. *Ibid.*, p. 254.
47. Sydney Redesdale to Jessica Mitford, 26 June 1948. Jessica Mitford Correspondence, Ohio State University, Special and Rare Manuscripts, 0089, Box 204, Folder 11.
48. Diana Mosley to Nancy Mitford, 5 August 1946. C Mosley (ed.), *The Mitfords: Letters*, p. 229.
49. Nancy Mitford to Diana Mosley, 29 July 1946. Mosley (ed.), *Love from Nancy*, p. 172.
50. Deborah Devonshire to Diana Mosley, 1 December 1946. Mosley (ed.), *The Mitfords: Letters*, p. 232.
51. Nancy Mitford to Diana Mosley, 29 July 1946. Mosley (ed.), *Love from Nancy*, p. 172.
52. Nancy Mitford to Gaston Palewski, 23 September 1946. Mosley (ed.), *Love from Nancy*, p. 175.

53. Nancy Mitford to Diana Mosley, 2 October 1946. Mosley (ed.), *The Mitfords: Letters*, p. 230.
54. Hastings, *Nancy Mitford*, p. 173.
55. Nancy Mitford to Diana Mosley, 22 November 1948. Mosley (ed.), *Love from Nancy*, p. 223.
56. Hastings, *Nancy Mitford*, p. 185.
57. Jessica Mitford, *A Fine Old Conflict*, p. 198.
58. Lord Redesdale to Sydney Redesdale, 7 June 1954. Jessica Mitford Correspondence, Ohio State University, Special and Rare Manuscripts, 0089, Box 205, Folder 1.
59. Sydney Redesdale to Diana Mosley, quoted in Hastings, *Nancy Mitford*, p. 176, note 1.
60. Budworth, *Never Forget*, p. 562.
61. Sydney Redesdale to Jessica Mitford, 4 February 1946. Jessica Mitford Correspondence, Ohio State University, Special and Rare Manuscripts, 0089, Box 204, Folder 11.
62. Jessica Mitford, *A Fine Old Conflict*, p. 124.
63. Nancy Mitford to Sydney Redesdale, 3 May 1948. Mosley (ed.), *Love from Nancy*, p. 208.
64. Lovell, *The Mitford Girls*, p. 406.
65. Interview with Constancia Romilly, 1 August 2024.
66. Jessica Mitford to Sydney Redesdale, 27 March 1944. Jessica Mitford Correspondence, Ohio State University, Special and Rare Manuscripts, 0089, Box 203, Folder 6.
67. Jessica Mitford, *A Fine Old Conflict*, p. 125.
68. Interview with Constancia Romilly, 1 August 2024.
69. Jessica Mitford, *A Fine Old Conflict*, p. 19.
70. *Ibid.*, p. 126.
71. Lovell, *The Mitford Girls*, p. 435.
72. Jessica Mitford, *A Fine Old Conflict*, p. 126.
73. Interview with Constancia Romilly, 1 August 2024.
74. Jessica Mitford to Aranka Treuhaft, 3 May 1948. Sussman (ed.), *Decca*, p. 130.
75. Lovell, *The Mitford Girls*, p. 407.
76. *Ibid.*
77. Jessica Mitford to Sydney Redesdale, 3 May 1948. Jessica Mitford Correspondence, Ohio State University, Special and Rare Manuscripts, 0089, Box 204, Folder 11.
78. Mosley (ed.), *The Mitfords: Letters*, p. 214.
79. Nanny Blor to Jessica Mitford, 24 June 1948. Jessica Mitford Correspondence, Ohio State University, Special and Rare Manuscripts, 0089, Box 203, Folder 6.
80. Jessica Mitford, *A Fine Old Conflict*, p. 127.
81. Jessica Mitford to Sydney Redesdale, 11 June 1948. Jessica Mitford Correspondence, Ohio State University, Special and Rare Manuscripts, 0089, Box 204, Folder 11.
82. Lovell, *The Mitford Girls*, p. 412.
83. Mosley, *A Life of Contrasts*, p. 208.
84. Guinness, *The House of Mitford*, p. 443.
85. Mosley, *A Life of Contrasts*, p. 208.

86. Lovell, *The Mitford Girls*, p. 413.
87. Sydney Redesdale, *The Daily Mail*, 2 June 1948, quoted in Pryce-Jones, *Unity Mitford*, p. 261.
88. Mosley, *A Life of Contrasts*, p. 208.
89. Nanny Blor to Jessica Mitford, 24 June 1948. Jessica Mitford Correspondence, Ohio State University, Special and Rare Manuscripts, 0089, Box 203, Folder 6.
90. Sydney Redesdale to Jessica Mitford, 26 June 1948. Jessica Mitford Correspondence, Ohio State University, Special and Rare Manuscripts, 0089, Box 204, Folder 11.
91. Sydney Redesdale to James Lees-Milne, 18 June 1948. James Lees-Milne Papers, Beinecke Library, Sydney, Lady Redesdale Series, Gen. Mss. 42, Box 13, f. 628.

Chapter 15: The Last Goodbye

1. Jessica Mitford to Sydney Redesdale, 11 June 1948. Jessica Mitford Correspondence, Ohio State University, Special and Rare Manuscripts, 0089, Box 204, Folder 11.
2. Mosley, *A Life of Contrasts*, p. 208.
3. Nanny Blor to Jessica Mitford, 24 June 1948. Jessica Mitford Correspondence, Ohio State University, Special and Rare Manuscripts, 0089, Box 203, Folder 6.
4. Jessica Mitford, *A Fine Old Conflict*, p. 125.
5. Mosley, *A Life of Contrasts*, p. 278.
6. Guinness, *The House of Mitford*, p. 558.
7. Interview with Constancia Romilly, 1 August 2024.
8. Jessica Mitford to Nancy Mitford, 16 November 1971. Mosley (ed.), *The Mitfords: Letters*, p. 568.
9. Jessica Mitford to Nancy Mitford, 13 October 1971. *Ibid.*, p. 555.
10. Interview with Constancia Romilly, 1 August 2024.
11. Sydney Redesdale to Jessica Mitford, 9 September 1960. Jessica Mitford Correspondence, Ohio State University, Special and Rare Manuscripts, 0089, Box 205, Folder 1.
12. Sydney Redesdale to Jessica Mitford, 16 September 1960. Jessica Mitford Correspondence, Ohio State University, Special and Rare Manuscripts, 0089, Box 205, Folder 1.
13. Mosley (ed.), *The Mitfords: Letters*, p. 265.
14. Jessica Mitford, *A Fine Old Conflict*, p. 126.
15. Jessica Mitford to Sydney Redesdale, 23 February 1955. Sussman (ed.), *Decca*, p. 149.
16. Lovell, *The Mitford Girls*, p. 434.
17. Mosley (ed.), *The Mitfords: Letters*, p. 265.
18. Sydney Redesdale to Jessica Mitford, 26 February 1955. Jessica Mitford Correspondence, Ohio State University, Special and Rare Manuscripts, 0089, Box 205, Folder 1.
19. Lovell, *The Mitford Girls*, p. 428.
20. Jessica Mitford to Nancy Mitford, 16 November 1971. Mosley (ed.), *The Mitfords: Letters*, p. 565.
21. Interview with Constancia Romilly, 1 August 2024.

22. Jessica Mitford to Robert Treuhaft, 12 November 1955. Sussman (ed.), *Decca*, p. 161.
23. Interview with Constancia Romilly, 1 August 2024.
24. Sydney Redesdale to Jessica Mitford, 26 March 1956. Jessica Mitford Correspondence, Ohio State University, Special and Rare Manuscripts, 0089, Box 205, Folder 1.
25. Nancy Mitford to Deborah, Duchess of Devonshire, 6 September 1955. Mosley (ed.), *The Mitfords: Letters*, p. 286.
26. Sydney Redesdale to Jessica Mitford, 28 November 1955. Jessica Mitford Correspondence, Ohio State University, Special and Rare Manuscripts, 0089, Box 205, Folder 1.
27. Jessica Mitford, *A Fine Old Conflict*, p. 28.
28. Sydney Redesdale to Jessica Mitford, 7 August 1958. Jessica Mitford Correspondence, Ohio State University, Special and Rare Manuscripts, 0089, Box 205, Folder 1.
29. Guinness, *The House of Mitford*, p. 444.
30. Nancy Mitford to Diana Mosley, 15 January 1954. Mosley (ed.), *The Mitfords: Letters*, pp. 278–9.
31. Lord Redesdale to Sydney Redesdale, 21 February 1954. Jessica Mitford Correspondence, Ohio State University, Special and Rare Manuscripts, 0089, Box 205, Folder 1.
32. Sydney Redesdale to Lord Redesdale, 24 February 1954. Jessica Mitford Correspondence, Ohio State University, Special and Rare Manuscripts, 0089, Box 205, Folder 1.
33. Sydney Redesdale to Jessica Mitford, 8 November 1957. Jessica Mitford Correspondence, Ohio State University, Special and Rare Manuscripts, 0089, Box 205, Folder 1.
34. Mosley, *A Life of Contrasts*, p. 241.
35. Sydney Redesdale to Jessica Mitford, 30 March 1958. Jessica Mitford Correspondence, Ohio State University, Special and Rare Manuscripts, 0089, Box 205, Folder 1.
36. Sydney Redesdale to Jessica Mitford, 18 July 1958. Jessica Mitford Correspondence, Ohio State University, Special and Rare Manuscripts, 0089, Box 205, Folder 1.
37. Lovell, *The Mitford Girls*, p. 462.
38. Nancy Mitford to Sydney Redesdale, 30 May 1959. Mosley (ed.), *Love from Nancy*, p. 375.
39. Sydney Redesdale to Jessica Mitford, 21 October 1958. Jessica Mitford Correspondence, Ohio State University, Special and Rare Manuscripts, 0089, Box 205, Folder 1.
40. Sydney Redesdale to Jessica Mitford, 18 July 1958. Jessica Mitford Correspondence, Ohio State University, Special and Rare Manuscripts, 0089, Box 205, Folder 1.
41. Jessica Mitford to Sydney Redesdale, 19 March 1958. Sussman (ed.), *Decca*, p. 174.
42. Jessica Mitford to Marge Frantz, 10 June 1959. *Ibid.*, p. 218.
43. Lovell, *The Mitford Girls*, p. 462.
44. Jessica Mitford to Aranka Treuhaft, 1 June 1959. Sussman (ed.), *Decca*, p. 216.

Chapter 16: The Final Voyage

1. Nancy Mitford to Madeau Stewart, 17 July 1968. Madeau Stewart Letters, Redesdale Stewart Correspondence, Oxfordshire History Centre, P/143/12/C1/003.
2. Nancy Mitford to Diana Mosley, 29 July 1946. Mosley (ed.), *Love from Nancy*, p. 172.
3. Diana Mitford to Madeau Stewart, 17 October 1969. Madeau Stewart Letters, Redesdale Stewart Correspondence, Oxfordshire History Centre, P/143/12/C5/002.
4. Nancy Mitford to Diana Mosley, 15 November 1955. Mosley (ed.), *The Mitfords: Letters*, p. 291.
5. Jessica Mitford, *A Fine Old Conflict*, p. 21.
6. Jessica Mitford to Sydney Redesdale, 2 April 1960. Jessica Mitford Correspondence, Ohio State University, Special and Rare Manuscripts, 0089, Box 205, Folder 1.
7. Sydney Redesdale to Jessica Mitford, 11 June 1958. Jessica Mitford Correspondence, Ohio State University, Special and Rare Manuscripts, 0089, Box 205, Folder 1.
8. Sydney Redesdale to Jessica Mitford, 14 June 1956. Jessica Mitford Correspondence, Ohio State University, Special and Rare Manuscripts, 0089, Box 205, Folder 1.
9. Guinness, *The House of Mitford*, p. 522.
10. Sydney Redesdale to Jessica Mitford, 12 May 1957. Jessica Mitford Correspondence, Ohio State University, Special and Rare Manuscripts, 0089, Box 205, Folder 1.
11. Jessica Mitford to Marge Frantz, 23 May 1959. Sussman (ed.), *Decca*, p. 212.
12. Sydney Redesdale to Jessica Mitford, 14 October 1959. Jessica Mitford Correspondence, Ohio State University, Special and Rare Manuscripts, 0089, Box 205, Folder 1.
13. Jessica Mitford to Sydney Redesdale, 28 November 1959. Jessica Mitford Correspondence, Ohio State University, Special and Rare Manuscripts, 0089, Box 205, Folder 1.
14. Sydney Redesdale to Jessica Mitford, 27 March 1960. Jessica Mitford Correspondence, Ohio State University, Special and Rare Manuscripts, 0089, Box 205, Folder 1.
15. Sydney Redesdale to Jessica Mitford, 21 April 1960. Jessica Mitford Correspondence, Ohio State University, Special and Rare Manuscripts, 0089, Box 205, Folder 1.
16. Sydney Redesdale to Jessica Mitford, 10 April 1960. Jessica Mitford Correspondence, Ohio State University, Special and Rare Manuscripts, 0089, Box 205, Folder 1.
17. Jessica Mitford, *A Fine Old Conflict*, p. 230.
18. Anthony Quinton, 'Girl of the Golden Left', *The Observer*, 27 March 1960.
19. 'Wealth and Ease, Beauty, Youth', *The Times Literary Supplement*, 1 April 1960.
20. Diana Mosley, 'Letters to the Editor. Hons and Rebels', *The Times Literary Supplement*, 8 April 1960.
21. Violet Hammersley, 'Hons and Rebels', *The Times Literary Supplement*, 15 April 1960.

22. Sydney Redesdale to Jessica Mitford, 10 April 1960. Jessica Mitford Correspondence, Ohio State University, Special and Rare Manuscripts, 0089, Box 205, Folder 1.
23. Sydney Redesdale to Jessica Mitford, 10 April 1960. Jessica Mitford Correspondence, Ohio State University, Special and Rare Manuscripts, 0089, Box 205, Folder 1.
24. Lovell, *The Mitford Girls*, p. 467.
25. James Lees-Milne, 'Lady Redesdale', *The Times*, 28 May 1963.
26. Nancy Mitford, 'Blor', *The Water Beetle*, pp. 3–14.
27. Interview with Charlotte Mosley, 9 August 2024.
28. Nancy Mitford to Jessica Mitford, October 1971. Mosley (ed.), *The Mitfords: Letters*, p. 554.
29. Sydney Redesdale, 29 August 1962. Mosley (ed.), *Love from Nancy*, p. 406.
30. Sydney Redesdale to Nancy Mitford, 18 August 1962. Mosley (ed.), *Love from Nancy*, p. 404.
31. Nancy Mitford to Deborah, Duchess of Devonshire, 23 August 1962. Mosley (ed.), *The Mitfords: Letters*, p. 376.
32. Diana Mosley to Deborah, Duchess of Devonshire, 26 August 1962. *Ibid.*, p. 377.
33. Diana Mosley to Deborah, Duchess of Devonshire, 15 December 1976. *Ibid.*, p. 638.
34. Jessica Mitford to Robert Treuhaft, 12 August 1959. Sussman (ed.), *Decca*, p. 227.
35. Devonshire, *The House*, p. 128.
36. Jessica Mitford to Deborah, Duchess of Devonshire, 25 May 1963. Mosley (ed.), *The Mitfords: Letters*, p. 396.
37. Deborah Devonshire to Diana Mosley, 20 April 1976. *Ibid.*, p. 620.
38. Sydney Redesdale to Jessica Mitford, 24 June 1957. Jessica Mitford Correspondence, Ohio State University, Special and Rare Manuscripts, 0089, Box 205, Folder 1.
39. Sydney Redesdale to Jessica Mitford, 25 January 1958. Jessica Mitford Correspondence, Ohio State University, Special and Rare Manuscripts, 0089, Box 205, Folder 1.
40. Sydney Redesdale to Jessica Mitford, 29 January 1961. Jessica Mitford Correspondence, Ohio State University, Special and Rare Manuscripts, 0089, Box 205, Folder 1.
41. Sydney Redesdale to Jessica Mitford, 4 March 1961. Jessica Mitford Correspondence, Ohio State University, Special and Rare Manuscripts, 0089, Box 205, Folder 1.
42. Diana Mosley to Madeau Stewart, 2 June 1963. Madeau Stewart Letters, Redesdale Stewart Correspondence, Oxfordshire History Centre, P/143/12/C5/1-2.
43. Email from Jonathan Guinness, January 2025.
44. Mosley, *A Life of Contrasts*, p. 242.
45. Mosley, *Loved Ones*, p. 188.
46. When he stood in Kensington in 1959, he received 8 per cent of the vote. Sussman (ed.), *Decca*, p. 207.
47. Interview with Charlotte Mosley, 9 August 2024.
48. Interview with Ben Treuhaft, 9 August 2024.

49. Pamela Jackson to Madeau Stewart, 8 June 1963. Madeau Stewart Letters, Redesdale Stewart Correspondence, Oxfordshire History Centre, P/143/12/C2/005.
50. Quoted in de Courcy, *Diana Mosley*, p. 309.
51. Sydney Redesdale to Jessica Mitford, 2 January 1961. Jessica Mitford Correspondence, Ohio State University, Special and Rare Manuscripts, 0089, Box 205, Folder 1.
52. Jessica Mitford, *A Fine Old Conflict*, p. 184.
53. Lovell, *The Mitford Girls*, p. 474.
54. Sydney Redesdale to Jessica Mitford, 22 May 1957. Jessica Mitford Correspondence, Ohio State University, Special and Rare Manuscripts, 0089, Box 205, Folder 1.
55. Jessica Mitford, *A Fine Old Conflict*, p. 185.
56. Lovell, *The Mitford Girls*, p. 438.
57. *Ibid.*, p. 439.
58. Diana Jackson to Madeau Stewart, 8 June 1963. Madeau Stewart Letters, Redesdale Stewart Correspondence, Oxfordshire History Centre, P/143/12/C2/005.
59. Sydney Redesdale, 'London–Oban Sleeper Service', *Oban Times and Argyllshire Advertiser*, 25 January 1958.
60. Budworth, *Never Forget*, p. 566.
61. *Ibid.*, p. 530.
62. Jessica Mitford to Robert Treuhaft, 12 November 1955. Sussman (ed.), *Decca*, p. 161.
63. Sydney Redesdale to Jessica Mitford, 24 June 1957. Jessica Mitford Correspondence, Ohio State University, Special and Rare Manuscripts, 0089, Box 205, Folder 1.
64. Mosley (ed.), *Love from Nancy*, p. vii.
65. Nancy Mitford to Deborah, Duchess of Devonshire, 27 August 1958. Mosley (ed.), *The Mitfords: Letters*, p. 309.
66. Mosley (ed.), *Love from Nancy*, p. vii.
67. Diana Mosley to Deborah, Duchess of Devonshire, 15 December 1976. Mosley (ed.), *The Mitfords: Letters*, p. 638.
68. Jessica Mitford to Doris Brin Walker and Mason Roberson, 11 September 1955. Sussman (ed.), *Decca*, p. 152.
69. Lovell, *The Mitford Girls*, p. 438.
70. *Ibid.*, p. 474.
71. Email from Marina Guinness, 7 August 2024.
72. Jessica Mitford to Barbara Kahn, 11 May 1959. Sussman (ed.), *Decca*, p. 209.
73. Jessica Mitford to Robert Treuhaft, 19 April 1959. Sussman (ed.), *Decca*, p. 199.
74. Interview with Ben Treuhaft, 9 August 2024.
75. Jessica Mitford to Margaret Fratz, 8 August 1959. Sussman (ed.), *Decca*, p. 225.
76. Jessica Mitford to Pamela Mitford, 6 August 1991. Mosley (ed.), *The Mitfords: Letters*, p. 732.
77. Sydney Redesdale to Jessica Mitford, 27 July 1957. Jessica Mitford Correspondence, Ohio State University, Special and Rare Manuscripts, 0089, Box 205, Folder 1.
78. Budworth, *Never Forget*, p. 575.
79. Diana Mosley to Madeau Stewart, 2 June 1963. Madeau Stewart Letters, Redesdale Stewart Correspondence, Oxfordshire History Centre, P/143/12/C6/003.
80. Budworth, *Never Forget*, p. 613.

81. Sydney Redesdale to Madeau Stewart, 1 July 1961. Madeau Stewart Letters, Redesdale Stewart Correspondence, Oxfordshire History Centre, P/143/12/C5/1-2.

82. Budworth, *Never Forget*, p. 613.

83. Mosley, *Loved Ones*, pp. 50–1.

84. Sydney Redesdale to Jessica Mitford, 10 January 1958. Jessica Mitford Correspondence, Ohio State University, Special and Rare Manuscripts, 0089, Box 205, Folder 1.

85. Violet Hammersley to Jessica Mitford, 28 May 1963. Jessica Mitford Correspondence, Ohio State University, Special and Rare Manuscripts, 0089, Box 205, Folder 1.

86. Sydney Redesdale to Jessica Mitford, 24 June 1957. Jessica Mitford Correspondence, Ohio State University, Special and Rare Manuscripts, 0089, Box 205, Folder 1.

87. Jessica Mitford to Aranka Treuhaft and Margaret Lourie, 11 July 1962, p. 288.

88. Sydney Redesdale to Jessica Mitford, 23 June 1961. Jessica Mitford Correspondence, Ohio State University, Special and Rare Manuscripts, 0089, Box 205, Folder 1.

89. Sydney Redesdale to Jessica Mitford, 16 March 1960. Jessica Mitford Correspondence, Ohio State University, Special and Rare Manuscripts, 0089, Box 205, Folder 1.

90. Email from Marina Guinness, 7 August 2024.

91. Jessica Mitford to Robert Treuhaft, 11 August 1959. Sussman (ed.), *Decca*, p. 226.

92. Jessica Mitford to Robert Treuhaft, 22 April 1959. Sussman (ed.), *Decca*, p. 201.

93. Sydney Redesdale to Jessica Mitford, 10 April 1960. Jessica Mitford Correspondence, Ohio State University, Special and Rare Manuscripts, 0089, Box 205, Folder 1.

94. Nancy Mitford to Mark Ogilvie-Grant, 16 April 1958. Mosley (ed.), *Love from Nancy*, p. 372.

95. Sydney Redesdale to Jessica Mitford, 14 May 1960. Jessica Mitford Correspondence, Ohio State University, Special and Rare Manuscripts, 0089, Box 205, Folder 1.

96. Mosley, *A Life of Contrasts*, p. 241.

97. Deborah, Duchess of Devonshire to Diana Mosley, 6 September 1961. Mosley (ed.), *The Mitfords: Letters*, p. 357.

98. Sydney Redesdale to Jessica Mitford, 21 October 1962. Jessica Mitford Correspondence, Ohio State University, Special and Rare Manuscripts, 0089, Box 205, Folder 1.

99. Nancy Mitford to Jessica Mitford, 19 May 1963. Mosley (ed.), *The Mitfords: Letters*, p. 394.

100. Sydney Redesdale to Jessica Mitford, 28 April 1963. Jessica Mitford Correspondence, Ohio State University, Special and Rare Manuscripts, 0089, Box 205, Folder 1.

101. Mosley, *A Life of Contrasts*, p. 255.

102. Sydney Redesdale to Madeau Stewart, 21 April 1963. Madeau Stewart Letters, Redesdale Stewart Correspondence, Oxfordshire History Centre, P/143/12/C6/013.

103. Lovell, *The Mitford Girls*, p. 475.

104. Madeau Stewart to Jessica Mitford, 17 June 1963. Jessica Mitford Correspondence, Ohio State University, Special and Rare Manuscripts, 0089, Box 205, Folder 1.

105. Devonshire, *Wait for Me!*, p. 246.
106. Madeau Stewart to Jessica Mitford, 17 June 1963. Jessica Mitford Correspondence, Ohio State University, Special and Rare Manuscripts, 0089, Box 205, Folder 1.
107. Acton, *Nancy Mitford*, p. 152.
108. Nancy Mitford to Mark Ogilvie-Grant, 14 May 1963. Mosley (ed.), *Love from Nancy*, p. 417.
109. Mosley, *A Life of Contrasts*, p. 256.
110. Nancy Mitford to Jessica Mitford, 14 May 1963. Mosley (ed.), *The Mitfords: Letters*, p. 393.
111. Deborah, Duchess of Devonshire to Jessica Mitford, 13 May 1963. Mosley (ed.), *The Mitfords: Letters*, p. 392.
112. Devonshire, *Wait for Me!*, p. 246.
113. Lovell, *The Mitford Girls*, p. 475.
114. Jessica Mitford to Peter Nevile, 20 November 1991, quoted in Lovell, *The Mitford Girls*, p. 476.
115. Jessica Mitford to Nancy Mitford, 16 November 1971. Mosley (ed.), *The Mitfords: Letters*, p. 565.
116. Mosley, *A Life of Contrasts*, p. 257.
117. Nancy Mitford to Gaston Palewski, 21 May 1963. Mosley (ed.), *Love from Nancy*, p. 417.
118. Madeau Stewart described her as this in letters to the sisters after Sydney's death and they agreed. Diana Mosley to Madeau Stewart, 2 June 1963. Madeau Stewart Letters, Redesdale Stewart Correspondence, Oxfordshire History Centre, P/143/12/C5/1-2.

Bibliography

Acton, Harold, *Nancy Mitford: The Biography* (London: Gibson Square Books, 2010).

Bowles, Geoffrey, *Writings of a Rebel* (London: The Sterling Press, 1944).

Budworth, Julia M., *Never Forget: George F.S. Bowles: A Biography* (privately published, 2001).

Cowles, Virginia, *Looking for Trouble* (London: Faber and Faber, 2021).

Dalley, Jan, *Diana Mosley: A Life* (London: Faber and Faber, 1999).

Davison, Neil R., 'The Jew as Homme/Femme Fatale: Jewish (Art)ifice, "Trilby" and "Dreyfus"', *Jewish Social Studies, New Series*, Vol. 8, No. 2/3 (Winter/Spring 2002), pp. 73–111.

De Courcy, Anne, *Diana Mosley* (London: Vintage, 2004).

Devonshire, Deborah, Duchess of, *The House: A Portrait of Chatsworth* (London: Macmillan, 1982).

——, *Wait For Me! Memoirs of the Youngest Mitford Sister* (London: John Murray, 2011).

Donaldson Jordan, H., 'Review of "The Irrepressible Victorian: The Story of Thomas Gibson Bowles" by Leonard E. Naylor', *Victorian Studies*, Vol. 10, No. 3, March 1967, pp. 318–19.

Evans, Richard J., *Hitler's People: The Faces of the Third Reich* (London: Allen Lane, 2024).

Franks, John, 'Jews in "Vanity Fair"', *Jewish Historical Studies*, Vol. 35, 1996–98, pp. 199–229.

Gibson Bowles, Thomas, *Flotsam and Jetsam: A Yachtsman's Experience at Sea and Ashore* (New York: Funk and Wagnalls Publishers, 1883).

——, *The Log of the Nereid* (London: Simpkin, Marshall and Co., 1889).

Gottleib, Julie V., *Feminine Fascism: Women in Britain's Fascist Movement* (London, New York: I.B. Tauris, 2003).

——, *'Guilty Women': Foreign Policy, and Appeasement in Inter-War Britain* (Basingstoke: Palgrave Macmillan, 2015).

Griffiths, Richard, *Fellow Travellers of the Right: British Enthusiasts for Nazi Germany 1933–1939* (London: Faber and Faber, 2010).

——, *Patriotism Perverted: Captain Ramsay, the Right Club and British Anti-Semitism, 1939–1940* (London: Faber and Faber, 2010).

Guinness, Jonathan, with Catherine Guinness, *The House of Mitford* (London: Hutchinson, 1984).

Hastings, Selina, *Nancy Mitford* (London: Vintage, 2002).

Heffer, Simon, *Sing as We Go: Britain Between the Wars* (London: Hutchinson Heinemann, 2023).

Jaconelli, Joseph, 'The "Bowles Act" – Cornerstone of the Fiscal Constitution', *The Cambridge Law Journal*, Vol. 69, No. 3, November 2010, pp. 582–608.

James, Lawrence, *Aristocrats: Power, Grace and Decadence* (London: Abacus, 2009).

Lees-Milne, James, *Ancestral Voices and Prophesying Peace: Diaries 1942–1945* (London: John Murray, 1977).

——, *Another Self* (Norwich: Michael Russell Publishing, 2003).

——, *A Mingled Measure: Diaries 1953–1972* (London: John Murray, 1977).

Lovell, Mary S., *The Mitford Girls: The Biography of an Extraordinary Family* (London: Little Brown and Co., 2001).

Lownie, Andrew, *Traitor King: The Scandalous Exile of the Duke and Duchess of Windsor* (London: Blink Publishing, 2021).

Mitford, Jessica, *A Fine Old Conflict* (London: Michael Joseph, 1977).

——, *Hons and Rebels* (London: Weidenfeld and Nicolson, 2007).

Mitford, Nancy, *Christmas Pudding and Pigeon Pie* (London: Vintage Books, 2013).

——, *Highland Fling* (London: Capuchin Classics, 2010).

——, *The Pursuit of Love and Other Novels* (London: Penguin Random House, 2000).

——, *The Water Beetle: Essays by Nancy Mitford* (New York: Atheneum, 1986).

——, *Wigs on the Green* (London: Penguin Books, 2015).

Mosley, Charlotte (ed.), *The Letters of Nancy Mitford and Evelyn Waugh* (London: Penguin, 2010).

——, *Love from Nancy: The Letters of Nancy Mitford* (London: Hodder and Stoughton, 1993).

——, *The Mitfords: Letters Between Six Sisters* (London: Fourth Estate, 2007).

Mosley, Diana, *A Life of Contrasts* (London: Gibson Square, 2018).

——, *Loved Ones: Pen Portraits by Diana Mosley* (London: Sidgwick and Jackson, 1985).

——, *The Pursuit of Laughter* (London: Gibson Square, 2008).

Murphy, Sophia, *The Mitford Family Album* (London: Sidgwick and Jackson, 1985).

Naylor, Leonard E., *The Irrepressible Victorian: The Story of Thomas Gibson Bowles* (London: MacDonald and Co., 1965).

Osborne, John B., '"Governed by Mediocrity": Image and Text in *Vanity Fair*'s Political Caricatures, 1869–1889', *Victorian Periodicals Review*, Vol. 40, No. 4 (Winter 2007), pp. 307–31.

Picardie, Justine, *Coco Chanel: The Legend and the Life* (London: HarperCollins, 2023).

Pryce-Jones, David, *Unity Mitford: A Quest* (London: Weidenfeld and Nicolson, 1976).

Pugh, Martin, *'Hurrah for the Blackshirts': Fascists and Fascism in Britain Between the Wars* (London: Pimlico, 2006).

Roberts, Andrew, *Churchill: Walking with Destiny* (London: Allen Lane, 2018).

BIBLIOGRAPHY

Spicer, Charles, *Coffee with Hitler: The British Amateurs Who Tried to Civilise the Nazis* (London: Oneworld, 2022).

Sussman, Peter Y. (ed.), *Decca: The Letters of Jessica Mitford* (London: Weidenfeld and Nicolson, 2006).

Taylor, D.J., *Bright Young People: The Rise and Fall of a Generation 1918–1940* (London: Vintage Books, 2008).

Thompson, Laura, *The Six: The Lives of the Mitford Sisters* (New York: Picador, St Martin's Press, 2015).

Young, Lauren, *Hitler's Girl: The British Aristocracy and the Third Reich on the Eve of World War Two* (London: Harper Collins, 2022)

Acknowledgements

Since I was a teenager captivated by Nancy Mitford's stylish novels, I have been fascinated by the real people behind the colourful characters. As I grew older and became a parent myself, I became increasingly intrigued by Muv, the Mitford girls' long-suffering mother. I wanted to find out more about her and how she coped with her unruly brood. Thanks to the help and support of many people, I have been able to satisfy my curiosity by writing this book.

My starting point was the other excellent books written about the Mitfords. Mary S. Lovell's *The Mitford Girls*, Jonathan and Catherine Guinness's *The House of Mitford*, and Julia M. Budworth's *Never Forget* were essential reading to provide an insight into the family dynamics. Jonathan Guinness, Lord Moyne, has generously allowed me to quote from *The House of Mitford*, while Julia Budworth's sons, Adam, Ben and Richard Budworth, have kindly allowed me to use material from their mother's book. Individual biographies of the daughters are also important sources. Particularly informative are Anne de Courcy's *Diana Mosley*, David Pryce-Jones's *Unity Mitford: A Quest* and Selina Hastings's *Nancy Mitford*. As the Mitford sisters were such brilliant writers themselves, I have drawn extensively on their memoirs and letters. Nancy's novels have also been enlightening to re-read, providing not only her perspective on the family, but also a good laugh.

I would like to thank the Dowager Duchess of Devonshire's Discretionary Settlement 2009 for allowing me to quote from the Duchess of Devonshire's memoir, *Wait for Me*, and Constancia Romilly and Ben Treuhaft for permission to use their mother Jessica Mitford's memoirs, *Hons and Rebels* and *A Fine Old Conflict*. Charlotte Mosley's insightful editing of the letters between the sisters has enabled me to hear their distinctive voices and feel as though I was eavesdropping on their chats. I am grateful to the Dowager Duchess of Devonshire's Discretionary Settlement 2009 for allowing me to quote from this collection. Thanks are also due to Phoebe Wyatt at Rogers, Coleridge and White for all her hard work in liaising with the relevant literary estates.

Unpublished sources have given me new information on the family relationships. Particularly important has been the extensive correspondence between Jessica Mitford and Lady Redesdale in Jessica Mitford's papers at the Thompson Library Special Collections, Ohio State University. I would like to thank the library for their help and Constancia Romilly and Ben Treuhaft for kindly allowing me to quote from Jessica Mitford's letters, while the Dowager Duchess of Devonshire's Discretionary Settlement 2009 has given permission to quote from Lady Redesdale's letters to her daughter in this collection. I am also grateful to the Special Collections, Cadbury Research Library, Birmingham University, for sending me Lady Redesdale's correspondence in the Oswald Mosley Collection; the Beinecke Rare Book and Manuscript Library, Yale University, for Lady Redesdale's correspondence in the James Lees-Milne Papers; Oxfordshire History Centre for Lady Redesdale's and her daughters' correspondence with Madeau Stewart in their Madeau Stewart Papers. The Dowager Duchess of Devonshire's Discretionary Settlement 2009 has allowed me to quote from these letters. Allen Packwood, Director of the Churchill Archives Centre, Cambridge, has given permission for me to quote from a memorandum from Winston Churchill to the Home Secretary, which is Crown Copyright.

Although written sources are essential, as a biographer, nothing compares to speaking to the people who really knew your subject. I would like to thank Lady Redesdale's descendants for their help. Lady

Redesdale's grandchildren Lord Moyne, Constancia Romilly and Ben Treuhaft, her grand-daughter-in-law Charlotte Mosley, and great granddaughter Marina Guinness generously shared their memories with me. Lord Moyne's daughter Diana Moores has also patiently helped me to liaise with her father.

To provide a balanced portrayal of Lady Redesdale's life involves setting her in the historical context of her era. I would like to thank Professors John Plunkett and Richard Toye of Exeter University, Allen Packwood, Director of the Churchill Archives Centre, Cambridge University, Professor Simon Heffer, Lord Andrew Roberts and Andrew Lownie for their help. The excellent studies of the interwar politics by Martin Pugh, Richard Griffiths, Julie Gottlieb, Lauren Young and Charlie Spicer have also been invaluable. I have drawn on their research and expertise, but the conclusions made in relation to Lady Redesdale and her family, and any errors, are my own.

Producing a book is always a team effort. My appreciation goes to my former literary agent Heather Holden Brown at HHB for being so enthusiastic about the initial idea, and since her retirement to her successor, Elly James, for helping me bring this project to fruition. As always, I could not ask for a more supportive publisher than Laura Perehinec at The History Press. Her team have also, once again, been a pleasure to work with. Finally, none of my books could be written without the love and support of my family, Bridget, John, Becky and Christopher.

I have made every effort to trace copyright holders. I greatly regret any omissions. These will be rectified in future editions.

Index

INDEX